APOSTLES
PROPHETS
AND THE
COMING MOVES OF GOD

God's End-Time Plans for His Church and Planet Earth

D0104821

APOSTLES
PROPHETS
AND THE
COMING MOVES OF GOD

God's End-Time Plans for His Church and Planet Earth

by
Dr. Bill Hamon

Foreword by
C. Peter Wagner

CHRISTIAN INTERNATIONAL
P.O. Box 9000
Santa Rosa Beach, FL 32459
(904) 231-2600

First Printing 1997:   15,000 Third Printing 1999:   15,000
Second Printing 1997: 15,000 Fourth Printing 2002: 20,000

Destiny Image® Publishers, Inc.
P.O. Box 310
Shippensburg, PA 17257-0310

"We Publish the Prophets"

ISBN 0-939868-09-1

Library of Congress Catalog Card Number: 97-65682

For Worldwide Distribution
Printed in the U.S.A.

This book and all other Destiny Image, Revival Press, MercyPlace, Fresh Bread, Destiny Image Fiction, and Treasure House books are available at Christian bookstores and distributors worldwide.

For a U.S. bookstore nearest you, call **1-800-722-6774**.
For more information on foreign distributors,
call **717-532-3040**.
Or reach us on the Internet: **www.destinyimage.com**

DEDICATION

This book is dedicated to the great company of Prophets and Apostles that God is bringing forth in these last days. May it be enlightening and enabling to all those who are called and chosen to co-labor with Christ in fulfilling the coming moves of God. It is for all those who are committed to making ready a people, preparing the way by restoring all things. This will enable Christ Jesus to be released from heaven to return for His Church and establish His kingdom over all the earth.

APPRECIATION

Appreciation is given to my CI Board of Governors who, by their dedicated ministry and support, made it possible for their Bishop to take the time from his active traveling ministry to fulfill his commission from Christ and stay home to finish this desperately needed book. Heartfelt appreciation is given to my wife, Evelyn, for her encouragement to me to finish the book, and to the CI staff and CINC ministers for carrying on the ministry while their Bishop was writing.

CAPITALIZATION

Dr. Hamon has taken the *author's prerogative* in capitalizing certain words that are not usually capitalized according to the standard grammatical practice. This is done for the purpose of clarity and emphasis. References to the Church/Bride **are** capitalized because of her union with Deity through Jesus Christ. The word Scripture is capitalized only when referring to the whole Bible. Church is used when referring to the whole Body of Christ; church when referring to a denominational or local church. Logos/Word is used when referring to the whole Bible; rhema/word when referring to individual scriptures or prophetic words.

The references to apostles and prophets are capitalized and bolded many times to give greater emphasis to the main subject of this book.

CONTENTS

A Local Church With All Fivefold Ministers
Personality Profiles for Apostles and Prophets
Two Prideful Extremes to Be Avoided
The Mighty Hand of God

COMMENDATIONS

ORAL ROBERTS, Oral Roberts University,
Tulsa, Oklahoma

"I want to confirm my love for you and confidence in you as you walk in holiness and divine guidance before the Lord. You have a tender heart yet a strong presentation of your knowledge and experience with the use of the ministry gifts of apostles and prophets, how they are linked together and how they are linked with the fivefold ministry gifts.

"Bill, you are bringing much-needed truths to the Body of Christ. The Lord's hand is surely on you. I admire you for being bold, in His name, about what you feel is going to be done through His apostles and prophets in the move of God. I pray that God will multiply your ministry, which is so urgently needed today."

DR. HENRY RAMAYA, Grace Assembly, Fasan, Malaysia

"It is an honor and privilege to write this on behalf of the Asian Church. The global recognition and acceptance of Bishop Bill Hamon as Father of the Apostolic-Prophetic Movement speaks for itself.

"The boldness of the lion has ushered the Apostle Prophet Statesman into audience with Presidents, Prime Ministers and Kings with the 'Thus saith the Lord' for the nations.

"His thorough historical and Biblical research in this book will help the dust of doubt and caution to settle and allow the global activation and submission to the emerging apostolic prophetic leadership.

"The apostle is God's vehicle of invasion like light invading darkness, and the prophet is God's ultimate weapon of warfare. This end-time Apostolic-Prophetic Movement will climax into the apocalypse with a spontaneous outburst of joy because the missionary mandate will be fulfilled."

CINDY JACOBS, Generals of Intercession,
Colorado Springs, Colorado

"This revelation from God, *Apostles, Prophets and the Coming Moves of God*, is a cutting edge and vanguard word to prepare us for the new millennium. Bishop Hamon has been used by God to 'put together the pieces' so those who are called to function as apostle/prophet can fulfill their office with knowledge and understanding."

APOSTLE EMANUELE CANNISTRACI, Senior Pastor,
Evangel Christian Fellowship, San Jose, California

"Bill Hamon has done it again! His book, *Apostles, Prophets and the Coming Moves of God*, is an overview of the climactic adjustment that must take place in the Church, which will complete and perfect the Church, hastening the coming of the Lord Jesus Christ for the Bride—adorned in holiness, purity, and righteousness—ready to rule and reign. This book will inspire and challenge anyone who longs to see divine order in the Church."

TAN KHIAN SENG, Christian Growth Ministries,
Singapore

"Based on many years of experience as an anointed Apostolic-Prophet, Bishop Bill Hamon combines Biblical insights with personal rhema to give a balanced thesis on the offices of Apostles and Prophets. Scholarly and thorough in its content, *Apostles, Prophets and the Coming Moves of God* is written with clarity and sensitivity that is easily understood by ministers and laymen. The reader is protected by the wisdom of this book as both offices (Apostles and Prophets) are presented in tandem with the other fivefold offices. This will save the Body of Christ, preventing many headaches in excesses that new moves tend to produce. Rich with many life-transforming present truths, this book stands head and shoulders above the rest. A must-read for every Christian, it is destined to be a classic along with the four other major books written by Bishop Hamon."

RICHARD SHAKARIAN, President, Full Gospel Business
Men's Fellowship International

"Dr. Hamon rings the bell with this book...exciting revelation of the Apostolic and Prophetic Gifts. Dr. Hamon, who developed one of the best correspondence universities...takes this same in-depth approach, and with his prophetic gifts...he reveals to the Body of Christ the next wave of Glory.

"The 'Apostolic Gift' upon ordinary men as in the time of Christ...."

ROGER WHEELER, Pastor, Santa Maria Foursquare Church,
Santa Maria, California

"Dr. Bill Hamon has given the Church a priceless gift of prophetic insight for the coming Apostolic age of ministry. His undeniable scholarship in the area of Church history has uniquely qualified him for the task of interpreting the former historical moves of God's Spirit, but his office gifting of Prophetic-Apostle has allowed the end-times Eternal Church to receive a road map for the exciting and challenging journey that lies immediately ahead. Pastors and leaders who care about the future and destiny of the Church need to get a copy of this book and devour its contents."

DR. FRED ROBERTS, Pastor, Durban Christian Center Network, Durban, South Africa

"Dr. Bill Hamon first came to South Africa in 1982. While ministering at our church he prophesied that we would buy land next to a main freeway and build a great rounded domed building seating a minimum of five thousand people. We are now on our new land by the freeway. We are in the process of finalizing the building that fulfills the prophecy in detail. In 1992, Dr. Hamon came when the nation was facing the possibility of great revolution and much bloodshed. Prophet Hamon prophesied in the major churches throughout South Africa that if the church would do intercessory warfare prayer and praise, God would cause a bloodless, non-revolutionary governmental transition. It happened just as he had prophesied.

"Dr. Bill Hamon is a present-day Apostle-Prophet fully qualified to write a book on the restoration of apostles and prophets and the final climactic moves of God that shall bring back Jesus as King over all His creation. It is a desperately needed book for this day and hour."

DR. RON SAWKA, Japan Ministries, Director of CI of Asia

"Dr. Hamon has demonstrated the office of the Prophet and Apostle for many years. His new book will help bring revelation and activation of God's Prophets and Apostles throughout the continent of Asia. God's restored Prophets and Apostles will be instrumental in transforming the church in

Asia and bringing in the great harvest of souls destined to be reaped in these last days."

DR. DAVID CANNISTRACI, Co-Pastor, Evangel Christian
Fellowship, San Jose, California

"There are few men alive who possess the keen prophetic awareness that Dr. Bill Hamon has demonstrated over the past several decades. This insightful volume is sure to stand out as a clear signpost for the ongoing journey of the Apostolic and Prophetic Movements."

—•••••—

FOREWORD BY C. PETER WAGNER

—•••••—

The days in which we live are not normal times. The extraordinary works of God in every continent of the world have caused me, along with many other leaders, to lift our voices in praise for the supreme privilege of being a Christian in this remarkable generation.

One of the principal figures whom God has been using to shape such a generation of believers is my friend, Bishop Bill Hamon. I must confess that I still feel a sense of awe when I call Bill Hamon a "friend." For years and years he was, for me, a distant Christian celebrity, whose name I knew and heard frequently, whom I greatly admired, and whose books had been among the most influential in nurturing me through what I refer to as my "paradigm shift" from traditional Christianity to an openness to the person and to the full ministry of the Holy Spirit. I never was presumptuous enough to imagine that I would ever meet him personally, much less develop the strong relationship that we now have.

His book, *Prophets and Personal Prophecy*, was the only book I could find during the 1980's that, to me, made Biblical and practical sense of the gift and office of prophet in the

Church today. My copy is as scratched up, underlined and dog-eared as any book in my library. I have referred to it often in my writings and I recommend it highly to my students.

Bishop Hamon's new book, *Apostles, Prophets and the Coming Moves of God*, is a thrill to read. It is so timely! God has not been standing still. His purposes and works in the 1990's are not the same as they were in the 1980's. The Holy Spirit continues to speak to the churches, and Bill Hamon is one who has special spiritual ears to hear what He is saying. Just as the 1980's was a decade initiating the renewal of the Biblical gift and office of prophet, the 1990's is shaping up to be the decade in which God is renewing the gift and office of apostle.

As a professional in the field of church growth, it has become obvious to me that the fastest growing cutting edge of worldwide Christianity in our times is what I like to call the New Apostolic Reformation, previously referred to by some as independent churches or nondenominational churches or postdenominational churches or grass-roots churches or other kinds of names. Whatever the name, the fact of the matter is that we are seeing, before our very eyes, the most radical change in the way of doing Christianity since the Protestant Reformation. The changes are obvious on every continent, and there are many commonalities.

As the name would imply, one of the chief features of the New Apostolic Reformation, setting it apart from the more traditional versions of Christianity, is the emerging recognition of the role of apostles in the Body of Christ. Because this is such a key to advancing the Kingdom of God and because the notion of contemporary apostles is so new to many of us, including myself, an urgent need of our times is wise and recognized leadership by those through whom God has been speaking and working along these lines for some time. Bill Hamon is one whom God has raised up to meet this need. Just as he helped us understand the role of the prophet a decade ago, he now helps us understand the role of apostle today.

As you read this book, you will sense an excitement about what God is doing to and through His people. Before you finish, you will not want to be simply a spectator, but you will want to launch out personally into this new stream of the Holy Spirit. You will not find a better navigator for this exhilarating trip than Bill Hamon.

C. Peter Wagner
Fuller Theological Seminary
Colorado Springs, Colorado

INTRODUCTION

Christians in the Body of Christ have a desperate need to know what the Holy Spirit has been commissioned to accomplish within the Church. A major restorational work is taking place now. Christ Jesus is moving His Church along progressively toward an ultimate goal. The Church is not drifting toward eternity but is being directed according to God's eternal purpose. Jesus has predestined that His Church/Bride will be glorious and victorious when He returns for Her to co-reign with Him. It is essential that Christians understand Christ's progressive and ultimate purpose for His Church and planet Earth.

The Church has been in a continual state of restoration since the "Period of the Great Reformation" began some five hundred years ago. Detailed descriptions of the presently restored ministries and truths are found in the book on Church restoration called *The Eternal Church*. The reader who is not familiar with the Holy Spirit's ministry of restoration within the Church should read the book to benefit from this foundational reality.

Christ's Church has two restorational movements that are restoring two major ministries back into the Church. Jesus gave the Prophet and the Apostle ascension gifts of Christ to be a vital part of His Church until His Second Coming. Nevertheless, church theologians who did not have an understanding of God's full purpose for Apostles and Prophets took them out of the present Church. They put them into a nonfunctional foundation of the Church. They dispensationally depleted them from being active in the Church. Within this book we cover all the religious thinking that caused them to make this decision. Nevertheless, the New Testament scriptures do not deplete them. Therefore the Holy Spirit is taking this present time in Church history to reinstate the Prophet and Apostle into the Church as Christ originally intended for them.

I encourage those who are not familiar with present-day apostolic and prophetic terminology, such as "Fivefold Ministers" to review the section in the back of this book entitled "Explanation and Definitions of Present-Truth Prophetic and Apostolic Terms."

This book will cover what is happening in the Church today. It gives explanation concerning the difference between a Sovereign Refreshing Move of the Holy Spirit and a Restorational Move of God. Both kinds of a sovereign move are taking place today within the Church. I believe all Christians need to be partaking of both the refreshing and the restoration. God has a divine purpose for the Refreshing Move of the Holy Spirit. It is reviving the saints, bringing inner cleansing and healing, and renewing the joy of the Lord and a greater love and appreciation for the supernatural presence of God. However, the Refreshing Move is not designed to be a temporary fix but to prepare the saints for the next Restorational Move of God.

Most Christians do not have a good comprehension of God's progressive and ultimate purpose. The section on the coming moves of God enlightens and envisions for the reader what is going to be happening in the Church as we progress to the end of the mortal Church Age.

I believe God wants this truth made known throughout the church world. I pray that all who read will have ears to hear what the Holy Spirit has to say to them from the contents of this volume. May the prayer that Paul prayed for the Christians at Ephesus be fulfilled in your mind, heart and whole being (Eph. 1:18-23).

Dr. Bill Hamon

1

WHY A BOOK ABOUT APOSTLES?

Why Does There Need to Be a Book on Apostles? Why has the Holy Spirit been commissioned at this time to fully restore prophets and apostles with their powerful prophetic and miraculous ministries? There are many reasons about which we will give abbreviated statements in this initial chapter. In the body of the book, scriptural proofs and detailed coverage will be presented.

Jesus chose from among His many disciples twelve whom He called APOSTLES. They were given a special mission and destiny to fulfill in Christ's Church (Eph. 4:11-13). They were an extension of Christ Jesus, the Great Apostle. Apostles express the apostolic nature, power and anointing of Jesus Christ just as pastors, prophets, evangelists and teachers each manifest their respective fivefold ascension gift nature of Christ.

Apostles were a new ministry that had never before been named or demonstrated. Therefore God majored on the ministry of the apostles in "The Acts of the Apostles," which depicts the historical activities of the first-century Church. Jesus gave five ascension gifts to certain believers to represent His fivefold nature of apostle, prophet, evangelist, pastor and teacher.

1

The apostles, along with the other four, were given to the Church until it reaches the fullness of Christ's ministry and maturity. Jesus cannot return to translate His Church until it obtains and fulfills all that the prophetic scriptures declare. This will not be accomplished until the last decade of the mortal Church. Apostles play a vital role in this ministry to the Church (Acts 3:19-25).

The apostle was the first fivefold minister to be placed in the Church and the last to be restored with full recognition, acceptance, placement and power. They are being restored according to the divine principle that the "first will be last, and the last first" (Matt. 19:30, NKJV).

When apostles were active in the first-generation Church, a great harvest of souls was brought in. When the apostles are fully restored, there will be the greatest harvest of souls ever. I believe more souls will be saved in the last one hundred years of the Church than have been saved during all the other years of its existence. "The glory of this latter house [last-century Church] shall be greater than of the former [first-century Church]" (Hag. 2:9).

The whole world will be affected when the apostles and prophets are fully restored. Their supernatural prophetic and apostolic words will signal the rise and fall of many nations and people. They will be instrumental in determining goat and sheep nations so that when Jesus Christ comes He can put the sheep nations on His right and the goat nations on His left.

It will not be long until Christians realize the tremendous ways the restoration of prophets and apostles will affect them and the corporate Church. When the truth fully dawns upon them, millions of saints will begin to make a continuous cry to heaven, "God, reactivate Your prophets and apostles into Your Church so that all things can be made ready and a people prepared for Your second coming."

All fivefold ministers will soon be restored and united in spirit and truth. They will relate together as five expressions of their one Lord and Savior, Christ Jesus. They will function knowing they are interdependent, and not independent of each other. When they reach this stage, it will release the next three moves of God, which will climax with Jesus coming and setting up His kingdom over all the earth.

By the time you have finished this study on God's end-time apostles and prophets, a cry will start arising within your heart for the Holy Spirit to escalate His restorational process of God's holy apostles and prophets.

The Church is beginning to acknowledge the need for Apostles and Prophets. Articles have appeared in several Christian magazines asking questions such as: Where are the modern-day apostles? Who are they? Were they removed from the Church or are they still active in the Church today?

Just as I was finishing writing this book, an article written by Jim Buchan appeared in the magazine *Ministries Today*. It was entitled "Where Are the Apostles Today?" The three and one-half pages revealed the interest of the Church in the present-day ministry of apostles. He gave a very good presentation of six key functions and ministries of Biblical apostles. Buchan then challenges the readers to evaluate whether these apostolic ministries are needed today.

Six Main Functions of First-Century Apostles

1. Taking the gospel to unreached areas (Rom. 15:20, NIV).

2. Planting churches upon the foundation of Christ and helping established churches return to this scriptural foundation (1 Cor. 3:10,11; Gal. 1:6-10; 3:13; Rev. 2:15).

3. Appointing and training the initial leaders of a church (Acts 14:21-23; Titus 1:5).

4. Dealing with specific problems, false doctrines or sins (1 Cor. 1:1–16:24; Acts 15).

5. Promoting unity in the Body of Christ and networking churches (Eph. 4:1-16; Acts 11:27-30; Rom. 15:25-27; 1 Cor. 16:1-4; 2 Cor. 8:9).

6.　Demonstrating and imparting the supernatural dimension of the kingdom of God (2 Cor. 12:12; Acts 4:33; 8:4-20; 10:44-46; 19:16; 2 Tim. 1:6-7).

Apostles Mentioned in the Bible.

The following people in the New Testament are recognized as apostles by being called apostles by name or identified by association, implication or root meaning of words.

The Original Twelve Apostles Commissioned by Christ Jesus

1. **Andrew**, the apostle, who brought his brother, Simon Peter, to Christ.

2. **Bartholomew** or **Nathaniel**, the apostle won by a word of knowledge.

3. **James**, the son of Alphaeus, the younger Apostle James who did obscure services.

4. **James**, the son of Zebedee, the elder Apostle James who was John's brother.

5. **John,** the beloved, the prophetic apostle, who wrote the book of Revelation.

6. **Judas Iscariot**, the apostle who betrayed Christ, and lost his apostleship.

7. **Matthew**, the apostle who wrote the first gospel book in the New Testament.

8. **Peter**, the quick-to-respond apostle, whose name Jesus changed from Simon.

9. **Philip,** the friendly apostle who brought resources and people to Jesus.

10. **Simon**, the Zealot apostle with enthusiastic zeal, revolutionary for change.

11. **Thaddaeus**, also called **Judas** and **Lebbaeus**, the young, obscure apostle.

12. **Thomas,** the devoted, melancholy apostle; "show and prove and I'll believe."

The Expanded Circle of Other Apostles of the Lord

1. **Matthias,** the disciple chosen as apostle to fill the vacated apostleship of Judas.

2. **Barnabas,** the networking apostle, who brought Paul to the Twelve and to Antioch.

3. **Paul,** the supernaturally chosen apostle to the Gentiles, given revelation of the Church.

4. **James,** Jesus' half brother, apostle (pastored the church in Jerusalem; wrote the book of James).

5. **Silas,** the established prophet, first to have a dual ministry of prophet-apostle.

6. **Apollos,** the eloquent apostle; apostle by association of "we" and "us."

7. **Andronicus,** a noteworthy apostle among the brethren.

8. **Epaphroditus,** the faithful, sacrificial apostle, overseer of the Philippian church.

9. **Junias,** the only woman apostle mentioned (based on interpretation of the name).

10. **Timothy,** the apostle trained and commissioned by Apostle Paul.

11. **Unnamed Apostle,** "Whose praise is in the gospel throughout all the churches" (2 Cor. 8:18b).

12. **Unnamed Apostle,** "Whom we have oftentimes proved diligent in many things" (2 Cor. 8:22b).

The Lord Jesus Christ, the Only Apostle of Apostles and the True Example for All God's Holy Apostles. Jesus loves His fivefold ministers as Himself. He has invested all of His ministries for the Church to these ministers. Even so, He continues His ministry of making intercession for all His saints (Rom. 8:34).

Books have been written revealing the end of each of the original Twelve Apostles and Apostle Paul. Historical tradition and legend declare that all these apostles were martyred in the different nations where they ministered. Paul was beheaded at Rome.

The two exceptions are Apostles John and Judas Iscariot. Apostle Judas betrayed the Lord for thirty pieces of silver, lost his apostleship and died by hanging himself. Apostle John was put in a big pot of oil to be boiled to death. It is said that he swam around in it like a refreshing bath while at the same time it renewed his youth. He was then banished to the Isle of Patmos where he received and wrote "The Revelation." He then escaped and returned to Ephesus where he died a natural death in his 90's. Apostles truly fulfilled in their day the prophecy that Jesus gave, "I will send them prophets and apostles, and some of them they will kill and persecute" (see Matt. 23:34).

Now we have an introduction to all the apostles mentioned in the Bible. If one wants to do a further study with all the scriptural references, historical background and meanings of the names of the apostles, details are in Herbert Lockyer's 270-page book entitled *All the APOSTLES of the Bible*. It is published by Zondervan and should be available in all major Christian bookstores.

Let us now find out what is presently happening in the Church throughout the world. There are specific things that God is doing in preparation for the full restoration of His apostles.

We all need to continue on until we are established in all present truth and the present ministry of the Holy Spirit within the Church.

2

WHAT IS HAPPENING NOW?

The kingdom prayer of Jesus is in its last stages of fulfillment. "Thy kingdom come. Thy will be done in earth, as it is in heaven" (Matt. 6:10). His kingdom is being established first in the Church. We are to give Him the full domain as King and Lord of our lives. The Refreshing Revival is activating our first love for our King Jesus and His personal presence. The Apostolic Movement will release the powerful domain of the King. When we allow the King to take His rightful domain within us, then His powerful dominion works will be manifested through us.

Holiness and Righteousness Are Being Laid to God's Plumb Line. The wind of God is blowing over the Church for more purposes than blessing and refreshing. The Holy Spirit has now been commissioned to start **separating** the **chaff** from the **wheat, profane** from **pure, flesh** from **Spirit** and the **false** from the **true.** God will be purifying the inward life and prophetic flow of the prophets and the apostles by separating man's religious ideas from heaven's pure words. He will be separating **self-activated actions** from **Holy Spirit manifestations, self-serving ministry** from **sacrificial ministry,**

personal kingdom ministry from **God's kingdom.** The present-truth Church will no longer be a mixed multitude but a disciplined army under dominion. It will be like the time of Israel after three months of sovereign deliverance from Egypt and supernatural manifestations such as the Red Sea being rolled back, healing at Marah and manna falling daily from heaven. They had to make the transition of being separated into tribes, put in divine order around the Tabernacle and everyone given direction and designation for his or her area of responsibility and ministry. During the first phase of God's great move they were a mixed multitude. They were joyful in their deliverance, signs, wonders and God's supernaturally supplying for all their needs. But they were wandering aimlessly without knowing what was coming next, what part they were to play or what God's progressive purpose was in all that was happening.

Now is the time of God's people camping around the Mountain of God until everyone knows his or her calling, placement, ministry and relationship to God's greater purpose within His local and universal Church. There are to be no more mixtures of flesh and Spirit in a person or prophetic flow. God is separating and calling His Church to come out of the Egyptian/Babylonian religious system to know their calling and membership ministry in God's spiritual Body of Christ, the Church.

A Restorational Move of God vs. a Holy Spirit Refreshing and Renewal. There is a different purpose for each of these divine visitations. A restoration movement is when God sovereignly chooses to restore certain major truths, ministries and spiritual experiences that have not been active since the early years of the Church. Holy Spirit renewal or refreshing is when God sends His refreshing spiritual rain to prepare His people for the next restorational move of God. These Holy Spirit moves are usually referred to as revivals, such as the Welsh Revival. It is called a "Renewal" when the Holy Spirit blows into every church denomination to update them into all presently restored truths, ministries and spiritual experiences, such as the Charismatic Renewal. Holy Spirit Refreshings and Renewals do not restore major truths or ministries to the corporate Church, but they do bring supernatural spiritual experiences into the lives of individual believers. Revivals, refreshings and renewals happen every so often in the Church, often just before a restorational movement.

The Holy Spirit is presently taking the Church through a process of transition, preparation and progression toward the Apostolic Movement and final restorational moves of God. All who are presently participating in the refreshing revival must maintain their joy, deliverance and divine transformation. At the same time proper response must be made to the Holy Spirit's challenge to be established in all the restorational realities that God has restored in the Prophetic and will restore in the Apostolic Movement.

Ministries Are Being Brought Forth to Further Fulfill Malachi 4:5-6.

The Promise Keepers ministry was born of the Holy Spirit to further fulfill God's prophetic purpose stated in Malachi. They are turning the hearts of men of all ages to God. This is causing the "hearts of the fathers [to turn] to the children, and the hearts of the children [to turn] to their fathers" (NKJV).

The Generals of Intercession ministry directed by Cindy Jacobs is also a part of the fulfillment of this prophecy. Cindy, often accompanied by Dr. C. Peter Wagner, and others are going to the nations teaching and activating thousands of ministers in "prophetic intercessory warfare prayer." They demonstrate to the national leaders how to discern the "strongman" over the nation and then destroy that ruling evil principality. This ministry helps that nation to become a sheep nation. It also causes the hearts of the leaders to turn to the people and the hearts of the people to turn to their leaders. Cindy, ministering with her powerful prophetic-apostolic anointing, has demonstrated that this works for regions, cities, national ministries and local churches.

Mass evangelism with the supernatural works of God has been reactivated by such men of God as Benny Hinn and Reinhard Bonnke. They are two of the best-known international ministers who have tens of thousands attending their evangelistic campaigns. Many national evangelists are doing the same things in their countries. They are preparing the way for the apostles to arise in every nation to establish the converts on a firm foundation and build them into a mighty Church for Jesus Christ.

A New Apostolic Reformation?

The National Symposium on the Post-Denominational Church convened by Dr. C. Peter Wagner at Fuller Seminary, May 21-23, 1996, was a historical occasion in God's annals of Church history. It was prophetically orchestrated by the Holy Spirit to fulfill God's progressive purpose of bringing His Church to its ultimate destiny. Numerous denominational representatives were present with many delegates from other nations. The consensus of the panelists was that there are still apostles and prophets in the Church, and that there is an emerging Apostolic Movement that will revolutionize the 21st-century Church. The last-generation Church will have an Apostolic Reformation that will be as great as the first-generation Apostolic Movement. The first-generation Church prophets and apostles laid the foundation of the Church. Now the last day Apostolic Reformation will put the final finishing touches on the Church.

It will also bring revolutionary changes like those the Protestant Movement brought forth in its day. The Protestant Movement started the era of the great reformation of the Church. The new Apostolic Movement will accelerate the final restorational work of the Holy Spirit, causing it to be accomplished in one generation. The Great Reformation started the Church on its process of restoration of all truths, life experiences and ministries that were in the early Church. God's purpose for the approximately five hundred years of the reformation was to bring the Church to a place of purity, ministry and maturity as declared in Ephesians 4:13; 5:25,27.

The work of restoration will continue until members of Christ's corporate Body are taught, trained, activated and matured in manifesting their membership ministries. There are multimillions of souls to be harvested for the purpose of incorporating them into the Body of Christ. God has predestined a certain quantity of members with Christlike qualities for the full functioning of His eternal Church. Jesus purchased, produced and is progressively perfecting His Church that He might present it to Himself as a glorious Church. His purpose is to use the Church to co-labor with Him in His eternal ministry (Eph. 3:21; Rom. 8:17).

Some of the Revolutionary Changes Perceived at This Point.

The new Apostolic Reformation will bring about the removal of many man-made traditions within the Church, such as the distinction between laity and clergy, spiritual and secular, members and ministers. There are Church members who are fulfilling their ministry as staff workers in a local church. There are those who are fulfilling their calling and ministry in the "secular" world. Regardless where members are functioning, they are ministers in the Body of Christ. Church government and fivefold ministries are not to be deleted, for there is structure and a chain of command in heaven as well as in the Church.

However, the position that is now called the "pastor" of a church will be redefined. Those who fill that position will function more like the coach of a sports team rather than the owner. The coach knows his calling is to teach, train, and equip each team member into their highest potential. He is to discover what team position each team member is best qualified to play. He develops the skills of each player while at the same time unifying them to play as one team. Their goal is not just to have fun but to enjoy fulfilling their part while playing to be winners over all the opposition.

The owner is more concerned about the team winning in order to bring in more paying participants. He is concerned about making payroll, making a profit and building bigger stadiums. Too many of today's preachers function more like a team owner than a coach. Owners are interested in having a winning team to bring in great numbers of people for a bigger audience. The coach wants the numbers to come in so that he can have a greater team. The owner is in the numbers game of having a bigger audience to make him more successful. The coach is interested in equipping every player on his team to fulfill their greatest potential. The Apostolic Reformation will make church leaders and pastors more committed to raising up an army of equipped saints than an audience of paying spectators and fans.

Church cell home groups will increase and transition into doing the work of the ministry. The pastor will make sure everyone works together in fulfilling the pastor's vision for that local church. The senior headship for the local church (pastor) will no longer be a one-man band but a band director. He will function as a choir director who makes sure all members not only sing their part well, but also are in harmony with all in the choir. The 21st-century Church will not function anything like the traditional church of today. Many leaders will not be able to make the transition because of their fear of losing control or lessening their authoritative position.

The Apostolic Reformation will cause believers to manifest the supernatural grace, gifts, and power of God. The one-man show will be over. A few great demonstrators of God's power will become the multimillions of demonstrators. The world will not exclaim "what a mighty man" but "what a mighty Church"! God will get all the glory through His Church, not just through a few great ministers around the world.

Who Will Be the Leaders in the New Apostolic Reformation?

The leaders will be all fivefold ministers who have progressed from "called to be" to "being commissioned" to their ministry. They will be mature, seasoned men and women who have God's heart and mind for His Church. The ascension gift of the apostle will be fully restored during the Apostolic Reformation, but apostles will not be the only leaders. There will be apostolic and prophetic leaders who walk in present truth. They will have integrity and Christlike character with powerful supernatural ministries conducted in wisdom and maturity. There are those who have many revelations and prophecies confirming that they are "called to be an apostle" but they will not initially be the apostolic leaders. The apostolic fathers and leaders will be those whom God has commissioned to be apostles, prophets, evangelists, pastors and teachers and who are walking in all that the Prophetic and Apostolic Movements have restored.

APOSTOLIC has a broader meaning than just those called to be apostles. Apostolic will include all presently restored truth and miraculous ministries with signs, wonders and miracles by ministers and church members. Apostolic fathers and leaders will be the ministers who have made the transition to the new divine order that God is establishing in His Church.

NETWORKING: There will be a new emphasis on prophetic and apostolic heads of denominations to network together. Networking does not imply that all groups should come under the headship of one great apostolic leader. Networking (a working net) is illustrated by a good fish net. Each network ministerial group or large church is like one of the knots that ties the lines together. Those who have vision, grace and wisdom to network with other networks will become the great fishing net that God will use to draw in the great multitude of souls.

The Post-Denominational Symposium or The New Apostolic Reformation Symposium has provided a place for all of these heads of networks, ministerial organizations and denominations to come together. This gives the Holy Spirit the opportunity to bring a greater unity and corporate vision within the Body of Christ.

The common meeting ground and corporate vision is reaping the great harvest and proclaiming Jesus as Lord over all the earth. The independent and denominational groups who believe the Apostles' Creed, the fundamentals of the Christian faith, and are walking in all restorational truth will be the ones with the greatest interest in networking. The religious Christian groups who are seclusive and exclusive, believing they are God's only true people, will not be interested in networking with other Christian groups. Also, those who are more interested in indoctrinating people in their religious, "Christian" beliefs than in winning them to Jesus Christ will not be interested in networking. But there are many Christian groups who are interested in establishing God's kingdom more than their own. The Holy Spirit will draw those of like vision together to form a networking relationship to fulfill God's eternal purpose for the Body of Christ and planet Earth.

The networking could be multilevel and worldwide. These same networks could be in each nation and continent on earth. There could be a national meeting of all these different networks from all levels of networking. There could also be an international meeting of all these heads of networks for unifying our corporate vision. Networking will promote unity in the Body of Christ by connecting groups through intermediaries. Where two groups could not walk together a third may step into the gap and form a buffered link between them.

Every God-ordained network within the Body of Christ will have its part to play in fulfilling the overall vision of Jesus Christ, the Head of the Body. Some networks would have more of a hand ministry, others the eye, some the ear, feet, heart, etc. Each major member (network) of the Body would have its own contribution to make for the functioning of the whole. Those who know what part of the Body they are and what their part is in fulfilling the vision of the Head will not be competitive, jealous, envious or critical of the others. For in the body the eye cannot say to the ear, or the mouth to the hand, "I have no need of you." We need each other. One network or denomination can never be the whole Body of Christ. We are all members of the **one universal many-membered corporate Body of Christ** under **one sovereign headship of Jesus Christ our Lord**. We all have only one Church to fulfill and one kingdom to build and that is Christ's Church and God's kingdom.

We see a model for this networking of networks in technology. The Internet is being heralded as a revolutionary tool for the world. It came into being by networking, that is, by providing communication links between existing networks. These networks represent various sectors of society, such as government, the military, education, science, banking, manufacturing, etc. The same synergistic explosion of progress seen in the Internet can be experienced by the corporate Church as denominations, ministries, networks, camps, fellowships, etc. begin to link together.

Preparation for God's Progressive Purposes. The Charismatic Renewal was the outpouring of the Holy Spirit upon all denominations. It made them realize that there was more than historic and fundamental church life. It broke up their fallow ground and activated them into supernatural experiences such as speaking in tongues. They experienced God's presence in praise. It renewed their first love and gave a desire for more of God. The present revival being called "laughter, times of refreshing, floor time," etc. is a preparatory move of the Holy Spirit, the same as in the Charismatic Renewal. The Charismatic Renewal was God preparing the Church for the Prophetic Movement. Now the present Refreshing Move of the Holy Spirit is preparing the Church for the great Apostolic Movement. Hundreds of ministers walking in present truth are already proclaiming and demonstrating that there are apostles in the Church today. The full restoration and demonstration of apostles is at hand.

The Timely Process for "GIDEON'S 300 Warrior Group" Is Now Taking Place in the Church. We are now in the progressive stage where God is taking the Church to the refreshing river of testing and separation unto a greater responsibility of maturity and ministry. Hundreds of thousands have come and will continue to come to the present river of refreshing and blessing. Those who have been saturated with His presence will be challenged and tested at the river. Drinking at the refreshing river is not an end in itself. It is like Gideon's "river," which was a place of testing one's personal commitment, motive and character. The challenge is to maintain the **personal blessing** while moving into **corporate building**. We retain what we have while at the same time making the transition from **soaking** to **sending**, from **floor time** to **flowing**

time, from just **soaking up His presence on the floor** to **taking up our warriors' weapons.**

From the thirty-two thousand who came to Gideon's refreshing-revival, less than one third continued on to the river of testing. Out of the ten thousand who drank at the river, only three percent passed the test to become soldiers in Gideon's army. Less than one percent of the original participants made the transition and moved on to become part of God's chosen three hundred mighty warriors.

From the thousands who are participating in the present Refreshing Move of the Holy Spirit, only a small percentage will make the transition to become God's end-time prophetic/apostolic warriors. Nevertheless, God will bring forth the "Gideon's 300" that He plans to use to put the enemy on the run. Jesus will choose those drinking at His river, who have the right spirit and attitude, to be a part of His "Gideon's Army." They are being prepared for the great end-time battle against the "Midianites" that are encamped against His Church.

A Personal Prophetic Vision of the Last Chapter of God's Book of His Mortal Church.

The Lord Jesus gave me a vision while seeking Him with prayer and fasting. He showed me a great Book. Its title was *The Book of the Mortal Church on Earth.* He flipped through the Book until He came to a page entitled "The Last Chapter of the Mortal Church." He then turned a page at a time for me to see the page and paragraph headings. On some pages I was able to read most of the contents under the headings and on other pages only enough time was given to read the bold headings.

He said **some of His ministers** would only be shown one **page** or **paragraph**, which would become their major message and ministry. They would have the anointing and responsibility to demonstrate and establish that part of the "Last Chapter" of His mortal Church.

He said He was showing me an **overview** and **highlights of the whole chapter** because He was giving me the responsibility of keeping an overall perspective and making the progressive purpose of God known to His corporate Church. My personal ministry would major in the headings dealing with the full restoration of fivefold ministers and their ministry of equipping the saints. However, the panoramic picture and destiny for Christ's corporate Church would be my message and part to fulfill during "The Last Chapter of the Mortal Church."

Following are some of the things I was allowed to see, especially those that the Holy Spirit is presently working with and implementing into the Church.

The Last Chapter Church—Divine Decrees and New Directives Being Made in Heaven.

New Assignments of the Angelic Host. More appearances of God's holy angels and the devil's demonic manifestations are decreed to begin now and continue escalating until the coming of the Lord Jesus. There will be more and more discussions about angels and the spirit world on television talk shows until the world becomes obsessed with the idea of "other world" spirit beings.

God has released the Holy Spirit to bring His revelations and activation to the end-time Church. This will bring forth the last generation of mortal **people**, unlimited **power**, new **products** and more **places** dedicated to fulfilling God's present-truth purposes.

Delay shall be no longer concerning the final preparation necessary for the kingdoms of this world to become the kingdoms of Christ Jesus and His Church (Rev. 10:7; 11:15).

God is activating the second phase of apostles and prophets and is fully restoring them to their rightful place of power and function. **The Holy Spirit will intensify the maturing process for those who will be the participants.**

Jesus is maturing and motivating His fivefold ministers to intensify their training, and equipping those who will be the soldiers in God's end-time army.

Local pastors must implement ministries that will reach the lost and establish and activate the saints while equipping them for their membership ministries in the Body of Christ.

The Holy Spirit Has Been Commissioned to Accelerate His Restorational Work in the Church. Here is a general overview of what accelerating restoration means: Restorational movements since AD 1500 have accelerated in their frequency of occurrence from three hundred years apart to one hundred to fifty to every ten years during the last half of the 20th century. Each prepared the way for the next over the past five hundred years. The Protestant Movement prepared the way for the Holiness Movement and so on, the Pentecostal for the Latter Rain Restoration for the Charismatic Renewal and Faith Movement for the present Prophetic Movement, which is now preparing the way for the Apostolic Movement, which will in turn prepare the way for the Saints Movement, which enables the saints of the Most High to fulfill Daniel 2:44; 7:18,22,27; and Revelation 11:15; 1:5-6; 5:9-10.

Apostles and Prophets Arising in the World of Administration and Finances.

It is now time to activate the Joseph and Daniel Company of apostles (Joseph) and prophets (Daniel) within the business field and political arena. The Esther and Deborah Company is arising right along with them. God is preparing an apostolic and prophetic company of Christian business people. They will not only bring the wealth of the wicked into the Church, but will also affect the economy in many nations of the world. God is bringing the full transition of His "Joseph Company" from the status of prisoner to prime minister, and His "Daniel Company" from the lion's den to the right hand of the king.

The First Shall Be Last and the Last Shall Be First. What happened at the beginning of the Church will happen at the end of the Church Age. In fact, Scripture says, "The glory of this latter house [last-days Church] shall be greater than of the former [early Church]" (Hag. 2:9). Jesus chose twelve men from the business world and ordained them as apostles. He did not choose men from the religious Rabbinical Schools or the Levitical Priesthood. Jesus made no distinction in calling and commissioning based on one's past professions or position in life. Revelation regarding God's thoughts concerning fivefold ministers is going to revolutionize the present thinking and function of the old church order. No scripture declares that a person must be the pastor of a church or have his own non-profit organization to be called as an apostle or prophet in the Body of Christ. The U.S. government and religious leaders have designated who can be recognized as a minister within the church. God is raising up and giving recognition to His company of Joseph/Daniel-apostles/prophets. The old order Church system or the government may never recognize them for who they are, but God is giving them His recognition and power to prosper. In the beginning of the Dark Ages of the Church, religious men segregated God's people into **secular** and **spiritual**, **clergy** and **laity**, **business** and **church**. Everyone does not have to have a pulpit ministry to be a valid minister in the Body of Christ. By the end of this century, there will come revolutionary adjustments to the way God's Church functions on earth.

Apostles and Prophets to the Nations. Prophets and apostles will continue going to the nations of the world. They will be some of the main instruments God uses to reap the great end-time harvest. However, the primary anointing of the prophet is not manifested through mass evangelism or missions. That is the main mission and anointing of the evangelist. Prophets and apostles are divinely sent to give God's revelation and prophetic word for that nation. How that nation responds to God's Word will determine whether they become a goat or sheep nation. God will continue increasing His ministry of separating sheep nations from goat nations. (CI prophets have now gone to forty nations, and in many of them God's prophetic word was spoken to the head of that nation. Many other prophets from other camps are doing the same things.)

The Realignment of Nations. The shifting and realignment of nations as allies and enemies is taking place now. Secret meetings are now going on behind closed doors to bring these things to pass. China and some Islamic nations are part of this process. The secret things will soon become public knowledge. Unless a tremendous revival happens within these nations, a great war between East and West will take place around the turn of this century. God will be progressively realigning the nations of the world in preparation for the final global conflict. The end result will be the exaltation of the righteous nations, while the wicked nations are subdued and come under the rule of the righteous.

Racial Strife and Rioting Reactivated! The devil has plans to reactivate racial issues, not only black versus white, but other races and religions such as Jews versus Christians. Islam and other cultic religions, and occultic and humanist beliefs will try to make Christianity look like the problem and not the solution. They, of course, present themselves as the true group to resolve all the problems. The white supremacist and separatist group will continue to spark the flame that will start the

fire roaring. Islamic radicals have plans to disrupt and hope-
fully overthrow and take over America by raising up a black
militant Islamic following. Black and white Christians walking in present truth will become more unified while the anti-
Christ religious system will propagate division, disunity,
hatred, anger and rebellion. Prophetic intercessory prayer and
warfare praise can stop, overturn and reverse the plans of the
enemy. One international prophetess said that God revealed to
her that if America as a nation does not turn to God like she
should, then God was going to allow America to be ruled by
Islam for a period of time. That would be worse than communism taking over.

Church Transitioning Toward Translation. A greater measure of revelation, faith and overcoming grace is being released
in the Church. The mortal Church is in transition and preparation for becoming the immortal Church. The resurrection-
translation of the saints that brings about the redemption of
their mortal bodies into immortal, indestructible bodies will
take place so that God can fulfill His greater purpose for and
through His Church. There is a last-day ministry designed for
the overcoming Church to accomplish in the heavenlies and
on earth that will require the saints to have their bodies redeemed. The redemption of the Body is the last act of redemption and **the last page of "The Last Chapter of the Mortal
Church."** To be in the first phase of God's end-time purpose
will require complete death to self and full life in Christ Jesus.
This includes dying to old religious traditions and living in all
present truth. Submit to the death/life process that is being intensified in Christ's Church.

—••●●●●●••—

3

BIBLICAL PERSPECTIVES
OF THE MINISTRY OF APOSTLES

—••●●●●●••—

Of all the fivefold ministers, there are more scriptures in the New Testament about apostles and the apostolic ministry. The English word "apostle(s)" is used eighty-three times, "evangelist" three times, "pastor" one time and "teacher" thirteen times. "Prophet" is mentioned one hundred seventy-two times, but only about twenty-five percent of those times are in reference to an active prophet in the New Testament. However, if one takes the original Greek term for these ministries and the different terms they use to convey the same ministry, it would change some. For instance, if we apply the word "shepherd" to being the ministry of the pastor, we find it is used twenty-four times in the New Testament. But most of them are not describing a pastor or the work of his ministry. Also, of the one hundred seventy-two times that "prophet" is used, the majority of times it is in reference to what the prophets in the past have prophesied. The writer is quoting their prophecies to prove a New Testament truth. There are also many demonstrations of the prophet's ministry in the book of Acts, which is the Bible's history book of the first-century Church.

Why are there so many references to Apostles and illustrations of their ministries in comparison to the other fivefold ministers? There are several reasons:

1.   Jesus chose twelve disciples and named them apostles. They were personally trained by Jesus for three years and then, after His resurrection, He commissioned them to go into all the nations preaching the gospel and bringing in those that would become members of Christ's Church. They were then to bring them to the stature of Christ's maturity and ministry. They were to present the Church to Christ Jesus in all His glory without spot or wrinkle, as a properly prepared Bride adorned for marriage to her Bridegroom.

2.   Most of the references to apostles come from the four Gospels where continual reference is made to the twelve apostles.

3.   This was the introduction of a new ministry. The title "apostle" had never before been taught, described, designated or demonstrated. The religious leaders of God's people, Israel, were familiar with the ministry of the prophet as well as the priest, which is typical of the New Testament pastor; the Levite, which is typical of the New Testament evangelist; and the scribe, which is typical of the New Testament teacher. But no one had heard of Apostles being ministers in the ministry of the Tabernacle. Therefore it was necessary that apostles be mentioned and demonstrated more than the rest.

In this chapter we are going to give different aspects of the ministry of the "apostle" as stated and demonstrated in the Scripture. To keep the reader from thinking we are making the apostle the all-powerful, all-knowing, superior minister because of all the things the scriptures reveal that he is and can do, the following insight is needed. There are no statements in Scripture describing what any one of the fivefold ministers can do that the others cannot do. There is no scriptural statement saying apostles do this but pastors cannot do this, or prophets can do this or that but the others cannot, etc.

All fivefold ministers are extensions of Christ's fivefold nature of apostle, prophet, evangelist, pastor and teacher. All five are to be born of the Holy Spirit and empowered as New Testament ministers of the Spirit and Word of God. All are to be able to preach the Word and minister the supernatural gifts of the Holy Spirit, such as healing the sick, casting out demons and revealing the mind of Christ concerning specific areas in the life of God's people. In fact, Jesus declared that even the New Testament believers are to cast out demons, heal the sick, speak with new tongues, prophesy and proclaim and demonstrate the gospel of Jesus Christ.

Since this is all true, then why does Scripture designate different ministry titles in the Church, such as the fivefold ministers, bishops, elders, deacons and members? Why didn't Christ have all those who would be extensions of Himself to the Church just be called "MINISTERS" without any differences in title? Wouldn't that have caused more unity with less comparison between ministries? Wouldn't it have eliminated the concern, "Which am I—apostle, prophet or pastor?" Or who has authority over whom, or which ministry is first and last or least and greatest? In every discussion or in every book that is written on the fivefold ministry these issues always arise. Jesus never intended for there to be competitive comparison of His gifted ministers. These fivefold ministries are five different expressions of the one Christ. So is Christ divided? How can He be in conflict and competition with Himself? (1 Cor. 3:1-9) All fivefold ministers are Christ's ascension gifts to His Church. They were given to complement each other and to co-labor together in building Christ's Church. Though all ministers and members are to do many of the same things, the fact still remains that Christ Jesus divided and designated His one personal ministry into five with descriptive names of the apostle, the prophet, the evangelist, the pastor and the teacher.

> *And He Himself gave some to be apostles, some prophets, some evangelists, and some pastors and teachers, for the equipping of the saints for the work of ministry, for the edifying of the Body of Christ* (Eph. 4:11-12, NKJV).

> *And God hath set some in the church, first apostles, secondarily prophets, thirdly teachers, after that miracles, then gifts of healings, helps, governments, diversities of tongues. Are all apostles? are all prophets? are all teachers? are all workers of miracles? have all the gifts of healing? do all speak with tongues? do all interpret? But covet earnestly the best gifts...* (1 Cor. 12:28-31).

The "best gifts" that every believer needs to covet earnestly are the ones that Jesus and His Holy Spirit have chosen for them to possess and manifest.

First Corinthians 12:28 emphatically declares that Jesus set in the Church apostles, prophets and teachers (representatives from fivefold ministers). He set gifts of healing, miracles and tongues (representatives of the nine gifts of the Holy Spirit). He also set helps and administrations (representatives of the many ministries within the church). In First Corinthians 12:28 Paul was not giving a pyramid list of the greatest and the least ministries within the Body of Christ, but a simple summarization of his discussion and understanding of the fivefold gifted ministers of Christ that he shared with the Ephesian church (Eph. 4:11), the nine gifts of the Spirit he had just covered in his letter to the Corinthian church (1 Cor. 12:8-10) and some of the ministries of the Church that he shared in his letter to the church at Rome (Rom. 12:3-8).

All fivefold ministers have a similarity in their ministries and yet have a specific anointing, ministry, power and authority that go with their individual calling. The ministries of the pastor, evangelist and teacher have been accepted and recognized by those names as valid ministries within the Church ever since the Protestant Movement of the 1500's. During the last decade, many books have been written on the ministry of the prophet. Now many books are being written on the apostle. Still, the church world has very little understanding about the calling and ministry of the apostle. Therefore it is necessary that a Biblical presentation of the apostle be given to enhance our understanding of apostles.

What the Bible Has to Say About Apostles.

Jesus established the ministry of apostle when He called His many disciples together and chose twelve of them and named them APOSTLES. That is the name that Jesus chose to designate those twelve whom He specially selected for His own purpose. A study of how the word "apostle" was used during that time and what its root meaning was in the Greek will help us to better understand the apostle. But how the Greeks used it in their language does not give the complete picture of what Jesus meant for the word to portray.

It takes a complete study of the New Testament examples of apostles to understand the full meaning of this gifted ministry that Christ placed within His Church. It is not just what the root meaning was when Jesus chose the word, but what He made it to become. It is like the word "ECCLESIA" that Jesus chose to identify His chosen people, the Church. The root meaning of the word simply means a group of people called out of their homes to gather at a special assembly. But Jesus and Apostle Paul gave the word CHURCH (ECCLESIA) much more meaning and significance than how the Greeks used it in their language. Therefore we must go to the Bible to find out what Jesus meant for the word "apostle" to mean and to include. Part of the purpose of this study is to bring Biblical clarity so that when reference is made to APOSTLES, a full comprehension of the calling, character and ministry of Church apostles flashes into one's mind. "And when it was day, He called His disciples to Himself; and from them He chose twelve whom He also named apostles" (Luke 6:13, NKJV).

The Twelve Apostles of the Lamb. The English word "apostle" comes from the Greek word "APOSTOLOS," which carries the meaning of "one being sent forth for a specific purpose or commissioned to accomplish a specific task or ministry." Those who faithfully fulfill their commission to the end of their mortal life will be placed in positions of ruling and reigning with Christ in His eternal kingdom. The original twelve spoken of in the Gospels had a destiny and purpose to fulfill in God's eternal city. They are called Apostles of the Lamb and seem to have a destiny that other church apostles do not have. "Now the wall of the city had **twelve foundations**, and on them were the names of the **twelve apostles of the Lamb**" (Rev. 21:14).

The Twelve's Overcomer's Reward. Those who faithfully followed Jesus Christ during His three-and-a-half years of ministry on earth and continued until the end of their lives were promised a great "overcomer's" reward. They were promised the position of being the head of one of the twelve tribes of Israel. Each would receive a throne and reign as king over one of the twelve tribes of Israel. Some do not take this as literal, but regardless of whether it is or not, Jesus clearly declared that they had been called and commissioned to fulfill a specific work for Christ. For their faithfulness they would be given the reward of a special position and ministry in God's eternal kingdom. "And Jesus said unto them, Verily I say unto you, That ye which have followed Me, in the regeneration when the Son of man shall sit in the throne of His glory, ye also shall sit upon twelve thrones, judging the twelve tribes of Israel" (Matt. 19:28). "That ye may eat and drink at My table in My kingdom, and sit on thrones judging the twelve tribes of Israel" (Luke 22:30).

Dispensational theologians who are natural-religionists teach that the twelve Apostles of the Lamb were the only truly valid apostles. They believe that when the apostles cast lots to determine who would take Apostle Judas' position as one of the Twelve after Judas forsook his apostleship, they were premature in their actions. They teach that God intended the Apostle Paul to fill that position. They say that the Twelve (including Paul) were chosen to lay the foundation of the New Testament Church and to write the Bible. After that was accomplished, there was no longer a need for apostles (they also include prophets as no longer being needed). They dispensationally deplete them into a non-active foundation. They also declare that there was no longer a need for the supernatural works of the Holy Spirit. They further state that miracles, healings, speaking in tongues, casting out devils—in fact, all supernatural manifestations—were to confirm the validity of the Church as an institution ordained of God. They conclude that, after the New Testament Church was established in the first century and the Bible was written, there was no further need of apostles and prophets or supernatural manifestations.

Praise God that born-again, Spirit-filled church theologians believe that the life and ministry of Jesus and all that happened in the book of Acts are the blueprint and pattern for the Church from the day of Pentecost to the Second Coming of Jesus. The works that Jesus did we are to do also, and even greater works (John 14:12). Jesus Christ is the same yesterday, today and forever (Heb. 13:8). All that was in the book of Acts is to be happening in the Church today. Jesus only has one Church.

The Church is still under the headship of Christ and is the same corporate Church Body that He birthed on the day of Pentecost. All fivefold ministers that were actively ministering then are to be actively ministering now. All the supernatural manifestations that were active then are to be manifested now in the present Church.

Body of Christ Members Who Are Apostles. There are more apostles of the Church than the original twelve Apostles of the Lamb. The Scriptures state that all true Christians are members of Christ's Church, which is called the Body of Christ. All are members but not all have the same calling and ministry. Some have special names that designate their position and function within the Body of Christ.

When people speak of the eye of the human body, they know its position in the body and its function. The same would be true if one said hand, nose, heart, foot or any other well-known member of the body. God made some of the members of the Body of Christ to be apostles. They are to have a certain position and function in the Body. They are a vital part of its life and function. They have been hidden members for centuries within the Church. The rest of the Body of Christ is not familiar with their position or function. God is in the process of revealing the function of the apostles and placing them back into their proper position within the Body of Christ. Please take note that GOD is the one who set the ministry of APOSTLES and PROPHETS in His Church, not theologians or church leaders. God set them in and He has never removed them. They are now in the process of being fully restored to their rightful recognition, function and position within the Church. Apostles are valid members and ministries within the Body of Christ. "Now ye are the body of Christ, and members in particular. And **God hath set** some in the church, first apostles, secondarily prophets..." (1 Cor. 12:27-28).

After Christ Jesus was resurrected, He ascended back to heaven and birthed the corporate Body of Christ called "the Church." He gave all the life, power and ministries that He had manifested in His personal body while on earth to that corporate Body. He told them that He was sending them forth into the world with the same authority and commission that the Father had given Him (John 17:18). To some He gave the divine enablement to be and to manifest His headship ministry. He gifted some to represent His apostolic office and anointing as He had gifted some to be and manifest His pastoral office and anointing.

Technically speaking, the fivefold ministries are not gifts of the Holy Spirit but gifts of Christ Himself to His Church. These ministers do not just have a gift but become the very embodiment and manifestation of that nature and grace of Christ. He gave some to BE apostles, not just have an occasionally functioning gift of an apostle. Apostles are to minister as ambassadors of Christ—being the apostolic ministry that Jesus would be if He were here personally. They are representing His apostolic ministry to the Church here on earth.

These five mentioned are referred to as fivefold ministers or ministries, administrative offices, governmental ministries, headship ministries and ascension gift ministries.

> *But to each one of us grace was given according to the measure of **Christ's gift**. Therefore He says: "When He ascended on high, He led captivity captive, and gave gifts to men." ... And **He Himself gave** some to be **apostles**, some **prophets**, some **evangelists**, and some **pastors** and **teachers*** (Eph. 4:7-8,11, NKJV).

Special Ministries and Abilities of Apostles.

Apostles Are Special Ambassadors for Christ. Apostle Paul declared, "We are ambassadors for Christ" (2 Cor. 5:20). Generally speaking, all Christians are to be ambassadors for Christ representing His saving grace. However, the word "apostle" has the meaning of an official ambassador of Jesus Christ. Paul introduced most of his epistles as "Paul, an apostle of Jesus Christ by the will of God..." (Col. 1:1; Eph. 1:1). It would have been the same if he had said, "Paul, an ambassador of Jesus Christ by the authorization of God Himself."

An Apostle is a Special Commissioner of Christ Jesus.
Apostles have the delegated authority to represent the kingdom of God in a governmental, official capacity. It is not a religious hierarchical authority given by man but a spiritual
authority given by Christ. The spirit realm recognizes this
authority within the apostles who are not just "called to be"
but who have matured to the place of wisdom and ministry
and have been divinely commissioned to the office of apostle.
This is one reason why the demonic spirit world will fight
with all they have to keep the apostles from coming forth.

They especially do not want the apostles and prophets,
who have a similar commission and much of the same anointing and authority, to be fully restored and joined together in
unity. Hell shudders at the very thought of such a thing happening. And they become frantic when they think all fivefold
ministers would unite together against the forces of hell. They
throw up their hands in despair when they think of all Church
members and all fivefold ministers becoming unified in Jesus
Christ to fulfill His purpose. These three steps of unity are
predestined to happen and when they do, all demons will be
cast into the lake of fire and the kingdom of God will be established on planet Earth and in all the heavenly realms around
the earth.

Apostles Are Miracle Workers With Signs and Wonders.

*Truly the **signs of an apostle** were wrought among you
in all patience, in signs, and wonders, and mighty
deeds* (2 Cor. 12:12).

*And fear came upon every soul: and many **wonders
and signs** were done by the **apostles*** (Acts 2:43).

*And **with great power gave the apostles witness** of the
resurrection of the Lord Jesus: and great grace was
upon them all* (Acts 4:33).

> *And by the **hands of the apostles** were many **signs and wonders** wrought among the people...* (Acts 5:12).

The apostles who have been commissioned by Jesus and released into their apostolic calling will have miracles, signs and wonders following their ministry. The only possible exceptions would be those who are still in the stage of "called to be" but have not "become" mature enough in their faith, character and ministry for God to commission them to "be" an apostle. It is like a girl who is "called to be" a mother but will not have the recognition and signs of motherhood until she attains maturity, marriage, conception and births a baby. Anyone who has had prophetic utterances over them declaring they have the calling of an apostle or an apostolic anointing should make manifestations of the miraculous a priority in their life. They should not begin to think about their title or position but about the power of God. Their thinking should not be, "Who am I to father in the Lord?" or "Over how many churches am I to be the overseer?" A young apostle's privileges, position, recognition and prestige will not come by promoting the fact that he is called to be an apostle but by his ability to demonstrate the wisdom, power and wonders of God. Likewise, older apostles who have attained a high position of leadership and administration in the Body of Christ should not rely on their position in the church world to maintain their apostleship before God but continue manifesting the miraculous.

Any apostle who is not believing for signs, wonders, and miracles in his ministry is walking short of his apostolic authority and anointing. Part of the Biblical meaning that the Apostle Paul gave to the word "apostle" is miraculous manifestations, and they are embodied within the name. It is like saying, "I have the gift of the Holy Spirit but cannot speak in other tongues," or a person saying, "I have been born of the Holy Spirit but I don't have any fruit of the Holy Spirit in my life."

Over the last 40 years I have prophesied to hundreds of ministers that their calling is that of an apostle. Many are now ministering in the mighty anointing of the apostle. Some of them have a worldwide ministry and are seen regularly on Christian television. Others are pastoring large churches and some of them are overseers of many ministers. Some heard the personal prophetic word and believed it was God; but because of a lack of understanding and recognition of the apostolic ministry, they have not pressed on to seeing a complete fulfillment of their apostolic calling.

Regardless of what type of an apostle one may be, the "signs of an apostle" should be manifest. A person claiming to be an apostle who cannot demonstrate supernatural miracles in his ministry is like a person claiming to be a prophet but can't prophesy; claiming to be an evangelist but can't preach the gospel or win souls to Jesus; or claiming to be an anointed minstrel but can't play any musical instrument or sing. The new breed of Joshua Generation apostles will move in the miraculous and definitely manifest the signs of the apostle. Paul said that those "signs" included patience, humility and wisdom in the person's character and the miraculous in his or her ministry.

Apostolic Maturity vs. Apostolic Ministry.

I believe that sufficient scriptural examples have been given to prove that the supernatural should be manifested in every true apostle. Like coins or paper currency they must have both sides complete to be usable money. There is the miraculous ministry side and the manhood maturity side. Both are equally important for manifesting the fullness of whatever God ordains for a person. Christlike character is absolutely essential for eternal relationship with Jesus Christ. One can make it to heaven without manifesting miracles, but not without the righteous character of Christ. This should be understood by all as a basic reality. At this point, we are not discussing the differences between earthly ministry manifestations and heavenly reward, but the present requirements to be a true apostle of Jesus Christ.

Fruits and Gifts Come From the Same Holy Spirit. However, gifts are given and fruit is grown. Gifts are given fully complete and ready for manifestation. Though the gift is complete, the person receiving it must know all its uses and then become proficient in using the gift. It is like receiving the gift of a computer from someone. The computer is complete and ready for use but the person receiving it must become knowledgeable of its abilities and then practice until he or she is capable of manifesting all the abilities of the gift received. It is the same for the gift of eternal life, gifts of the Holy Spirit and the fivefold ascension gifts of Christ. Gifts of God are manifested the same way they are received, by the unmerited grace of God and the faith of the person to receive. They are not given or manifested on the basis of the person's worthiness. Divine gifts are received and manifested by grace and faith alone. The ideal would be for gifts to operate from the fruit of the Spirit, and miraculous ministry from Christlike character. The reality is that God put these divine gifts in earthen vessels that are imperfect (2 Cor. 4:7). Apostle Peter manifested the miraculous for years before his doctrine and character were perfected.

How Can These Things Be? One of the biggest dilemmas in the Church is how saints and ministers can manifest the miraculous and yet be unrighteous in areas of their life. I have had hundreds of people ask, "How can these things be?" How can spiritual gifts and supernatural manifestations of God operate in imperfect people? Some could understand God's using people who are immature, but people practicing immorality was another thing. During almost half a century of involvement with saints and ministers who manifest the supernatural,

I became knowledgeable of the following. Many ministers were successful in mighty ministries but had on-going problems with such things as adultery, drunkenness, sexual perversion, dishonesty, pride and every work of the flesh mentioned in the Bible. How does this work? We must understand the basics of how this works if we are to be able to discern between the false and the true. Just because a person can manifest the supernatural in prophetic and apostolic ministry does not guarantee that his or her doctrine is right or personal life is Christlike. Never be swayed to believe that a man's teaching and revelations are all correct just because he can manifest the miraculous. There have been evangelists who have had millions saved through their ministry while at the same time they were committing immoral acts in their personal life. Pastors have nurtured and blessed many while during the same time they were struggling with an ungodly habit. Prophets have prophesied to hundreds, giving them accurate words from God, while at the same time having serious character flaws in their lives.

Remember that Balaam prophesied true words from God to Israel and gave the only Messianic prophecy in the book of Numbers. He was true in his ministry but false in his personal life. Apostles can build mighty works with their supernatural ministry and gifted ability but have ungodly activities in their lives. I knew a mighty apostle in the 1960's who oversaw four hundred ministers, was married with four teenage children, and spoke at conferences around the world, but it was revealed and proven that he had a serious problem with homosexuality. How can these things be? It would require a whole book to cover this from every area but let us look at a couple of reasons why these things can and do go on in the church world.

God Confirms His Word Not Ministers! "And they went forth, and preached every where, the Lord working with them, and **confirming the word** with signs following. Amen"

(Mark 16:20). God confirms His Word with salvation of souls, prophetic utterances and apostolic ministry, but that does not mean that He is confirming that the minister is right in all of his life and doctrine.

God backs up His Word regardless of the person that is speaking it. He confirms His Word not the worker. The Holy Spirit works with God's Word regardless of the person speaking the Word. The gospel of Jesus Christ, not the person speaking it, is the power of God unto salvation (Rom. 1:16). **Ministers should never assume that God is pleased with their lifestyle and beliefs just because they are having successful ministry of salvations, miracles and financial prosperity.** God will confirm His Word for whoever will preach the truth. This is one insight into how these things can be happening in the Church without God bringing immediate exposure and judgment.

Tares and wheat grow together in one person until the time of harvest. Judgment is now beginning at the house of God and individual temples (1 Pet. 4:17). Ministers will either allow God to take the tares and bad fish out of them or He will take the ministers out of His ministry (Matt. 13:30).

Gifts Are Given Not Loaned. Several Scriptures emphatically declare that gifts are given. It never says that they are lent. A divine gift given to a person is God putting into that person's spirit a supernatural ability, whether it is one of the nine gifts of the Holy Spirit or one of the ascension gifts of Christ. It is a supernatural grace (divine enablement) given to the person. Just as the natural body was given special abilities to hear, see, think, use muscle power, etc., in like manner God gives to the spirit of man certain abilities to prophesy, work miracles, heal the sick and preach. When God gave me the ascension gift of "prophet" He enabled my spirit to have the ability to perceive the heart and mind of God and to speak it forth. It became a part of my being, my new man in Christ Jesus. It is the same with giving His gift of the apostle. The ability abides there twenty-four hours a day, seven days a week. The Holy Spirit gave me the **gift** to pray with my spirit directly to God without my natural understanding directing it. This gift can be used anywhere at any time I feel it is appropriate and timely. My spirit has been given that gifted ability. Apostle Paul declared that when he prayed in his unknown tongue, it was his divinely enabled spirit praying (1 Cor. 14:14-15).

Fruit Is Given as a Seed. The measure (seed) of faith is given to every Christian. All the fruits of the Holy Spirit are impregnated into the Spirit-born Christian. It is our responsibility to water that seed with prayer, to cultivate it with obedience, and to activate and exercise that fruit until it becomes a fully ripened fruitful character of Christ in our lives. All plant, animal and human life starts as a small seed, grows to sprouting or birthing and then proceeds to full maturity. New Testament ministers of the Spirit and life of God can lay hands on saints and impart, from the anointing within, the various graces and gifts of God. But ministers cannot lay hands on saints and impart mature character of faithfulness, patience, wisdom, love and all the fruits of the Spirit and character of Christ. If I had that power every pastor and Christian leader would be calling me to come and impart that to their elders, deacons and saints. Mature fruit comes only after many seasons of life experiences and providential happenings in our lives (Rom. 12:3; Gal. 5:22; 2 Cor. 3:6).

An Example: In the late 1970's God supernaturally provided the down payment for us to buy some property for our ministry headquarters. One year later we were not able to meet the annual payment. All of it reverted back to the previous owners. I went through six months of self-incrimination and discouragement.

Like Elijah, I was in the cave of despair. God would speak "through me" to people but He wouldn't talk "to me" during that period of time. Finally, after many months of condemning and blaming myself for losing that property, and asking God numerous times why it happened that way, He answered with this word. He said, "Bill Hamon, that property and money were the tuition price I paid for your schooling for wisdom and maturity. I can give you land, property and money overnight. But I cannot give you wisdom and maturity overnight. I can give you popularity and success in a short time but I cannot instantly give you the wisdom and maturity to handle that success and popularity." He went on to explain to me how godly wisdom, character, integrity and maturity come through a process of time and providential life experiences. The thing that clinched it and delivered me from self-condemnation was when He said that if it had been property and buildings worth millions of dollars, He would have gladly sacrificed it all for my wisdom and maturity in Him. Hallelujah, the truth makes one free.

The Spirit and Character of Last-Day Apostles. Many books will be written on the spirit, attributes, character and ministries of true apostles. Let it suffice to say here that the new breed of apostles will be motivated by the Spirit of Wisdom as described in James 3:17. They will minister in the faith that works by love (Gal. 5:6). Their character will be in line with the fruits of the Holy Spirit (Gal. 5:22). Their attitudes, actions and relationships with others will be according to the attributes of agape-love as revealed in First Corinthians 13. All of their "10 M's" of Manhood, Ministry, Message, Maturity, Marriage, Methods, Manners, Money, Morality and Motive will be working in their lives according to God's divine order. It would require several books to cover every point in all these categories just mentioned. The true apostles and prophets arising in this new day and hour will have most of these Biblical realities within their life and ministry.

Mature Apostles Are Fathers: Mature human fathers are more concerned about their children's well-being and success than their own. True prophetic and apostolic fathers are more interested in seeing those they are fathering come into their ministry than in magnifying their own ministry. The apostles with a true fathering anointing are selfless and self-sacrificing for those who look to them as their spiritual overseer. The true apostles will be more "other" oriented than "self" oriented.

When I was a young minister in my twenties, I used to wonder what those older ministers meant by the word "maturity." I felt I was as mature as most ministers. I could preach, prophesy, and had revelation and anointing. I was steadfast in my calling and never wavered from pursuing my destiny. Now some forty years later I believe there is a better comprehension of maturity. Basically it is the difference between a young single man and one who is married with several children. It is the difference between a child and an adult. The differences between one who is striving to be and one who has become.

The difference in all of these illustrations of maturity is whether the person is in chapter 6, 7 or 8 of Romans. They are the three "S" chapters of "Sin, Self and Spirit." Those who are not mature fathers are still stuck in chapter 7 where in twenty-six verses the "SELF" pronouns of "Me, My, Myself and I" are repeated more than fifty times. Those who are still children in ministry and Christian maturity are still in the "My" syndrome. Their concerns and conversations center around I, Me and My. They continually talk about "My Ministry," and I want to do this and I want to do that. I have my rights. I have to find myself. Give me room to find my ministry. There is no condemnation for a person being in that growing-up stage of their life. It becomes a real problem when older saints and ordained ministers never grow out of that stage of their life. Those who must have everything and everyone revolving around them to help meet their need for their personal desires and ambitions will not be the apostolic fathers who will be God's designated leaders in these last days. They must come out of the self chapter and enter into chapter 8 where in thirty-nine verses there are only two self pronouns and the Godhead of Father, Son and Holy Spirit are mentioned fifty-seven times. Let us all strive to become more oriented in God and others than in self. May God raise up millions of mature fathers of the Faith to nurture the multimillions that are coming into the Church. May He raise up apostolic fathers who will be true fathers to the great company of fivefold ministers that are being brought forth to equip His Church.

—●●●●●●●—

4

APOSTLES AND CHURCH DOCTRINE

—●●●●●●●—

Holy Apostles Determine and Establish Correct Doctrine.

And they continued steadfastly in the apostles' doctrine... (Acts 2:42).

Read Acts 15:1-35. (You must read all these verses to get the complete picture of what happened and what contribution Peter, Paul and James made that helped establish the truth on this doctrinal issue.)

And certain men came down from Judea and taught the brethren, "Unless you are circumcised according to the custom of Moses, you cannot be saved." Therefore, when Paul and Barnabas had no small dissension and dispute with them, they determined that Paul and Barnabas and certain others of them should go up to Jerusalem, to the apostles and elders, about this question. ... And when they had come to Jerusalem, they were received by the church and the apostles and the elders; and they reported all things that God had done with them. But some of the sect of the Pharisees who believed rose up, saying, "It is necessary to circumcise them, and to command them to keep the law of Moses."

Now the apostles and elders came together to consider this matter (Acts 15:1-6, NKJV).

They settled the issue after a long discussion. They gave doctrinal directives and made it into a letter. Trustworthy men with proven ministries, who had participated in the decision-making process, were chosen to deliver the letter and exhort the Antioch church concerning its content. They designated four men whom they felt were capable of laying this doctrinal stone in the foundation of the New Testament church at Antioch. The four ambassadors of truth were made up of two apostles, Barnabas and Paul, and two prophets, Judas-Barsabas and Silas.

Then it pleased the apostles and elders, with the whole church, to send chosen men of their own company to Antioch with Paul and Barnabas, namely, **Judas** *who was also named Barsabas, and Silas,* **leading men among the brethren.** *... We have therefore sent Judas and Silas, who will also report the same things by word of mouth. For it seemed good to the Holy Spirit, and to us, to lay upon you no greater burden than these necessary things: ... Now* **Judas and Silas,** *themselves* **being prophets** *also, exhorted and strengthened the brethren with many words* (Acts 15:22, 27-28, 32, NKJV).

Who Is James? Who Are the Apostles and Elders?

THE APOSTLES: At this time in the history of the Church most of the Twelve Apostles were still headquartering in Jerusalem. So it is fairly safe to say that they were the majority of the apostles to whom the delegation from Antioch came to present this controversy concerning a major doctrinal issue.

JAMES: He was not one of the Twelve but the natural brother of Jesus. He is referred to as an apostle by Paul, "But I saw none of the other apostles except James, the Lord's brother"

(Gal. 1:19, NKJV). He was senior pastor of the Jerusalem church. This shows the respect and position he had attained since Peter and many of the other twelve probably made that their local church home. He is the one who wrote the book of James in the New Testament. He became a believer when Jesus appeared to him after His resurrection (1 Cor. 15:7). He had years of proven ministry and was held in great esteem by all the other apostles and elders.

THE ELDERS: The scriptures do not give a detailed accounting of the names of the elders present and what fivefold ministry they represented. One reason might be that there was no understanding of the fivefold ministry at that time. Paul didn't write the Ephesus letter until many years later. Paul is the only New Testament writer who seems to have had a revelation on there being five separately named eldership ministries. The Twelve Apostles were viewed by the Church as the standard bearers of what the Church was supposed to be, do and teach. No doubt all fivefold ministers were present. We know there were major prophets there because Prophet Judas and Prophet Silas were chosen to accompany Paul and Barnabas back to Antioch to deliver the decree from the church council at Jerusalem. All translations bring out that they were recognized as major leaders with the apostles and elders in Jerusalem. So we do not want to be guilty of saying apostles are the only ones qualified to make decisions on major issues that affect the corporate Church of Jesus Christ. It is definitely not a ministry for novices regardless of their fivefold calling. It is reserved for men and women of maturity with years of proven ministry who meet all the qualifications of ministerial elders.

Apostles, Prophets, Fivefold & Elders Determining Doctrine.

Those who have been involved in the ministry for decades have discovered several guidelines with regard to apostles, fivefold eldership ministers and doctrine. Let us now discover what part all these apostles, prophets, elders, visions and ministerial and life experiences play in determining major decisions that affect the foundation and function of the Body of Christ.

First of all, fivefold ministers are the headship directors for establishing Biblical principles, teachings and church doctrine. New Testament doctrine was established by proper revelation and application of the Logos Scripture, which was the Old Testament at that time. There was no collection of writings by the apostles or church prophets that was acknowledged as equal to the writing of the Old Testament prophets and the Law of Moses. Church order, doctrine and practices were not established by prophecy, visions, dreams or personal spiritual experiences of any private individual (2 Pet. 1:20). Doctrine that would be applicable to the whole Church was not determined by one great apostle, who could make papal decrees that would become binding doctrine for the whole Church. The scriptures dealing with the Council at Jerusalem show that apostles, prophets, visions and personal experiences are Biblical means that the Holy Spirit can use to gain our attention, enlighten our understanding or prepare us to receive a doctrinal truth that God is about to reveal. But such personal spiritual experiences should not be the sole basis for formulating a doctrine. Thank God! The Bible does give an example of how major doctrinal issues were settled.

The Church Council at Jerusalem: Consider the example of the first church council in Jerusalem, which met to resolve the doctrinal issue concerning whether Gentile Christians should be required to follow the Abrahamic covenant and Mosaic law of circumcision. God's process for the acceptance and establishment of this doctrine was as follows: Peter told them about the vision he had received while praying. That vision and

God's application to it adjusted Apostle Peter's attitude and opened up his spirit to do something contrary to his old religious convictions and beliefs. He then related to them how he went to Cornelius' Gentile household in obedience to the vision, the personal Rhema word of God and the coinciding invitation of the two men sent by Cornelius who had been instructed by an angel to ask for Peter (Acts 10:1-18).

Cornelius' household received the forgiveness of sins and the gift of the Holy Spirit, evidenced by speaking in unknown tongues just as the Jewish Christians had done. This sovereign spiritual experience convinced Peter they should also be baptized in water.

Then Paul and Barnabas shared what they had experienced while traveling together in ministry. They emphasized how God was sovereignly causing many Gentiles to respond to the gospel and how the Holy Spirit was enabling them to receive salvation, the gift of the Holy Spirit, healing and miracles without becoming proselyte Jews first.

Validated testimonies from reputable ministers do influence decisions being made on vital issues of the Church. At the council in Jerusalem, Peter gave his testimony of his vision and angelic visitation and the sovereign move of God at Cornelius' house. Barnabas and Paul gave their testimony of the Holy Spirit sovereignly bestowing all the benefits of Christianity on the Gentiles, apart from the Mosaic law. These testimonies, visions and supernatural experiences were eye openers and served as a witness and confirming evidence. But it was not until Senior Pastor Apostle James received a revelation and application of a scripture from the Logos that the issue was settled and written into established doctrine for the New Testament Church (Acts 15:1-35).

One Person Cannot Dictate Doctrine. No one man or ministry should establish a doctrine as essential belief and practice for all Christians. Paul declared that he received his revelation on this matter directly from God in the Arabian desert and was not given this truth from the original apostles. Paul was confident that the truth he was preaching was from God, but was not too proud or self-important to submit it to the recognized top leadership in the Church. He did not see himself as the only one who had the true message of the gospel. He did not preach it as an absolute church doctrine and send letters to establish it until he had met with the apostles and other fivefold ministers. No one should ever think of himself as so great or sovereign in the Body of Christ that he believes he doesn't have a need to submit his teachings and beliefs to other key present-truth apostles, prophets and other fivefold ministries (Gal. 1:11-18).

Apostolic Church Councils to Come in the 1990's. I personally believe that in the 1990's and into the 21st century, as prophets and apostles are being restored back to proper order and function within the Church, many of these church councils of leading present-truth ministers will be necessary. One particular apostle or prophet or camp will never receive the whole revelation for the establishing of prophets and apostles back into the Church.

Many will have visions (even of Jesus), dreams, rhemas, angelic visitations and supernatural personal experiences and sovereign moves of the Holy Spirit in their meetings. But doctrines that claim to be binding on all Christians must not be established by only one apostle, prophet or camp. There must be meetings of a church council with other leaders of past and present **restorational** streams of truth.

Five Principles for Establishing Doctrine. When the fivefold ministers come together to consider doctrines and practices this way, they will need to keep several areas of insight in mind: (1) the claimed revelation from God; (2) the fruit of the ministry among those who have received the doctrine or practice; (3) the supernatural working of God accompanying

it; (4) the Logos and Rhema word of God application and
authority for the doctrine or practice; and (5) the witness of
the Spirit and the unified consent of those present.

No Popes. In the meantime, we may say, "As for me and my
house"—declaring what our own fellowship or family will
believe and practice. But we must not present it in such a way
to imply that those who do not believe and worship the same
way are out of order or in error. This is not the prerogative of
one person—neither the Catholic pope nor a Charismatic,
Kingdom, Faith, Prophetic or Apostolic pope.

Each person and fellowship has a responsibility to follow
their own revelations, convictions and practices, but not to impose them upon the corporate Body of Christ. Such presumptuous declarations, teachings and actions cause divisions in
the Body of Christ. Every erroneous Christian religious group
has established certain doctrines and practices that are unique
to themselves. This then makes them an exclusive, seclusive,
"elected" group that sees itself as superior to all others.

Exclusivism Leads to Cults. The manifestations of this attitude are seen in the extreme groups that arose during the time
of the Holiness and Pentecostal Movements: Mormons, Christian Scientists and Jehovah Witnesses. But sad to say, there
are also some on the extreme right that are still counted as
"mainline" Christian denominations who believe they are the
only true people of God. They base this conviction on a certain baptism formula, way of worship, church order or some
other unique doctrine or practice.

No One Man or Group Has It All. The New Testament
Scriptures emphatically and repeatedly declare that Christ has
only one Church here on planet Earth. No denomination, fellowship or restoration camp makes up the entirety of the
Church. Every born-again, blood washed, sanctified child of

God is a member of Christ's Church. They may be Charismatic Catholics, Evangelicals, Pentecostals, Prophetic People or Present-Truth Apostolic people. We are only parts of the whole and members in particular of the corporate Body of Christ. All truth and life are found in the whole, not just in one particular part or member. We need each other and will never come to maturity and fullness of truth without each other. The new wine is in the cluster—not just in one individual grape (Is. 65:8).

5

APOSTLES & PROPHETS
AND FIVEFOLD MINISTRIES

The Relationship of the Apostles and Prophets to the Other Fivefold Ministers. The Lord revealed to me in the mid 1980's that many extremes would come in the swing of the pendulum of restoration truth concerning prophets and apostles. So I have been making an intensified study throughout Scripture, church history and present-day writings, joined with much prayer for illumination on Scripture and even revelation from Christ, concerning His proper order for the function and interrelationship of His fivefold ministers.

Most of the writings and teachings of this century are based only on the knowledge and experience of our present limited status—that is, with the majority of the church only recognizing three of the five offices: pastor, evangelist and teacher. All present ministerial church order, structure and relationships have been determined by that perspective. Now, however, sufficient room and proper structure must be made for the function and ministry of the apostles and prophets.

We Have Not Passed This Way Before. All present-day ministers, and especially those who will be moving in present-truth revelation, must be open, teachable and adjustable to the Holy Spirit educating us more perfectly in this way. We must follow the admonition of Joshua to the leaders and people of Israel when they were about to enter their promised Canaan Land. They were to sanctify themselves and watch for the moving of the ark of God by the priests. Then when they saw it begin to move, they were to "go after it"! (Josh. 3: 1-3) Joshua emphasized that they had to follow the leadership who was following the Lord so that they might know the way that they must go, "for ye have not passed this way heretofore" (verse 4). In the same way we, the present-day Church, have never passed this way in the history of the restoration of the Church. We have never functioned with the full restoration of all five offices—apostles, prophets, evangelists, pastors and teachers.

One Ministry Restored Each Decade. We explain in another chapter how the Holy Spirit has been commissioned to bring all five of Christ's ascension gift ministries to proper order, authority, position and ministry. We also show that the last fifty years of the 20th century were designated as the time for that to be accomplished, with each ten-year period being used to restore one of the five. During that decade a particular ascension gift ministry would be brought forth to be clarified, amplified and magnified within the Church. That fivefold ministry would be brought forth in one decade and fully established within the Church during the following decade. Then, each restored ministry would continue to grow and function until it was fully understood, accepted and established in its God-ordained role.

The First Shall Be Last and the Last, First. God revealed to me the reason for choosing the particular order in which He was restoring the fivefold ministers. His divine principle of "the first shall be last and the last, first" has determined the order of restoration (Matt. 19:30; 20:16; 1 Cor. 12:28). When

God first set the fivefold ministers in the Church, His chronological order of establishing them was this: **first apostles, second prophets, third teachers, fourth pastors** and **fifth evangelists**. Now during these five decades of reestablishing the fivefold ministries and setting them back in proper order, the Holy Spirit is starting with the last that was established and is step by step working His way back to the first: first, the evangelist in the 1950's; second, the pastor in the 1960's; third, the teacher in the 1970's; fourth, the prophet in the 1980's; and finally, the apostle in the 1990's.

God's First Order of Establishing the Fivefold Ministries.
When Christ originally established the ascension gift ministries in the Church, first came the **apostles** who followed Jesus for more than three years. Second, the New Testament **prophets** were brought forth, and together the two foundational ministries of the apostle and prophet laid the foundation of the Church with proper structure doctrinally and spiritually. Third, the **teachers** were set in to ground the saints in these truths until they were fully established as New Testament churches. Apostle and prophet teams then set **pastors** and pastoral elders over the churches to guard, feed and lead the flock of believers like a shepherd (Acts 15:32; 16:4,18,25; 2 Cor. 1:19; 2 Thess. 1:1; Acts 20:28). After the churches were doctrinally founded and structured into proper church order with a pastor, elders and deacons, then **evangelists** were sent out from the local church. They were sent forth by the Holy Spirit from the local church in a way similar to how Philip, "the deacon turned into an evangelist," went out from the church in Jerusalem to Samaria and conducted that great evangelistic campaign. The evangelists not only went to unreached areas but they also went to churches to encourage the saints and to keep them renewed in Christ's final commission on world evangelism and making disciples in all nations (Acts 8:15; 6:5; Matt. 28:19).

No Final Church Structure Until Apostles Restored. God's divine order and structure for the functioning, authority and relationship of the fivefold ministry will not be fully revealed and established until after that fifty-year period has brought forth the full restoration and unity of all five ministers. The reality of this revelation implies that not one minister alive today sees the whole picture in proper perspective. We each have and demonstrate only different pieces of the puzzle. The whole will not be fully seen, understood and established until every puzzle piece is placed in the picture. Only Jesus has the box cover with the whole picture on it. We are individual pieces in the box and on the table. The pastor, evangelist and teacher pieces have been placed in their general area on the table; the prophet pieces have been taken out of the box and are being examined to determine where they go; the apostle pieces are just now beginning to be brought out of the box in the 1990's. So all systems and structures established before the year 2000 will be limited and temporary.

Transition and Progression to Full Revelation. In the current situation, it is as if all the ministries were dominoes, and we each have a hand of them that represents our revelation of fivefold ministry structure and function. The Holy Spirit will tell everyone to lay down his or her own hand [fivefold ministry concept] so that He can transform them. Then we will all pick up the same hand so that we can then come forth with one revelation for structure rather than five. Consequently, we can expect a great deal of reshuffling and playing out those hands during the 90's and early part of the 21st century. Many ministers, and especially apostles, will come forth in the 90's to declare presumptuously that they have the perfect hand for playing out the role of fivefold ministries. But do not become bound or boxed in by one person's revelation. That person's hand of dominoes will have to be laid down and shuffled again before full and proper revelation comes in the beginning of the 21st century.

The Reshuffling Has Already Begun. Some ministers have already begun to establish guidelines and doctrines concerning proper structure and function for fivefold ministers. Many Pentecostal and Charismatic ministers are becoming nervous and concerned about the multitude of prophets and apostles that is arising. They do not know what to do with them and when, where and how to let them function, if at all. Some prophets are getting nervous and concerned about the restoration of apostles and are fearful that they will try to structure them into a restricted realm that God never intended. This situation is creating the potential for some extreme teaching within the Prophetic and Apostolic Movements. I hope I can offer some understanding and encourage some balance in this area. Another chapter in this book is devoted to bringing clarity to some of these potential controversies and extremes.

What Will Be the Role of the Apostles?

As we look forward to the full blossoming of the Apostolic Movement in the years to come, we need an understanding of the restored role of the apostle in the Church to help us avoid misunderstandings and extremes. In particular, we need insight into the nature of the apostle, the necessity of apostles today, the appropriate place of an apostolic ministry, the relation of apostles to doctrine and the relationship of the apostle to the other fivefold ministers.

The Nature of an Apostle. First of all, who is an apostle and what is his or her ministry? An apostle is just a person who has been divinely gifted with the nature and ability of Christ the Apostle. Jesus was able to manifest the miraculous, know the truths about His Church and the purposes of God His Father, operate in the gift of faith and discerning of spirits, lay the foundation and bring forth the revelation for His Church through His office of the apostle.

His ability to know the counsels and purposes of God for an individual life, such as Jesus did with Peter at Caesarea Philippi (Matt. 16:18), was an ability that came from His ministry as a prophet. When Christ Jesus calls and gifts a man or woman with that part of His ability, attributes and divine nature, then that person has been commissioned to the office of a prophet. Apostles will always have an ability to work miracles. They will vary in their gifts of the Holy Spirit, but they primarily move in the gifts of healing, faith, working of miracles, word of wisdom, discerning of spirits and sometimes prophecy.

The two apostles for whom we have the most examples of apostolic ministry are Peter and Paul. They both manifested the miraculous, which would be the power gifts. Ministers and other saints who are not called to the office of an apostle may manifest one or more of these gifts, but there is a difference in their anointing, authority and level of function. Apostles and prophets both prophesy the mind and counsel of God. However, a saint ministering with the gift of prophecy to a congregation is limited to the general activity of that gift, which is edification, exhortation and comfort (1 Cor. 14:3). Not everyone who prophesies is a prophet and not everyone who manifests the miraculous is an apostle. The apostles and prophets, when ministering within their gifted office and prophetic anointing, have the same authority for reproving, correcting, directing and instructing in the Rhema word of the Lord as the pastors, evangelists and teachers have in their teaching, counseling and preaching with the Logos Word.

How Does Someone Become an Apostle or Prophet? A person does not call or appoint him or herself to any of the ascension gift ministries. This is strictly the personal prerogative and gift of Christ Himself. Each minister needs to know what his or her ascension gift office is in the Body of Christ. After years of research, life experience, scriptural study and personal involvement in the ministry, I have concluded that a person initially has one major calling and divine enablement to fully manifest one of the five administrative offices of apostle, prophet, evangelist, pastor or teacher. Some ministers believe that you graduate from one fivefold ministry to another and I grant allowance for that possibility. That person may be required to do the work and fill the position of any of the other four at one time or another in his or her life. These other ministerial activities will be used by the Lord to mature that person in his or her specific calling.

Consider two examples from Scripture. Jeremiah was called to be a prophet from his mother's womb (Jer. 1:5). In the case of Paul, numerous scriptures state that he was "called to be an apostle." Ten of his epistles start with a statement acknowledging his call to be an apostle (for example, Eph. 1:1; Col. 1:1). He exhibited the fruit of an apostle. Yet he also held evangelistic campaigns and itinerated from church to church. He pastored for several months or years some of the churches that were established out of his ministry. He taught the Word of God better than most, and even wrote fourteen divinely inspired letters that became books of the New Testament. Despite these ministries, however, he never states that he was ever "called to be" a pastor, evangelist or prophet. He does declare that he was ordained as an apostle to be a preacher and a teacher of the Gentiles (1 Tim. 2:7; 2 Tim. 1:11).

One Calling or Many? When Paul was itinerating from church to church on his second journey, we would have introduced him in modern church terminology as "our visiting evangelist" or "Evangelist Paul." When he stayed in one church and taught them daily for several months, we would have referred to him as "our teacher." While he was taking the oversight of one of the churches for several months, we would have referred to him as "Pastor Paul." The fact remains, however, that though he did the ministerial work of evangelizing, teaching and pastoring—and even at times functioned like a prophet—he had one main Christ-gifted calling: that of the apostle. With few exceptions, each minister has one specific gifted calling but, at different times during a lifetime of ministry, may perform many of the fivefold ministerial functions.

My Personal Experience. Probably one of the reasons for this conclusion is that my personal experience bears out this principle. I **pastored** for six years, then traveled for three years in full-time **evangelism**, then was a **teacher** in a Bible College for five years, then founded and established the Christian International School of Theology during the mid-1960's (which some would call **apostolic** work). During all this time the **Prophet** Ministry was continually functioning within my life and ministry. I have received personal prophecies from many different people over the last forty-three years. Those which were recorded total more than one thousand pages of typewritten prophecies containing more than two hundred thousand words—enough to fill three volumes the size of this book.

These prophecies have not been from just one place or people. They have been received while ministering on almost every continent of the world. These words were prophesied by ministers representing all fivefold ascension gift ministries; by new converts and by ministers who have been ordained for more than fifty years; by male and female; by old and young. The prophecies have come from Christians in the historic denominational churches, classical Pentecostal churches, and different "camps" and fellowships, including those called by the names "Restoration," "Charismatic," "Faith," "Kingdom" and the "Prophetic." They have come from Christian men's and women's organizations such as the Full Gospel Businessmen's Fellowship International and Women's Aglow. And they have come from special ministry groups such as Teen Challenge and Maranatha Ministries. The amazing thing is that in all of these thousands of prophetic words through hundreds of people from all over the world during four decades, there has been no statement to contradict my main office and calling. For the first twenty years of ministry the prophecies spoke only of the office of a **prophet**. However, in the last twenty years there have been as many prophecies about being an **apostle** as about being a **prophet**. When I first started receiving prophecies about my having an apostolic anointing, a ministry of the apostle and many other similar expressions, I just figured they were prophesying that to me because of their understanding of what an apostle did and what a prophet did. The position I held as head of five major ministries and the preaching and teaching I was doing was more in line with what they thought only apostles did. But when the prophecies kept coming, even from people who did not know me personally, I had to start reevaluating my attitude and theology. I had to adjust my rigid stand on a person only having one of the fivefold ascension gifts. Though you may do the work and ministry of the other four at different times, initially you are only called to one of the fivefold, not three or five.

When God challenged me to accept the office and ministry of the apostle, I at first resisted it. I told the Lord that He was going to have to explain how this can be and how it works for it did not fit my theology concerning fivefold ministry calling and commissioning. This is what He revealed for it to be understandable and acceptable to me. Because I had been faithful to the ministry of the prophet and to raise up a company of prophets, prophetic ministers and prophetic people, He was giving me the office and anointing of the apostle to do the same thing. In 1994, I accepted His prophetic charge to be one of His apostles as well as His prophet.

To adjust my theology on the matter, He reminded me of His principle revealed in the use of one's talents (Matt. 25:14-30). The servants who were faithful to use and reproduce their talents were given equal and more to what they had. He revealed that because I had been faithful to use the office of the prophet and to multiply by reproducing hundreds of other prophets, He was going to make me a double-barreled shotgun. One gun barrel would be the prophet and the other the apostle. The Spirit would direct me concerning whether to pull the trigger that would release the apostle or the one that released the prophet, or whether both should be pulled at the same time. So whether we say apostolic-prophet or prophetic-apostle, or equally prophet-apostle, I know that God wants me to maintain the prophetic office and anointing while at the same time accepting and manifesting the ministry and office of the apostle.

An Apostle-Prophet? The Holy Spirit prophetically stated that this apostolic anointing was being granted for two reasons. The first reason was that I had been faithful in multiplying the prophetic anointing that had been given, so now that prophet anointing was being doubled by the addition of the apostolic anointing (Matt. 25:28-29). The second reason was that the apostolic anointing had been given for the purpose of pioneering, establishing and taking a fatherhood responsibility for the restoration and propagation of the office of the prophets and apostles.

Before I could fully accept the idea that one person could have the full anointing of two fivefold offices, the term "apostolic-prophet" was used to describe my ministerial position in the Body of Christ, specifically as it related to my position of oversight of more than five hundred ministers in our Christian International Network of Churches (CINC), vision-holder and headship of CI Network of Prophetic Ministries (CI-NPM), CI School of Theology (CIST), CI Business Network (CIBN), CI Family Church (CIFC), CI Family Worship Center (CIFWC)—Central U.S. headquarters for CI as well as our international headquarters in Canada, India, England and Japan. All of these organizations have a presidential director with his own staff to manage the ministry, but I serve as bishop over all of them.

Why Use the Term "Bishop"? The main reasons I accepted the title of bishop was because it is a Biblical term and it described my position as overseer of all the ministries of Christian International. When we started raising up hundreds of prophets, some wanted to call me "Papa Prophet," "Senior Prophet" or something similar. Now, in the Apostolic, some wanted to call me "Chief Apostle," "Master Apostle," "Patriarchal Apostle" or something similar to establish the position of leader and vision-holder for the ministry. These did not convey the position of the person with the vision and overseer, but rather came across as a superior, super prophet or apostle.

Motivated by Fear or Wisdom? We are not afraid to use the names of apostle or prophet. We introduce our speakers at conferences as Prophet Smith or Apostle Jones. We do this to let everyone know that we accept and boldly propagate the fact that there are present-day prophets and apostles in the Church the same as evangelists, pastors or teachers. It was not a matter of fear, unwillingness or false humility, but a matter of wisdom and maturity with a desire to protect the office of the apostle and prophet from a wrong conception or improper presentation.

Apostles-Prophets and the Written Word. Once we understand the nature of apostles and prophets, we must consider the fundamental issue of the need for apostles and prophets in the Church today. Some theologians question whether or not there is even a place or need for them in the modern Church. They believe that there are no continuing needs for prophets and apostles today because we now have the Bible. The Bible, they say, reveals all of God's principles, ways, wisdom, word, direction and revealed will for every person. There is no further need for their revelation and foundation-laying ministry, for now the Holy Spirit is the revealer and we have the written Word of God.

Their theology is that prophets were used to write the Old Testament and apostles were used to write the New Testament. Since we have thirty-nine books in the Old Testament and twenty-seven in the New Testament that have been canonized into one Bible, they claim there is no further need for prophets and apostles.

Apostles and prophets were used for much more than writing most of the books of the Bible. The majority of the apostles never wrote letters that became Biblical books. Of the original Twelve Apostles, only three authored books: Matthew, John and Peter. Those who were not of the Twelve but who wrote books of the Bible were Mark, Luke, James, Jude and Paul. The Apostle Paul wrote fourteen of the twenty-seven books, more than all the rest put together. The Bible does not identify Mark, Luke and Jude as apostles. If God only called the Twelve Apostles and the Church apostles to write the Bible, then most of them never fulfilled their calling. But Scripture reveals that apostles and prophets were called to a continuing ministry within the Church with many more responsibilities than writing books.

Logos Word vs. Rhema Word of Apostles and Prophets. To respond, we need only to ask a question: If a divinely inspired book of instruction eliminates the need for the prophet, then why didn't God do away with the office and ministry of the prophet after Moses wrote the Pentateuch (the first five books of the Bible)? The Pentateuch contains the Law of God with detailed instructions for every area of human life. Yet even though Israel had the Law, God still continued to raise up prophets to give specific messages to leaders, nations and individuals. The priests and the Levites taught the written Word of God, but the prophets did more than read and teach the written Word, the Logos. They spoke God's present Rhema word to specific situations and needs. In fact, the prophets were more numerous and they ministered more during the fifteen centuries of the Law than during any other time in Biblical history. Yet for that period of time, the Law of Moses was the complete revealed will of God, even down to the very details of humankind's relationship to each other and to God. It was the complete written Word, the Logos for the children of Israel during the Dispensation of the Law just as the New Testament is for the Dispensation of the Church. In both dispensations, God's prophets are needed.

Apostles continued to minister after the writing of all the Epistles that became canonized into books of the New Testament. Most important is the fact that no scriptures say apostles were given to write Scripture. In fact, it says Christ Jesus gave apostles and prophets the same as evangelists, pastors and teachers:

For the equipping of the saints for the work of ministry, for the edifying of the body of Christ, till we all come to the unity of the faith and of the knowledge of the Son of God, to a perfect man, to the measure of the fullness of Christ; that we should no longer be children, tossed to and fro and carried about with every wind of doctrine, by the trickery of men, in the cunning craftiness of deceitful plotting, but, speaking the truth in love may grow up in all things into Him who is the head— Christ—from whom the whole body, joined and knit

together by what every joint supplies, according to the
effective working by which every part does its share,
causes growth of the body for the edifying of itself in
love (Eph. 4:11-16, NKJV).

Does the Holy Spirit Replace Prophets and Apostles?
Some theologians imply that the Church does not need the
ministry of the prophet and apostle today because the Holy
Spirit has been sent. Each Christian now has the Holy Spirit
within, they insist, and He illuminates them with a Rhema
when needed. Consequently, the apostle and prophet with
their anointing to give revelation Rhema words are no longer
needed, except as an inspired preacher expounding upon the
already revealed and written Word of God. If we accept that
idea as proper theology, then it would be more realistic to say
that we do not need teachers to teach the Word of God, because each Church Age saint has the Holy Spirit and a Bible.
The Bible is self explanatory and there are numerous scriptures stating that the Holy Spirit shall teach you all things,
lead you into all truth, take the things of Christ and show them
to you and be your illuminator, director, counselor and enabler
(John 16:7-15). First John 2:27a states, "But the anointing
which you have received from Him abides in you, and **you do
not need that anyone teach you**" (NKJV).

It would be much easier to make a theological argument
for doing away with the office of the teacher in the Body of
Christ than those of the prophet and apostle. If these ministers
are not needed in Christ's Church because we now have the revealed will of God written for all to read and the Holy Spirit
to personalize that Word when needed, then the same reasoning would have to eliminate from the Church not only the
teacher, but eventually all the other fivefold ministers. They
could say we do not need the evangelist; we can just give everyone a Bible and let the Holy Spirit do the work of convict-
ing and converting.

Likewise, the Church would not need apostles to do their founding and establishing ministry, because the Church has already been established by the original Twelve Apostles. Nor would the Church need pastors, for the Holy Spirit and the Bible will give direction, and Jesus is the Good Shepherd to every one of His sheep.

All Fivefold Ministers Are Still Needed. The Word of God emphatically states that the resurrected Christ gifted individuals to be apostles, prophets, evangelists, pastors and teachers. There is not one scriptural indication anywhere that any of the five have been recalled, dispensationally depleted, or removed from their Christ-appointed ministry to the Church throughout her existence on earth. Ephesians 4 declares that the fivefold representation, manifestation and personified ministry of Christ in mortal bodies will continue until every member in the Body of Christ is fully matured and equipped in their ministries so that the whole Body is edified, built up and matured (Eph. 4:11-13). Only as all five of the ascension gift ministers function fully and equally in the Church will she enter her predestined purpose of coming into the "unity of the faith, and of the knowledge of the Son of God, unto a perfect man, unto the measure of the stature of the fulness of Christ: ... [and by] speaking the truth in love, [she] may grow up into Him in all things, which is the head, even Christ" (Eph. 4:13,15).

Apostles and Prophets Are Perpetual. Each age, dispensation and covenant of God has added and dropped terminology concerning certain ministries. There was first the time of the patriarchs. Then the Law defined priests, Levites, scribes and later on kings. In the New Testament we have mention of apostles, prophets, evangelists, pastors, teachers, elders, deacons, bishops and saints. We should note here that the only ministry that can be found consistently functioning with the same name in every age and dispensation from Genesis to Revelation is that of the prophet. The prophet is the one ministry that has never been limited to any particular dispensation, age or covenant of God. The man or woman who becomes the pure expression of the mind of God to humankind is the ministry mentioned and manifested more consistently throughout the whole Bible—and that ministry is the prophet.

Apostles were called and ordained by Christ Jesus to function here on earth, from the time He chose the Twelve and called them apostles until He comes again at the end of the age of His mortal Church. Apostles and prophets are now being restored, recognized and reactivated within Christ's Church. The Prophetic Movement has been active for the last ten years. **The Apostolic Movement is now emerging.** The Apostolic along with the Prophetic Movements are bringing revolutionary ministries and truths back into the Church. Ministers and saints are going to be challenged with the apostolic and prophetic ministries and truths. Old order pastors and denominational leaders always try to protect and warn their people against the new restorational truths, ministries and spiritual experiences that the Holy Spirit is bringing forth in Christ's Church. There are only three options for our response to new truth: We can persecute it, be passive about it or participate and propagate the new restorational truths and ministries. Personally, I never want to be found resisting or fighting any new thing that Christ Jesus is doing within His Church.

—••••••••—

6

CALLING VS. COMMISSIONING
OF APOSTLES OR PROPHETS

—••••••••—

"Behold therefore the goodness and severity of God"
(Rom. 11:22a). This scripture reveals the nature of God and
His dealings with His own children. His goodness and mercy
are shown in Him, sovereignly calling us into His kingdom. It
was God's love for the world and Christ's love and desire to
have a Church/Bride, consisting of multimillions of members,
that revealed the goodness of God. All of His members are to
work together to fulfill Christ's overall purpose for His
Church. The scriptures clearly teach that members of Christ's
Church do not choose their membership ministry within the
Body of Christ. Nor do ministers call themselves to a fivefold
ministry of their own choosing. Jesus told the Twelve Apostles: "Ye have not chosen Me, but I have chosen you, and ordained you" (John 15:16a).

The gifts and callings of God are based on His sovereignty,
not on human worthiness or persistence in requesting a position. Hours of prayer and weeks of fasting will show our desire and dedicated determination to be whatever God has

called us to be and to become. But it will not buy a certain position in the Body of Christ or force God to give us a ministry that He did not genetically design us to fulfill when He conceived and birthed us into His many-membered Church Body. The principle that Apostle Paul revealed when he said, "Behold therefore the goodness and severity of God," applies to all of God's children who have a membership ministry in His corporate Body. It also applies to His ascension gifts given to those who are to stand and minister in His office of apostle, prophet, evangelist, pastor or teacher.

The goodness of God is manifested in the **gifts and callings He freely gives**. Our gifts of eternal life, the Holy Spirit and membership ministry are not based on who we are or what we have done but who God is and what He has done for us. His **severity** is revealed in **the process of His severe training** to make us ready to be **commissioned** to our divine **calling**.

To Whom Much Is Given, Much Is Required. Jesus has an incredible love for all members of His Church. But there seems to be a special love and dedication to those whom He has called to represent Him in His fivefold ministry. The Lord Jesus Christ has invested much of Himself into them; He has given them of His own nature, grace, gifts and ministry. And to whom much is given, much is required (Luke 12:48). Those who are called to this realm of the ministry will go through a greater process of severe training before God commissions them to their fivefold office. They will also be judged by a much higher standard and more strictly than the regular members of the Body of Christ (James 3:1).

This principle seems to apply especially to those called to be **prophets** and **apostles**. Those apostles whom He has called to be special ambassadors for Him, and the prophets whom He calls to speak directly for God with a "Thus saith the Lord" are given a greater responsibility. Apostles and prophets have the dual ministry of laying the proper foundation for Christ's Church with the mutual divine enablement to receive supernatural revelation from God (Eph. 2:20; 3:5). But in the same way much more is required of them in obedience, integrity, righteousness and Christlikeness in all areas of their life. They are also required to minister more accurately and reveal God's specific word, will, and way more precisely than any other ministry in the Body of Christ.

Essentials for Apostles and Prophets. There is a key scripture that all Body of Christ members must embrace into their attitude and actions if they are to make it through God's process from calling to commissioning. This has a special application to those with the high calling of apostle or prophet. They must never assume they have already attained their commissioning simply because they have received several supernatural confirmations of their calling and are ministering some in that calling. After many years of ministry, Apostle Paul made the following as a cry to God and a charge to the Church.

> *But what things were gain to me, those I counted loss for Christ. Yea doubtless, and I count all things but loss for the excellency of the knowledge of Christ Jesus my Lord: for whom I have suffered the loss of all things, and do count them but dung, that I may win Christ, and be found in Him, not having mine own righteousness, which is of the law, but that which is through the faith of Christ, the righteousness which is of God by faith: that I may know Him, and the power of His resurrection, and the fellowship of His sufferings, being made conformable unto His death; if by any means I might attain unto the resurrection of the dead. Not as though I had already attained, either were already perfect: but I follow after, if that I may apprehend that for which also I am apprehended of Christ Jesus. Brethren, I*

*count not myself to have apprehended: but this one
thing I do, forgetting those things which are behind,
and reaching forth unto those things which are before,
I press toward the mark for the prize of the high calling
of God in Christ Jesus* (Phil. 3:7-14).

Paul declares that those who are going to make it from
calling to commissioning must do these things. First, count
everything as loss that would promote self-glory and self-
preservation; not only count the loss, but suffer the loss. Second, never assume you have already attained to everything
that God has called you to. Finally, forget all the successes and
failures of the past, and then PRESS with all that is within you
TOWARD THE MARK for the PRIZE of the HIGH CALL-
ING of God you have in Christ Jesus.

Many Are Called, But Few Are Chosen. It is interesting to
note the two occasions when Jesus made this statement in
Matthew 20:16 and 22:14. One was in reference to people's
attitude and the other was to a lack of proper preparation. The
first was a wrong attitude in relating to how God rewards His
laborers who work for different durations of time in His vine-
yard. The other statement was made at the end of His parable
about the person who had received the calling to be an atten-
dee at the king's wedding for his son, but did not make the
proper preparation to fulfill that calling. I understand in this
context that the word "chosen" is synonymous with the word
"commissioned" and it would therefore be hermeneutically
correct to make the following statement: "Many are called but
few are commissioned." In other words, there are many in the
Body of Christ who receive a high ministerial calling in Christ
Jesus, but because of their attitude and lack of proper preparation, never press all the way through to their commissioning to
that high calling. Therefore, it would be the same to say,
"Many are called but few ever reach their commissioning to

their high calling in Christ Jesus.'' The winning overcomers are not those who start the race at their CALLING but those who finish the race to their COMMISSIONING and remain FAITHFUL to it until the end. ''They that are with Him are CALLED, and CHOSEN, and FAITHFUL'' (Rev. 17:14).

God's Divine Process.

There are many examples of God's process of calling a person to the position of a prophet, apostle or king. In most cases there is a long period of apprenticeship, training, testing and trying before God commissions them to that calling. If there was greater understanding of this principle within the Body of Christ it would take much of the confusion out of those who are called, but who are not fully fulfilling what they know they are called to be and do.

A person receives a divine call from God usually by revelation knowledge, a vision, a dream, a deep conviction or a personal prophecy from a prophet or prophetic presbytery. The general assumption is that if God sovereignly reveals what we are called to be, such as an apostle, for example, the tendency is to immediately start trying to fulfill our concept of an apostle. This always brings much confusion and frustration to the individuals trying to be what they are not yet prepared to be. It not only affects them but their mate, family and anybody they are working with. A person trying to fulfill a ministry before God's timing is like an engine trying to run smoothly with the timing gear completely out of proper timing.

We must always remember that God is the one who gives a divine calling. He initiates it, not the person. Fivefold ministries, gifts of the Holy Spirit and ministries in the Church are not set out on God's ''smorgasbord table'' for us to pick and choose as we will. ''But now **God has set** the members...in the body just **as He pleased**'' (1 Cor. 12:18, NKJV). ''But one and the same Spirit works all these things, distributing to each one individually **as He wills**" (1 Cor. 12:11, NKJV). "And **God has appointed** these in the church: first apostles, second prophets..." (1 Cor. 12:28, NKJV). "But to each one of us **grace was given** according to the measure of **Christ's gift**. ... And **He Himself gave** some to be apostles, some prophets..." (Eph. 4:7,11, NKJV).

We cannot expect a positive response from God if we say, "I choose to be a pastor; I don't want to be a prophet," or "I want to be an apostle, not a teacher." God does the choosing and appointing. We do the responding with a yes or no, acceptance or rejection. However, if we reject, then God starts the process of making us willing to say yes. He will continue that for a period of time until He determines that we are not going to respond. At that time He transfers the calling and anointing to another vessel who is willing. There are examples in the Bible of this happening, as it did with Saul and David, or Esau and Jacob. If the person gives a positive response, then God directs the Holy Spirit to start the process of taking him or her from the state of "CALLED TO BE" to "COMMISSIONED TO BEING" an apostle and manifesting apostolic signs and wonders. The scriptures even declare that the angels are assigned to help those heirs of this great salvation and those who accept their calling to demonstrate their special portion of God's grace and glory (Heb. 1:14; Eph. 1:11).

Biblical Examples of God's Process for Taking a Person From Calling to Commissioning.

DAVID: The Shepherd Boy With a Prophetic Minstrel Anointing But Called to Be King Over All Israel. He is a good example of this process. Let us look at David's preparation between calling and commissioning.

He was called at approximately the age of thirteen. David was faithfully shepherding his father's sheep when he was summoned to appear before the Prophet, Samuel. God gave

David his kingly ministry calling through the laying on of hands and prophecy. At that time, Prophet Samuel anointed him with holy oil to be king and the Spirit of God came on him with a kingly anointing. Nevertheless, that did not put David in the position or ministry of being a king. It did not make his brethren recognize him as a king. David did not make his name cards with the title "King David" and a statement on it declaring, "I have been prophesied a kingship calling and have been anointed to be a king, call me if you need the ministry of a king." I have seen some young ministers who received a prophecy that they were called to be prophets. They immediately made name cards "Prophet So-and-So" with a statement on it saying, "I have been called and anointed to be a prophet. Call me if you need the ministry of a prophet."

Called to Be an Apostle? What does one do when the revelation comes that one is called to be an apostle? That person should say to God, "Lord, I accept the calling of an apostle. Now I give You my full permission for You to start the intensified process of training me from 'called to be' to Your commissioning for me to BE the apostle You want me to be." That is the first thing anyone can do at that stage of his or her life and ministry.

It would not be wise to immediately start doing certain things. First, do not get the 'Moses Syndrome' and begin arguing and debating with God. Do not make statements that imply God didn't really evaluate you before He revealed such a calling. Do not start making excuses about why you cannot be and do what He has prophesied to you. Do not try to explain to the all-knowing and all-powerful God why it couldn't happen. Do not make such insulting remarks to God. God does not call the qualified but qualifies the called. The Bible reveals that those who argue and debate with God at their calling rarely ever fulfilled their ultimate destiny.

During the last few years, I have seen some young pastors of small churches receive prophecies that they are called to be apostles. Some immediately changed their name cards from "Rev." or "Pastor" to "Apostle" and began trying to plant churches and solicit other ministers whom they can father. Some want to begin writing their book on the ministry of the apostle right away. Usually these called ones are very sincere and are doing what they think they are supposed to do. But most times the called one has a lack of proper understanding. They have more presumption than faith, more zeal than wisdom, more revelation than reality and more gifted ministry than manhood maturity. This type of person usually makes the wrong response and causes an improper representation of the divine ministry of an apostle.

So What Is the Process and Why Does God Choose to Do It This Way? One reason is that God must make the man before He can release the ministry. The Christlike character of the person called to a ministry is the foundation for the quality, quantity and lasting ability of the ultimate ministry of the called one. For instance, if a person lays a two-foot foundation for a three story house, then that is all he can build. If he takes a longer time, uses more material and effort to go down two or three stories underground in laying his foundation, then he can build a thirty- to fifty-story building. If he wants to build a one hundred-story building, then much more preparation is required. In other words, provision is based on preparation. The height of the building is based on the quality of the foundation. If a fifty-story building was suddenly placed on a five-story building foundation, it would crush it and the building would crumble to the ground.

As an example, when I was a twenty-year-old pastor, I prayed, fasted and begged God to give me a powerful ministry and anointing that would affect the whole church world. Without knowing it I was asking God to do for me then what He is doing now. However, if God had dropped on me back then this "multi-story building" ministry that I have now, it would have crushed me. My foundation of preparation, experience and maturity of manhood and ministry was just a basic one-story foundation at that time. Over the last forty-three years of ministry there have been four major times when God has torn down my manhood and ministry building, ripped out my limited foundation and dug deep down into my earth, removing it and pouring in His cement while replacing my old structure with His greater steel beams. I am convinced that God has given the Holy Spirit the same prophetic ministry that He gave to Prophet Jeremiah: "...To root out and to pull down, to destroy and to throw down, to build and to plant" (Jer. 1:10, NKJV). Notice that there are twice as many words devoted to the preparative process as there are to the building and planting. The greater and more in-depth the preparation, the greater the man and the mightier the ministry can be. It is the law of cause and effect, preparation and provision, calling and commissioning at work.

The books of First and Second Samuel record the life of David from his calling to be king of Israel to his inauguration as king over all Israel and his following forty years of kingship ministry. He was "**called to be**" at age thirteen but it was seventeen years later before he had a partial fulfillment of that prophecy. He was made king over the tribe of Judah when he was thirty years old, but it was more than seven years after that before he became king over all Israel. He had a twenty-four-year process of going from "called to be a king" to "being a king." Most of the Psalms are prayers that David prayed while he was going through stages of ministry and God's preparative process. Let's now look at the different processes David had to go through and the ministries that he had to be faithful in before God fulfilled his personal prophecy of being a king.

1. David was faithful in shepherding his father's sheep before and after his anointed calling.

2. He was faithful in his bear- and lion-killing ministry of protecting his father's sheep.

3. He willingly ministered to the needs of his brothers who were already in their soldiering ministry.

4. He boldly fulfilled his giant-killing ministry. (He didn't get exalted with people's praises.)

5. He was faithful in his music ministry to King Saul. (He didn't say, "I am sorry, but I wasn't called to sing for the king; I was called to be a king!")

6. He was faithful in his position when Saul made him captain of a thousand soldiers. David had an appreciative and humble attitude. He did not say, "My prophecy from Prophet Samuel said nothing about being a lowly captain. I'm called to the position of king."

7. He stayed true to God during his time of having to run and hide from the persecution of Saul. He could have developed a spirit of rejection, a persecution complex, a sense of abandonment and bitterness against leadership. The records in First and Second Samuel and the Psalms reveal the attitude David took that kept this from happening. It is not just what one goes through that causes the inner problems that need inner healing much later, but the attitude we take and our response toward them.

8. He was faithful and true to God while giving his best service to the heathen headship he was under when he had to go outside of Israel and live in the land of the Philistines for a period of time. David went from his closest possibility for his prophecy being fulfilled to the furthest and most remote possibility of it ever being fulfilled. The old saying, "It is the darkest just before the dawn" is very applicable to a person who is about to come into his or her ultimate calling and prophesied destiny. This is exemplified in the life of Joseph, David and Jesus, as well

as in Moses' seeking to fulfill his prophetic word concerning bringing Israel out of Egypt.

9. He did not give up during his darkest hour when all of his wives and children and those of his six hundred men were captured and all their possessions taken from his headquarters at Ziklag. For the first time in his life, his own men were turning against him and blaming him for their grief and loss. But David "encouraged himself in the Lord," rallied his men together, pursued the enemy, recovered all and distributed it equally among his men. Those who stayed behind guarding the stuff received the same portion as those who went to the battle. He manifested fairness, equity, unselfishness, courage and faith to pursue, attack and take back all that was his plus all the possessions of those who had stolen from him. Those who give in to discouragement during their darkest hour before the dawn of prophetic fulfillment will miss their day of opportunity and not fulfill their ultimate ministry.

10. While David was going through his lowest ebb and greatest test of his life, the person who was occupying his prophesied position was killed in battle. After the position of king was vacated because of the death of Saul on the battlefield, the elders of Judah called David to come and be king over the tribe of Judah. This was David's heritage, for he was a descendant of Judah. When we maintain our integrity and faith during our greatest trial, God makes a way for us to take dominion over our heritage.

The other tribes put one of Saul's sons as king over them. The position that rightly belonged to David was temporarily given to someone who had no divine right to it. God had already declared through Prophet Samuel that Saul's posterity had been cut off from ruling over Israel. God had already canceled Saul's continued kingship over Israel because he had not taken seriously the prophet's personal prophecies to him and had failed on two occasions to do everything the prophecies told him to do (1 Sam. 13:13-14; 15:28-29; 16:1).

Though David knew that he rightfully belonged in the position as king over all Israel, he did not demand his own rights or try to make the elders vote him in as king over all the tribes. He waited more than seven years for God's timing and providential workings for all the tribes to request him to take his place as king over all Israel. He did not take advantage of his opportunity to remove King Saul by killing him while being persecuted in the wilderness. He even blessed the seed of Saul who had forced him to remain in a wilderness area and seemingly been a hindrance to David's seeing the fulfillment of his prophecies for many years. There are many checkpoints and tests during the process from people's prophetic calling to their commissioning to their ordained major ministry. How one responds and adjusts to these processes of God will determine the degree of prophetic fulfillment.

11. Finally, after twenty-four years of God's progressive preparative process David realizes the complete fulfillment of his personal prophecy concerning being king over all Israel. What a joyful sense of destiny and fulfillment it brings when God's prophesied purpose actually comes to pass. David was finally commissioned to the office of king according to God's full purpose. It launched him into forty years of successful ministry as king over all Israel. Do not settle for partial fulfillment of God's prophetic destiny for your life. Be patient, enduring and persevering until you receive and fulfill all that God has prophetically promised. "Be [not] weary in well doing: for in [God's] due season we shall reap, if we faint not" (Gal. 6:9). "Therefore do not cast away your confidence,

which has great reward. For you have need of endurance, so that after you have done the will of God, you may receive [your prophetic] promise" (Gal. 6:9; Heb. 10:35-36, NKJV).

More Examples.

There are several more biblical examples that we will use to illustrate this truth concerning the lengthy period of time between calling and commissioning. A divinely called one cannot bypass God's process. You can pray, prophesy, decree and confess your way through, but there is nothing you can do to exempt yourself from it. Paul and Peter declare that this fiery process must try every person's works and attitudes. Everything that is wood, hay or stubble shall be burnt up but that which is gold and silver will be brought to a higher grade of purity. The trying of your faith is more precious than gold to God. Therefore, don't think it strange concerning the fiery process that shall try all of us, but rejoice knowing that tribulation develops patience and produces that which makes us not ashamed to believe, endure and press on until we receive our ultimate ministry and fulfill our ultimate destiny (1 Cor. 3:13; 1 Pet. 1:8).

ELISHA: Called to Be a Prophet to Israel. Elisha had to spend a twelve-year apprenticeship from his calling to his commissioning. After Elijah came out of his cave of despair, God spoke to him to anoint Hazael to be king over Syria, Jehu to be king over Israel, "And Elisha the son of Shaphat of Abel Meholah you shall anoint as prophet in your place" (1 Kings 19:16b, NKJV). He found Elisha plowing in the field with twelve yokes of oxen. Elijah came to him and threw his mantle upon Elisha. Elisha knew from this act that he had just been called to be Elijah's apprentice to inherit his prophetic anointing. He sacrificed two of his oxen as an offering unto the Lord and had a feast for his people, then kissed his father and mother goodbye. "Then he arose and followed Elijah, and became his servant" (1 Kings 19:21c, NKJV). Notice that the prophetic call made a wealthy farmer be willing to forsake all of his wealth and prestige to become the servant of a major prophet. This reveals some of the qualities that he would need to press on to receive the double-portion anointing of his mentor.

For twelve years Elisha served Elijah by carrying his luggage, preparing his meals and doing all the other things that a servant would do for his master. There are no records that Elisha ever performed any miracles or prophesied to anyone during those twelve years. Finally the test came to see whether Elisha would make it over the last hurdle. The story unfolds in Second Kings chapter 2. Four times Elisha had the opportunity to miss out on his commissioning to be the prophet who would take Prophet Elijah's place as God's voice to Israel.

Elijah knew where the Lord wanted him to be when he was to be taken to heaven in a whirlwind and God's fiery chariot. He knew that Elisha had to be there to see him ascend to heaven in order to receive his prophetic mantle. Knowing this, Elijah gave Elisha his final exams before graduating him to his position. They stopped at Gilgal, Bethel, Jericho and the Jordan River. At each place Elijah told Elisha "Stay here, please, for the Lord has sent me on to..." but each time Elisha responded with settled determination in his voice, "As the Lord lives, and as your soul lives, I will not leave you!" God always checks us out to see how committed we are to going all the way with Him to receive everything that has been prophetically promised. Elisha had invested twelve years to come to this place and he was not about to allow anything to cause him to come short of God's ultimate for his life and ministry.

Not only did his master try to talk him into staying but his prophetic brethren tried to discourage him. Prophets came out of their school of prophets at Bethel and Jericho and before they crossed over Jordan saying to Elisha, "Don't you know that your master is going to be taken away from you today? Why do you continue to stick with him when he is going to be gone before the day is over?" Each time Elisha emphatically replied with determined finality, "Yes, I know; keep silent!" At the Jordan River, Elijah took his mantle and struck the water, and it parted. The pathway across Jordan dried up immediately and they crossed over on dry ground.

Make It to God's Appointed Place and Time. Elisha Made It! Then the revelation was given to reveal why it was necessary for Elisha to have stuck with him like a leach.

> *And so it was, when they had crossed over, that Elijah said to Elisha, "Ask! What may I do for you, before I am taken away from you?" Elisha said, "Please let a double portion of your spirit be upon me." So he said, "You have asked a hard thing. Nevertheless, **if you see me when I am taken from you, it shall be so for you; but if not, it shall not be so**"* (2 Kings 2:9-10, NKJV).

In other words, if Elisha had stayed anywhere along the way and not been there to see Elijah taken up to heaven, he would not have received the mantle of Elijah. This represented his double portion and commissioning to be the major prophet to Israel as Elijah had been. His twelve-year apprenticeship would have counted for nothing if he had not determinedly pressed on through that final day. He could have discouraged himself by thinking, "Elijah has not shared any of his anointing with me for these twelve years. I don't think he is going to follow through and let me have his mantle." I have seen many who had faithfully served a ministry for years hoping to inherit a leadership role or the mighty ministry of the man of God, but they became impatient, lost faith in the leadership and forsook the ministry and the man of God just before they would have received everything. Once you have been called and placed in a position of apprenticeship, stay with dedicated determination and stick-to-itiveness until you have received what you originally set out to receive.

Oh, the Joy and Reward of Ultimate Fulfillment. Elisha had stuck in there until he saw Elijah ascend to heaven. As he ascended up he threw his mantle back to Elisha. Elisha wanted to check it out to see if he had finally received what he had believed for all these years. He had just seen Elijah part the Jordan by striking it with the mantle he now held in his hands.

> *Then he took the mantle of Elijah that had fallen from him, and struck the water, and said, "Where is the Lord God of Elijah?" And when he also had struck the water, it was divided this way and that; and Elisha crossed over. Now when the sons of the prophets who were from Jericho saw him, they said, "The spirit of Elijah rests on Elisha." And they came to meet him, and bowed to the ground before him* (2 Kings 2:14-15, NKJV).

Those who had ridiculed him just a few hours before now acknowledged that Elisha had inherited Prophet Elijah's powerful anointing as God's major prophet to Israel. The records of the two prophets show that Elisha truly did receive the double portion, for he performed twice as many miracles in his ministry as Elijah did. After pressing through his darkest hour and greatest test, Elisha received the double-portion anointing and was launched into more than fifty years of successful ministry. There is no joy and sense of accomplishment like that of finally receiving what you have been believing and pursuing for many years.

JOSEPH: Called to Be a Ruler and a Savior. His life dramatically reveals the process God may take some through between their calling and commissioning to their supernaturally revealed destiny. Joseph received his calling through two prophetic dreams when he was seventeen years old (Gen. 37:2-11).

But it was thirteen years before he saw a partial fulfillment of his calling and another two years before he saw his dreams come to pass exactly as he had seen them. From the moment he received his dreams and revealed them to his brethren and father, things began to fall apart around him. He went from being his father's favored son with a royal robe to having that robe ripped off by his jealous brothers. They stripped him and threw him into a pit with the intent of letting him die there. But some Ishmaelite merchantmen came along, so his brothers sold Joseph to them for twenty pieces of silver. The Ishmaelites took him to Egypt and sold him to Potiphar, an Egyptian captain of the guards over all the prisons in Egypt.

Negative Circumstances vs. God's Presence and Will. It is good to know that our circumstances do not determine whether God is **with** us and directing the affairs of our lives. Thank God, the Bible declares:

*The Lord was **with** Joseph, and he was a successful man; and he was in the house of his master the Egyptian. And his master saw that the Lord was with him and that the Lord made all he did to prosper in his hand. So Joseph found favor in his sight, and served him. Then he made him the overseer of his house, and all that he had he put under his authority. So it was, from the time that he had made him the overseer of his house and all that he had, that the Lord blessed the Egyptian's house for Joseph's sake; and the **blessing of the Lord was on all that he had in the house and in the field. Thus he left all that he had in Joseph's hand, and he did not know what he had except for the bread which he ate. Now Joseph was handsome in form and appearance** (Gen. 39:2-6, NKJV).*

These scriptures reveal some of the attitudes and activities that Joseph experienced during his humbling and depressing process. He worked hard for his heathen master with a willing spirit and joyful attitude. Because of Joseph's calling, attitude and anointing, God blessed all that he did for Potiphar. God promoted him to be the overseer of all of Potiphar's business and household. This gave him a ray of hope that he might be progressing to the position where his prophetic dreams could be fulfilled.

Setbacks and Unjust Treatment vs. God's Process and Purposes. Suddenly all of Joseph's hopes and possibilities were dashed to pieces. Because Joseph was such a handsome and charming man, Potiphar's wife began to lust after him. She demanded that he commit adultery with her. Joseph exemplified a virtuous character. He declared to her that he could not do this for it would betray loyalty to his master and the trust that Potiphar had put in him. But most of all, it would cause him to sin against his God. Nevertheless, she persisted day after day until the opportunity arose when there was no one in the house but the two of them. She grabbed him by his tunic and tried to force him to bed with her. He pulled away but she held on. He got away but his tunic was left in her hands. **A person scorned and rejected becomes a bitter enemy.** She falsely accused Joseph of trying to rape her, showing her husband the tunic as proof. The husband believed her and became so angry with Joseph that he had him thrown into the prison where the king's prisoners were confined. Can God allow such things to happen to His chosen ones? Joseph was innocent and righteous in all his doings, but he was still unjustly treated, convicted and sentenced as though he was completely guilty. Why didn't God protect him and defend his righteous integrity? Could all of these negative experiences be providential in bringing Joseph to the place where his prophetic dreams would come to pass? Yes, for in this prison he made the contacts and had the experience that resulted in his being in position for commissioning to his ordained ministry. Righteous acts are not always immediately rewarded, but they keep us in good standing with God so that He can progressively move us on to our ultimate ministry. Joseph was unjustly thrown into jail, but the scriptures declare:

> *...And he was there in the prison. But the Lord was* **with** *Joseph and showed him mercy, and He gave him favor in the sight of the keeper of the prison. And the keeper of the prison committed to Joseph's hand all the prisoners who were in the prison; whatever they did there, it was his doing. The keeper of the prison did not look into anything that was under Joseph's authority, because the Lord was with him; and whatever he did, the Lord made it prosper* (Gen. 39:20-23, NKJV).

When Setbacks and Demotions Are Setups for Promotion. What we need to know more than anything else is if the Lord is **with** us. It's neither our apparent successes or failures nor our circumstances, but whether the Lord Jesus is **WITH US.** After about two years in this prison, God caused the king's butler and baker, who had been committed to the same prison, to each have a dream. Joseph's interpretation of these dreams was that the butler would be restored to his ministry with the king but the baker would be killed. He asked the butler to bring his name before the Pharaoh in hopes that he would release him from prison. But two more years passed by, for a total of four years, before the butler remembered him.

Pharaoh had a very disturbing dream that his psychics, astrologers, magicians and wise men could not interpret. The butler suddenly remembered Joseph and mentioned how he had interpreted their dreams and they had come to pass just as he had described their meanings. The Pharaoh summoned Joseph who then interpreted his dream as predicting seven years of plentiful crops and then seven years of famine. He then proceeded to give Pharaoh the wisdom as to what to do. He should select a discerning and wise man to set as lord over all the land of Egypt.

So the advice was good in the eyes of Pharaoh and in the eyes of all his servants. And Pharaoh said to his servants, "Can we find such a one as this, a man in whom is the Spirit of God?" Then Pharaoh said to Joseph, "Inasmuch as God has shown you all this, there is no one as discerning and wise as you. You shall be over my house, and all my people shall be ruled according to your word; only in regard to the throne will I be greater than you." ... Then Pharaoh took his signet ring off his hand and put it on Joseph's hand; and he clothed him in garments of fine linen and put a gold chain around his neck. And he had him ride in the second chariot which he had; and they cried out before him, "Bow the knee!" So he set him over all the land of Egypt. ... And Pharaoh called Joseph's name Zaphnath-Paaneah. And he gave him as a wife Asenath, the daughter of Poti-Pherah priest of On. So Joseph went out over all the land of Egypt. Joseph was thirty years old when he stood before Pharaoh king of Egypt... (Gen. 41:37-46, NKJV).*

Prisoner to Prime Minister in One Day. Thus, after thirteen long years, Joseph had progressed from "called to be" to "being," from calling to commissioning, from prisoner to prime minister. When Pharaoh put his signet ring and new clothing of fine linen on him, Joseph was launched into the full-time ministry that he had been called to fulfill. We see how important it is for one to keep the right attitude, resist temptation, retain integrity and never stop giving one's best in every unjust and humbling situation that seems to be a setback to the progress toward one's ultimate objective. God rewards faithfulness. Joseph's trouble started when he began his ministry of dreams and interpretations. But it was dreams and interpretation of dreams that made the way for him to be launched into his ministry. Never say, "I am never going to do this or that ministry again because it was what caused my brothers to turn against me and gave me thirteen years of horrible experiences." If so, you will miss the very thing that God had arranged for your deliverance.

Prophetic Dreams Are Finally Fulfilled. Nine years later, his brothers came to buy corn and fulfilled the first dream by bowing before him. Then Jacob and all his sixty-six descendants came and bowed before Joseph, which fulfilled his second dream. Joseph gave full forgiveness and restoration to his brothers who had so wronged him. He brought them to Egypt to be a part of his ministry and blessed them with the area of Goshen, the best pasture land in Egypt. After Jacob died at the age of one hundred forty-seven, Joseph's brothers came and begged him not to take vengeance on them. Because of the revelation he had received about all that had transpired, he was able to say with heartfelt conviction, "Do not be afraid, for am I in the place of God? But as for you, **you meant evil against me**; but **God meant it for good**, in order to **bring it about** as it is this day, to **save many people alive**" (Gen. 50:19-20, NKJV). Joseph received the same revelation that Apostle Paul shared with the Roman Christians. "And **we know that all things work together for good** to those who **love God**, to those who are the **called according to His purpose**" (Rom. 8:28, NKJV). This is a vital understanding and attitude for a person to have in order to make it through the process. Because Joseph maintained the proper attitude and took correct actions during his testing and trying process, he was commissioned to his exalted position of being the savior not only of his headquarters area in Egypt but also of his own kindred. He went from prisoner to prime minister in one day. At the age of seventeen, he was called; but at the age of thirty, he was commissioned and launched into eighty years of successful ministry, concluding it at the age of one hundred ten when he died.

ABRAHAM: Called to Be Father of Many Nations. His life also portrays this truth. Since I am in the process of writing a book on "Prophet Abraham, The Father of Us All," I will not give the details of his life. He was called at the age of around fifty to be the father of many nations. He was to leave all of his kindred and go stake out a land that God would give as his heritage. His first attempt at fulfilling this word fell short of the promised land. He took all his family and traveled to Haran in Mesopotamia, which was two hundred miles beyond Canaan. He stayed there for twenty-five years until his father died. He was seventy-five years old when he launched out again to fulfill his prophetic calling. This time he overshot the land of Canaan by around two hundred miles, ending up in Egypt. He finally came back from Egypt and stopped in the middle of the land of Canaan. There the Lord spoke to him that this was the land.

Trying to help God fulfill prophecy produces an "Ishmael" ministry or business. Abraham and Sarah decided to help God fulfill their prophecy after ten years in the land and not being able to produce a child. Trying to fulfill a calling with human reason and logic caused them to produce a child, Ishmael, which was not God's choice. Ishmael represents a ministry that is born of the flesh, brought into existence by man's manipulation and not by the Spirit and will of God. Then, fourteen years later, God told Abraham that he had missed it. Ishmael was not the son that God had promised him. God changed Abraham's status from "called to be" to "being" the father of many nations. After fifty years (Abraham one hundred, Sarah eighty-nine), Abraham had progressed from his calling to God's commissioning him by enabling Sarah to conceive and bring forth the promised son.

God's Progressive Prophecies and Testing Process. During his life Abraham received **eleven personal prophecies** and went through **seven major tests**. When he passed each test, God increased his prophetic promises. The last major test took place twenty-five years after Isaac was born. God asked him to take Isaac, his only son whom he deeply loved, and offer him as a burnt offering upon an altar. He took the wood and fire. He laid the wood on the altar and then tied Isaac on top of it. He took his knife and was ready to plunge it into Isaac's heart, when suddenly the angel of the Lord shouted for Abraham to stop! "And He said, Do not lay your hand on the lad, or do anything to him; **for now I know** that you fear God, since you have not withheld your son, your only son, from Me" (Gen. 22:12, NKJV).

There Is a Place Beyond Calling and Commissioning. When God saw the unquestioning obedience of Abraham to take what all his prophetic promises were wrapped in and destroy it, God changed His word to him from a conditional personal prophecy to a ratified oath. God swore on His honor and eternal name that nothing could keep all that He had promised Abraham from coming to pass.

> *"...By Myself I have sworn, says the Lord, **because you have done this thing**, and have not withheld your son, your only son—blessing I will bless you, and multiplying I will multiply your descendants as the stars of the heaven and as the sand which is on the seashore; and your descendants shall possess the gate of their enemies. In your seed all the nations of the earth shall be blessed, **because you have obeyed My voice.**" So Abraham returned to his young men, and they rose and went together to Beersheba; and Abraham dwelt at Beersheba* (Gen. 22:16-19, NKJV).

Obedience and Patience Appropriates. Thus, we find that it took a fifty-year process for Abraham to go from "called to be a father" to "being a father." It took another twenty-five years for God to take Abraham to the ultimate test that would bring him into a relationship and covenant with God that very few of God's people ever reach. As in natural schooling, the teacher cannot pass students on to the next grade level until they pass the test. The scripture in Genesis 22:1 says that God **tested** Abraham. We should understand the positive purposes of God's tests and not fear or resist them, for they are God's way of determining if we are ready for promotion. It is amazing that the eternal God, who knows all things, said to Abraham, after he had demonstrated that he would do anything, **"Now I know that you fear God."** Many are called, but few are chosen or commissioned. How we respond to God's preparative process of trying and testing determines if we will ever reach the status of being chosen and commissioned. Whether or not we pass the ultimate test determines whether our descendants will carry on our ministry. If we pass the ultimate test, then God will change our conditional prophecies to unconditional prophetic decrees that are backed by God's own sworn oath. He will personally make sure that every prophetic promise comes to pass.

JESUS CHRIST: Called to Be Redeemer, Head of the Church, King of the Universe. The prophets of old prophesied His ministry according to God the Father's will and purpose for Him. In the fullness of time, He was supernaturally conceived in the womb of Mary and then birthed into this world. He was the perfect and holy Son of God who lived a sinless life. He was called from His birth, but it was thirty years later before God commissioned Him to do the work that He had come to do on earth. He had thirty years of God's preparative process but only three-and-a-half years of ministry. Just think: Jesus spent thirty years of His life in God's preparatory process and only three-and-a-half years in His ministry. That is a ratio of about ten to one. If the Father felt that Jesus, the sinless Son of God, needed this much preparation before He could be commissioned to His preordained ministry, then how much more do you and I need to go through God's preparation process. Jesus had to go through the major test of fasting forty days and nights and then being tempted with the devil's greatest strategies and manipulating powers. After He passed this test, "…God anointed Jesus of Nazareth with the Holy Spirit and with power, who went about doing good and healing all who were oppressed by the devil, for God was **with** Him" (Acts 10:38). When Jesus was baptized in water, Father God said, "This is My beloved Son, in whom I am well pleased." But it was when Jesus passed the test in the wilderness that God commissioned Him to begin His miraculous ministry.

After Jesus fulfilled three-and-a-half years of ministry, God put Him to His ultimate test to see if He could be promoted to be head over all things to His universal Church. When He went through the Garden of Gethsemane, He suffered incomprehensibly in His soul and will. He cried out in heartbreaking anguish, "Father, if it be possible, let this cup of suffering pass from Me, nevertheless, not My will but Thine be done." He endured incredible physical suffering from the beatings, the crown of thorns, thirty-nine lashes on His back, and finally the most excruciating pain of being crucified on a wooden cross and hanging there until His body expired in physical death. He paid the highest price of personal suffering even unto death. Because He was willing and obedient to pay the extreme price He was exalted to the highest position heaven had to offer.

> [Jesus] *made Himself of no reputation, taking the form of a bondservant, and coming in the likeness of men. And being found in appearance as a man, He humbled Himself and became obedient to the point of death, even the death of the cross. Therefore God also has*

*highly exalted Him and given Him the name which is
above every name, that at the name of Jesus every knee
should bow, of those in heaven, and of those on earth,
and of those under the earth, and that every tongue
should confess that Jesus Christ is Lord, to the glory of
God the Father* (Phil. 2:7-11, NKJV).

The attainment of Jesus' ultimate position was dependent
upon His willingness to go through the ultimate testing process of suffering and death. He learned obedience and full
submission to God through the things He suffered while in His
mortal body. Those who fulfill their ultimate destiny will have
gone through all three phases of the overcomer. "And they
overcame him [the devil, who is the accuser of the saints] by
the blood of the Lamb and by the word of their testimony, and
they did not love their lives to the death" (Rev. 12:11,
NKJV). The only ones who will be exalted to the high position of ruling and reigning with Christ will be those who are
willing to suffer the complete death of the self-life, being fully
crucified with Christ, and not trying to preserve their lives but
laying them down at the foot of the cross of Jesus. Becoming
children of God by being washed in His blood and born of His
Spirit does not guarantee full heirship with Christ Jesus. "And
if children, then heirs—heirs of God and joint heirs with
Christ, **if indeed we suffer with Him,** that we may also be
glorified together. For I consider that the **sufferings** of this
present time are not worthy to be compared with the glory
which shall be revealed in us" (Rom. 8:17-18, NKJV). "To
him that **overcomes** I will grant to sit with Me on My throne,
as I also overcame and sat down with My Father on His
throne" (Rev. 3:21, NKJV). He that overcomes very little will
receive just a little reward, but those who overcome all things
will inherit all things (Rev. 21:7).

**THE TWELVE APOSTLES: Called to Establish the New
Testament Church.** They only had three-and-a-half years of

training from the time of their calling to their commissioning, but those were intensified years with Jesus working with them around the clock. Jesus was with them in person and teaching them by His words, life example and mighty demonstrations of His power and glory. This made it possible for them to go through God's preparative process in this abbreviated period of time. It still shows that there is a time of preparation and apprenticeship between one's calling and commissioning.

APOSTLE PAUL: Called to Reveal the Body of Christ, the Church. We have done a thorough research and study of the life and ministry of Paul. All indications are that there was a seventeen-year period between his supernatural conversion and call to be an apostle and his commissioning as an apostle. He had a miraculous conversion on the road to Damascus. He was struck blind by a blinding light from God. He was led to Damascus. A disciple named Ananias received a vision from God that revealed to him where Saul/Paul was staying, what he should do for him and what he should prophesy to him. Ananias prayed for him and Paul received his sight and was filled with the Holy Spirit. Ananias then prophesied to Paul about his apostolic calling to the Gentiles, kings and the children of Israel. Then he prophesied to Paul about the great sufferings Paul would go through for Jesus' name's sake. Paul immediately began to preach in Damascus that Jesus was the Son of God and the promised Messiah. A plot to kill him was discovered, so some Christian brothers took him by night and let him down through the wall in a large basket. He went back to Jerusalem and tried to join with the apostles and disciples there but they were suspicious of him and would not believe he was a disciple of Jesus Christ.

Barnabas came to Paul's rescue by taking him to the apostles. They allowed Paul to speak, so he declared to them how he had seen the Lord on the road, that Christ Jesus had spoken to him and how he had preached boldly in the name of Jesus.

They accepted Saul as a true disciple. He preached a few times in Jerusalem and disputed with the Hellenists, but they attempted to kill him. When the brethren found out, they took Paul down to Caesarea and then sent him on to Tarsus, his hometown. He went to Arabia for three years to spend time alone with Christ Jesus. He received his revelation that Jesus was choosing Jews and Gentiles into one corporate Body of Christ, the Church. He then progressed through fourteen years of making tents and preaching now and then.

Antioch, the Prophetic Activating Church. When the apostles heard that a church had started in Antioch, they sent Barnabas to find out what was happening. After Barnabas was there a short time, he left to find Paul. When he found him, he brought him back to Antioch where they ministered for a year. Then some prophets came from Jerusalem to Antioch. One of the prophets was Agabus, who prophesied that there was going to be a great famine throughout the world. They took up a big offering and delegated Barnabas and Saul/Paul to take it to the brethren in Judea. After delivering the offering, they returned to Antioch and continued to work with the church. God then set things in motion to commission disciple Saul into his apostolic calling, and change his name to Paul. "Now in the church that was at Antioch there were certain prophets and teachers: Barnabas, Simeon who was called Niger, Lucius of Cyrene, Manaen who had been brought up with Herod the tetrarch, and Saul" (Acts 13:1, NKJV). They did not know what fivefold ministry Saul was so they mentioned all these prophets and teachers, and Saul. "As they ministered to the Lord and fasted, the Holy Spirit said, 'Now separate to Me Barnabas and Saul for the work to which I have called them.' Then, having fasted and prayed, and laid hands on them, they sent them away" (Acts 13:2-3, NKJV).

Prophetic Presbytery Commissioning. There were several prophets headquartered in Antioch. When Scripture states that the "Holy Spirit said," it does not mean a mighty voice thundered from heaven. It implies that one of the prophets heard the thought and intent of the Holy Spirit and verbally expressed them. We who have ministered in the prophetic for years have developed certain terminology to specify different ways that God makes known His thoughts and words. A Rhema is when an individual receives prophetic insight and divine illumination from within. When an individual prophet speaks a prophetic word, we state that "the prophet spoke," or "a prophet spoke," or "Prophet Hamon prophesied." When two or more prophets prophesy to the same person, we refer to them as a "Prophetic Presbytery." After the word is confirmed and accepted as a Holy Spirit inspired word from God, then in future references to that word we normally just say, "God spoke thus and so" or the "Holy Spirit said." I believe this is what Luke, the author of the book of Acts, did in writing this account. Luke recorded this incident long after it had taken place. The prophetic word spoken had already been proven to be a Holy Spirit inspired word. Without going into detail to explain how God made His thoughts known, he just wrote that "the Holy Spirit said."

A prophetic presbytery of several prophets and teachers laid hands on Barnabas and Paul, prophesied to them and gave a prophetic charge that launched them into their apostolic ministry. For Paul especially, this transitioned him from "called to be an apostle" to officially becoming an apostle to the Gentiles with the revelation of Christ's corporate Church. These are some of the reasons why we call this laying on of hands anointing and prophetic activation into the apostolic ministry as a "prophetic presbytery commissioning." That is why we call Saul and Barnabas' anointing and prophetic activation into their apostolic ministry as a prophetic presbytery commissioning.

Prophets and Teachers Ministered to Apostles. It is interesting that the Holy Spirit did not speak to the apostles at

Jerusalem to lay hands on and commission Paul and Barnabas to their apostolic ministry while they were there. The Holy Spirit did not choose the apostles at Jerusalem to lay hands on Paul and Barnabas and commission them to their apostolic ministry, but the Holy Spirit directed it to be done by the prophets at Antioch. Regardless of any confusion over how God made His thoughts and desires known, this biblical example definitely contradicts the unscriptural teaching that only apostles can commission apostles.

The Process From Calling to Commissioning Took Approximately Seventeen Years. It took seventeen years for God to feel that Saul, the disciple, was now ready to become Paul, the Apostle of Jesus Christ and His Church. From then on, they were referred to as Apostles. "Which when the apostles, Barnabas and Paul, heard..." (Acts 14:14). Thus Paul was commissioned and launched into his Apostolic ministry to the corporate Body of Christ. In the opening greetings of most of Paul's epistles, he refers to himself as an Apostle. "Paul, a servant of Jesus Christ, called to be an apostle" (Rom. 1:1a). "Paul, called to be an apostle of Jesus Christ through the will of God" (1 Cor. 1:1a). "For I speak to you Gentiles, inasmuch as I am the apostle of the Gentiles" (Rom. 11:13a). "Whereunto I am appointed a preacher, and an apostle, and a teacher of the Gentiles" (2 Tim. 1:11). "Paul, an apostle of Jesus Christ by the commandment of God our Saviour, and Lord Jesus Christ" (1 Tim. 1:1a).

God's Preparation Process Is for All Who Are Called to Be His. We have found in the Old Testament and the New Testament that God has a preparatory process for taking His chosen servants from calling to commissioning. It can be a period of time from three to thirty years. If the called one is faithful to submit to all of God's dealings and passes all the tests God gives, then the day will come when that calling becomes a commissioning. The full manifestations of our ministry will not be manifested until we progress from the state of "called to be" to fully "being" that which God chose and ordained us to be. After divine commissioning the minister should have several decades of successful ministry. Joseph had eighty years of successful ministry, David had forty, Elisha had fifty, Paul more than thirty, and Jesus Christ three-and-a-half years on earth and an eternal ministry as head of His Church and the universe. If we could communicate with this great cloud of witnesses concerning the value of going all the way through the process from calling to commissioning, they would say, "It is worth everything you have to go through on earth to ful-fill God's destiny for your lives, which results in receiving that unfathomable joy of your eternal reward in Christ Jesus." There is an old gospel hymn that expresses how we will feel on that glorious day.

> *It will be worth it all*
> *When we see Jesus.*
> *Life's trials will seem so small*
> *When we see Christ.*
> *One glimpse of His dear face*
> *All sorrow will erase*
> *So bravely run this race*
> *Till we see Christ.*

We will find in the following chapter that God even has a process of calling to commissioning for His corporate Church. The Church was called forth on the day of Pentecost. It was birthed and seemingly grew to its apex within thirty years. It then went through its "David's Wilderness," "Joseph's Prison," "Abraham's Ishmael Ministry," and "Israel's Egyptian Bondage" for over a thousand years. The Holy Spirit was commissioned to bring full restoration to Christ's Church so that the corporate Church could be commissioned in AD 1500 to being fully restored and restoring all things. Finally, at

Christ's Second Coming the Church will be launched into its eternal ministry and destiny. All conditional prophecies will have come to pass, all temporal things made eternal. All who went through God's divine process on earth until they were conformed to the image of Jesus Christ will be commissioned to their joint heir ministry with Jesus Christ. It will launch them into a successful ministry that will continue throughout the endless ages of eternity. Apostle Paul received a glimpse of eternity and exclaimed that "the sufferings of this present time are not worthy to be compared with the glory which shall be revealed in us. To [Christ] be glory in the church...throughout all ages, world without end. Amen" (Rom. 8:18; Eph. 3:21).

7

GOD'S DESIRE AND PURPOSE FOR ESTABLISHING HIS CHURCH

To appreciate any progressive restorational move of God within the Church we must first know several things about **the Church,** which can be defined as **the one universal many-membered corporate Body of Christ.** One must understand how precious the Church is to Christ Jesus. It cost Him more to bring forth the Church than anything else that He had done throughout eternity.

When God created the **heavens and earth,** all He had to do was to think what He wanted and then speak His creative word and it came into existence. When God created **man,** all He had to do was to take up a handful of dirt and transform it into the human body of Adam. It was just by a little creative handiwork and then breathing some of His eternal Spirit into man that caused him to become a living soul. When God called forth **Abraham** to start the **Hebrew race,** which would bring forth His chosen nation of Israel, all He had to do was bring forth a revelation to Abraham and then watch over his descendants until they came back from Egypt to possess their promised Canaan land.

What Did It Cost God to Produce the Church? Now let us see what it cost the Godhead to bring forth the Church. Oh yes, all of the eternal Godhead became involved in producing the Church. Jehovah God gave His Son Jesus to the world for the redemption of humankind so that they could become members of Christ's Church. Jesus loved the Church and gave Himself for it, so that He might present it to Himself a glorious Church without spot or wrinkle (Eph. 5:25-27). Jesus gave the Holy Spirit to the Church for its empowerment, preservation and perfection. The Holy Spirit gives each individual member of the Church the ability to communicate with God in a new prayer and praise language of the Spirit, a dynamo generating inner life and power.

The Church Is as Eternal as Christ Jesus. The Church was not something that God decided to do after Israel rejected Him. The Church was conceived in the mind of God from eternity past. It was in the mind of the Eternal from the beginning and was planned and ordained before the foundation of the world (Eph. 1:4; Rev. 13:8). The concept of the Church is as eternal as Christ Jesus Himself. It was chosen in Him from the beginning. The **death of Jesus** on the cross **paid the redemptive price** for every person who would become a member of **the Church**. The resurrection of Jesus authorized the bringing forth of the Church, and the coming of the **Holy Spirit** on the day of Pentecost gave **birth to the Church**.

What Did It Cost Christ to Purchase and Produce the Church? His indescribable agony in the Garden of Gethsemane, a crown of thorns on His head, thirty-nine painful lashes upon His back, carrying that big wooden cross on His lacerated back and finally His horrible humiliation, suffering and shedding of the last drop of His life's blood while hanging on that cruel cross until His death—that was the purchase price He paid to have His Church. He battled the hordes of hell and arose victorious the third day from His grave. Yes, it personally cost God more than anything else He had ever done. It cost Him His very life. The Church means more to Christ than life itself for He gave His very life for it. No wonder the Church is so dear and precious to Jesus. The Church is more precious to Him than anything else in heaven or earth.

Did God Want the Church? If So, Why? Absolutely! He personally declared, "...**I will build My church**..." (Matt. 16:18). Notice the powerful implications of each word.

"I"   Jesus is personally committed to the building of His Church. He emphatically declares that He takes the place of personal ownership and Headship. His whole eternal life is committed to redeeming, placing and growing these members to full maturity.

"WILL"   When Jesus made this statement the Church had not yet been birthed, but was the sovereign will of Jesus Christ. "Will" indicates determination to produce and perfect regardless of time and effort required, even if it took two thousand years.

"BUILD"   Suggests a long, slow, drawn-out process (Eph. 2:20, literal translation: the Church is "being built"). He is building according to a plan. He will not stop building His Church until every member needed is placed in his or her proper position and the whole building finished to perfection.

"MY"   The Church is His personal property, pride, and possession (Acts 20:28). "Christ...gave Himself for it [the Church]" (Eph. 5:25b). "He hath purchased [it] with His own blood" (Acts 20:28c). Jesus is jealous over His position as owner and head of what He calls "MY CHURCH."

"CHURCH"   Establishes at once the distinction between this special, called-out company and every other classification of human beings. All heaven and even hell recognizes that the Church belongs to Jesus. All evil forces and humanistic people are trying to prevent Christ's Church from becoming all that God has preplanned for the quantity and quality of its members, the ultimate purpose and work it will do during the Church Age and throughout eternity.

Jesus, in His human body, purchased the Church, but it is through the work of His Holy Spirit that He is building the Church. A correlating analogy: David, God's prophet and king of Israel, received by divine revelation the blueprint for the Temple of God. He gathered gold, silver and brass and made provisions for all the other material needed to build the temple. He then gave it all to Solomon, who directed the building of the temple until it was finished. Jesus provided all things for the building of the Church (John 17:4; 19:30). He then commissioned the Holy Spirit to take His provisions, birth the Church and continue to work with the Church until every part is in place and the whole is perfectly complete. Jesus also gave His fivefold anointing of apostle, prophet, evangelist, pastor and teacher to special members of His Body for the purpose of building and perfecting His Church.

Apostles and prophets have a definite role to play in working with Christ Jesus in His Church. They are the foundation layers and they put the finishing touches to God's building, the Church. It was birthed on the day of Pentecost, but had to be built a certain way. It would be "...built upon the foundation of the apostles and prophets, Jesus Christ Himself being the chief corner stone; in whom all the building fitly framed together groweth unto an holy temple in the Lord: in whom ye also are builded together for an habitation of God through the Spirit" (Eph. 2:20-22). They not only laid the foundation, but they were set in the Church as permanent ministries during the whole Church Age. "And God hath set some in the church, first apostles, secondarily prophets, thirdly teachers, after that miracles, then gifts of healings, helps, governments, diversities of tongues" (1 Cor. 12:28). They were set in the Church to primarily work with the Church until every member is built up to the full stature and ministry of Jesus Christ.

> *And He gave some, apostles; and some, prophets; and some, evangelists; and some, pastors and teachers; for the perfecting of the saints, for the work of the ministry, for the edifying of the body of Christ: till we all come in the unity of the faith, and of the knowledge of the Son of God, unto a perfect man, unto the measure of the stature of the fulness of Christ* (Eph. 4:11-13).

These scriptures definitely state that apostles and prophets had a vital ministry in laying the foundation of the Church and they are to have a continuing ministry of bringing the Church to the fullness of truth, Christlikeness, maturity in ministry and manhood. The last generation of the mortal Church will reach all these characteristics, ministries and maturity. That is one reason why apostles and prophets are being restored back into the Church, for they play a vital role in this process of bringing the Church to the "fulness of Christ." God has preordained a work that the last generation will do that no other generation of the Church has ever done. To accomplish this task they will need all of that perfecting, edifying, unity of the faith and knowledge that the Son of God has, even the full measure of the maturity and fullness of Christ Himself. Since prophets and apostles are an essential part of that process, they must be restored, recognized and accepted so that they can do their part in ministering to the Church until it reaches God's predestined purpose for the Church. The cry needs to arise in the Church, "God, raise up Your last-day company of prophets and apostles."

Jesus wants to come back to earth and be joined with His Bride /Church. God wants to send Jesus Christ back to earth the second time, not to suffer, bleed and die, but to immortalize His beloved Church and be fully joined with her so that she may co-labor with Him in setting up His kingdom over all the earth. But He cannot yet for He is being held, restrained and kept in the realm of heaven until certain things take place on earth in His Church. "[God] shall send Jesus Christ, which before was preached unto you: whom the **heaven must receive until** the times of restitution [restoration] of all things, which God hath spoken by the mouth of all His holy prophets since the world began" (Acts 3:20-21).

The restitution/restoration of the Church started in AD 1517 after more than a thousand years of the Church's apostate condition, called the Dark Ages. On that date came "The Great Restoration of the Church," when the Protestant Movement was birthed. Beginning with that date there have been five major restorational movements: the Protestant, Holiness, Pentecostal, Charismatic and Prophetic Movements. Each movement restored several essential truths and ministries back into the Church that had been lost during its Dark Age.

For those interested in a more in-depth study of what each movement restored, a more detailed chart on the Restoration of the Church is found on pages 158, 309-310 in my book *The Eternal Church*. There is an updated chart found on page 52 of my book *Prophets and the Prophetic Movement*. The next chapter will cover the ten major things that the Holy Spirit restored to the Church with the Prophetic Movement.

—••◉◉◉◉••—

8

THE PROPHETIC MOVEMENT
AND WHAT IT RESTORED

—••◉◉◉◉••—

The Prophetic Movement served the same purpose as the previous restorational moves of God. Each movement took Christ's Church one step closer to its full restoration and maturity in preparation for its final end-time ministry. It was and is a divinely ordained work of the Holy Spirit to restore and reactivate certain truths, ministries, spiritual experiences and manifestations in the Church.

The Prophetic Movement met the seven principles or criteria that must be met by any truly God-ordained restoration movement. It fulfilled these seven conditions as the previous four movements fulfilled them. The seven principles are the following:

1.   Divine enlightenment and revelation knowledge of the new truths and ministries.

2.   The transition from occasional individuals to a consistent company.

3.   New divine authority and anointing for establishing the new truths and ministries.

4. A small beginning in an insignificant place and then covering the earth.

5. Power to reproduce by teaching, training, activating and maturing the saints in its truths and ministries.

6. Practiced and publicized until controversial, contested and then finally accepted.

7. New songs, choruses, and other music portraying the restoration message.

Detailed explanations and examples are given in forty-two pages of Chapter Seven of *Prophets and the Prophetic Movement*. All Holy Spirit orchestrated restorational movements that have taken place over the last five hundred years have met these requirements. Even the "Jesus the Messiah Movement" and the "New Testament Church Movement," as described in the Gospels and the book of Acts, met all these seven principles. The recent and continuing Prophetic Movement includes the seven principles of a true restoration movement.

Restorational movements. Church historians recognize the year 1517 as the official beginning of the period of Church restoration. There have been five major movements since that time: the Protestant, Holiness, Pentecostal, Charismatic and Prophetic Movements. The Holiness Movement actually covered a three hundred-year period and included three Christian truths and practices that were restored. The Charismatic Renewal covers a forty-year period when three distinct truths were restored by different movements within the time of the Renewal. If we categorize these individual movements according to the particular **century** and **decade** when each truth and ministry was restored, it is as follows:

RESTORATION

YEAR	MOVEMENT	MAJOR TRUTH RESTORED
1500	Protestant Movement	Salvation by grace through faith (Eph. 2:8-9).
1600	Evangelical Movement	Water baptism, separation of Church and state.
1700	Holiness Movement	Sanctification, the Church set apart from the world.
1800	Faith Healing Movement	Divine healing for the physical body, healing in the atonement.
1900	Pentecostal Movement	Holy Spirit baptism with speaking in tongues, gifts of the Spirit.
1950	Latter Rain Movement	Prophetic presbytery, singing praises and melodious worship.
1950	Deliverance Evangelism	**Evangelist** ministry and mass evangelism reactivated.
1960	Charismatic Movement	Renewal of all restored truth to all past movement churches. **Pastors** were restored to being sovereign head of their local churches.
1970	Faith Movement	Faith confessions, prosperity and victorious attitude and life. **Teacher** ministry reestablished as a major fivefold minister.
1980	Prophetic Movement	Prophetic, activating gifts, warfare praise, prophets to nations. **Prophet** ministry was restored and a company of prophets brought forth.
1990	Apostolic Movement	Miraculous signs and wonders, apostolic ministry, and unity, great harvest of souls, **Apostle** ministry being restored to bring divine order and structure, finalize restoration of fivefold ministers.

Prophetic Movement Restorational Truths and Ministries.

Since this book is about the restoration of prophets and apostles, we need to give a more detailed coverage of what truths, ministries, spiritual blessings and spiritual experiences were restored and activated into the Church by the Prophetic Movement.

1. PROPHETS RESTORED: God's main purpose was to bring about the full restoration of the fivefold ascension gift and office of the prophet. Prophets and prophecy are found in the Bible from its first book, Genesis, to its last chapters in the book of Revelation. Prophets have always been alive and active in every dispensation of God's dealings with humankind. But church theologians declared they were no longer an active ministry within the Church. So the Holy Spirit had to restore the reality of the existence of prophets in the present Church. Then there had to come the recognition and acceptance of the ministry of the prophet and his rightful position as a fivefold minister within the present-day Church. Many books have been written to scripturally validate the reality of Church prophets. Numerous seminars and conferences have been conducted since the early 80's to teach and demonstrate the ministry of the prophet. There are now thousands of prophets functioning within the Church in most nations of the world. A few key scriptures on the prophet include the following: Eph. 2:19; 3:5; 4:11; 1 Cor. 12:28; Amos 3:7; Ps. 105:15; 2 Chron. 20:20; Matt. 10:41; Luke 11:49; Rev. 10:7.

2. A COMPANY OF PROPHETS: Every restorational movement brings illumination and application to scriptures that were not understood or applied in that way prior to that time. The prophetic scripture in Malachi 4:5 was the key scripture for establishing the fact that God was bringing forth a company of prophets for a specific purpose. "Behold, I will send you Elijah the prophet before the coming of the great and dreadful day of the Lord: and He shall turn the heart of the fathers to the children, and the heart of the children to their fathers, lest I come and smite the earth with a curse" (Mal. 4:5-6). The revelation was that God fulfilled that prophecy in a singular way by the Prophet John the Baptist coming forth in the power and spirit of Prophet Elijah. He was the fulfillment of the prophecies in Malachi 4:5; 3:1; and Isaiah 40:3. John "prepared the way and made ready a people" for Jesus' first coming to earth as the Messiah of Israel and the Redeemer of the world (Luke 1:17,76; Matt. 10:9-14; 17:11.)

Notice in this last reference how Jesus responds to a question from Peter, James and John as they were coming down from the Mount of Transfiguration. They had just seen Jesus glorified and knew for sure now that Jesus was the manifested Messiah and God's only Son. This also puzzled them because of what the scribe theologians taught. "And His disciples asked Him, saying, 'Why then do the scribes say that Elijah must come first?' Jesus answered and said to them, 'Indeed, Elijah **IS COMING** first and **WILL RESTORE ALL THINGS**' " (Matt. 17:10-11, NKJV). Jesus said first, "Elijah IS coming." He then explained to them that it was timely for Him to be manifested as the promised Messiah. "But I say to you that Elijah **HAS COME** already, and they [scribes and Pharisees] did not know him" (Matt. 17:12a, NKJV). Jesus reassured His three special apostles that He was in prophetic order, for Elijah, through the ministry of Prophet John the Baptist, had already come and prepared the way for His first coming to earth to be the Messiah of humankind. He declared that the prophecy concerning Prophet Elijah coming first had already been fulfilled. **But there is still a future fulfillment** when Elijah will come to prepare the way for Christ's Second Coming. This time it would not be just one prophet but a great company of prophets that would not only prepare the way and make ready a people, but they would **RESTORE ALL THINGS**.

Peter declared to the Jews after Christ's resurrection, "But those things which God foretold by the mouth of all His prophets, that the Christ would suffer, He [Jesus] has thus fulfilled" (Acts 3:18, NKJV). Jesus could not leave earth until He had fulfilled all Messianic prophecies and He cannot come back to earth until the Church fulfills all restoration scriptures. He then told them to repent and be prepared for the times of refreshing (restoration) that were going to come from the presence of the Lord, "that [God] may send Jesus Christ, who was preached to you before, whom heaven **MUST RECEIVE** [keep, retain, hold] **UNTIL** the times of **RESTORATION OF ALL THINGS**, which God has spoken by the mouth of all His **HOLY PROPHETS** since the world began" (Acts 3:20-21, NKJV).

More Than One Type of Prophecy. There are several types of prophecies in the Bible: general prophecies, personal prophecies, Messianic prophecies and dualistic prophecies, just to mention a few. Dualistic prophecies are those that have more than one legitimate prophetic meaning or application.

Dualistic Prophecies. Example: Prophet Hosea prophetically described the deliverance of Israel out of Egypt. "When Israel was a child, I loved him, and out of Egypt I called My son" (Hos. 11:1, NKJV). But Apostle Matthew used this same phrase and prophetically applied it to Jesus coming back out of Egypt after Joseph had received instructions from God in a dream. "And [He] was there until the death of Herod, **THAT IT MIGHT BE FULFILLED** which was spoken by the Lord through the prophet [Hosea], saying, 'Out of Egypt I called My Son' " (Matt. 2:15, NKJV). This is a scriptural example of a dualistic prophecy.

The same prophetic phrase can be applied to the beginning of the great restoration of the Church, when Jesus called His

Child-Church out of its religious Egyptian bondage. Moses was the prophet who brought Israel out of Egypt fifteen hundred years before Christ's coming; Martin Luther was the prophet who brought the Church out of its Egypt fifteen hundred years after Christ came.

The same prophetic principle applies to Malachi 4:5. Prophet John fulfilled this prophecy of Prophet Malachi as one prophet preparing the way for Christ's first coming. Now there is a further fulfillment on a corporate scale through a company of prophets preparing the way for Christ's Second Coming.

This company is being brought forth with the same commission as Prophet John in the anointing of Prophet Elijah. Jesus said of Prophet John the Baptist that he was more than a prophet; he was a particular prophet that was fulfilling the prophecies concerning preparing the way and making ready a people for the Messiah to be manifest on Earth. The present-day company of prophets is preparing the way and making ready a people for Christ's return to earth again. This time Christ is not coming back to suffer and die at the cruel hands of men, but as the world's judge and the Church's conquering king.

They are preparing the way for Christ Jesus to establish His kingdom over all the kingdoms of this world. God declares that their ministry is so consequential that if they don't fulfill their prophetic destiny, God will have to curse the earth to utter destruction. The prophets are prophesying the mysteries of God and the time they are to be fulfilled (Rev. 10:7). The end result will be the fulfillment of Revelation 11:15, which says, "The kingdoms of this world are become the kingdoms of our Lord, and of His Christ; and He shall reign for ever and ever" (see also Mal. 4:5, cf. Matt. 11:9-14; Isa. 40:3-5, cf. Luke 1:16-17; Rev. 10:7, cf. 11:15; Matt. 17:11, cf. Acts 3:21).

**3. ACTIVATION OF SPIRITUAL GIFTS AND MINIS-
TRIES**: In the Pentecostal Movement there was a revelation of
not only the gift of the Holy Spirit with speaking in other
tongues, but also of the nine gifts of the Holy Spirit (Acts 2:1-39;
1 Cor. 12:7-11). They believed and demonstrated many of the
gifts, but taught that the gifts only operated when the Holy
Spirit sovereignly willed. They taught, preached, prayed and
ministered to believers to receive and manifest the Gift of the
Holy Spirit. But there was no open revelation for activating
the saints in the gifts of the Holy Spirit.

The Prophetic Movement brought with it the revelation of
how to teach, train, activate and mature the saints in their
spiritual gifts and ministries, just as the Pentecostal Movement brought the revelation of how to teach, pray and help
saints receive the gift of the Holy Spirit. The prophetic
preachers used the word "activate" and it became a controversial issue with some of the Pentecostal, Charismatic and Faith
Movement leaders. Nevertheless it has been proven to be a
true revelation, for tens of thousands of saints in several nations have been activated into their gifts, personal ministry
and the prophetic ministry. These pastors and leaders who
have been trained and activated are activating their saints the
same way they were activated.

Ministers of the Spirit. Another similar prophetic ministry
was to teach, train, activate and mature church ministers into
becoming New Testament ministers of the Spirit. People in
the world such as politicians, cultic leaders, all public speakers and church ministers can stand before an audience and
speak forth their convictions, philosophy and theology. But
only Spirit-born and Spirit-baptized ministers who have become New Testament ministers of the Spirit can manifest the
supernatural manifestations of the Holy Spirit. Church ministers who are not ministering the supernatural graces, gifts and

ministries of the Holy Spirit are living short of their God-ordained calling as ministers in Christ's Church. The revelation and application of Second Corinthians 3:6 has activated hundreds of ministers into being ministers of the Spirit as well as teachers and preachers of the Bible (1 Cor. 2:4; 14:6; 2 Cor. 3:6).

4. CROSSING JORDAN: The Prophetic Movement restorationally crossed the Church over its Jordan River just as the Protestant Movement brought the Church out of its religious Egyptian bondage, launching the Body of Christ on its journey to the promised Canaan land. The journeys of the children of Israel from Egypt to Canaan correlate with the restoration of the Church to its Canaan land destiny. Their major experiences correlate with the major restorational movements.

The Israeli Passover feast with the lamb slain and the blood applied to their houses is a type of the Protestant Movement truth, which proclaimed that the only cleansing from sin was by faith through application of the cleansing blood of Jesus, the Lamb of God. The crossing through the Red Sea and healing at the waters of Marah are types of the Holiness Movement truths of water baptism, sanctification and divine healing. The experience of supernaturally receiving life-giving water from the rock is a type of the Pentecostal Movement truth of the baptism of the Holy Spirit, which causes one to be filled with living water that flows out of one's innermost being. The experiences at Mount Sinai, their time of renewing and updating, and their challenges of faith at Kadesh Barnea are types of the Charismatic Movement truths of membership ministry, renewal, updating and faith.

They then wandered for thirty-eight more years until a new Joshua Generation arose who were challenged to cross over Jordan and start possessing their prophetically promised Canaan land. The Prophetic Movement, with its truths and ministries, activated the Joshua Generation and caused the Jordan

River to part. The way was made and a people prepared to cross over Jordan. The front-line pioneers and present-truth Joshua saints and leaders, like the Marines division of the military, have restorationally crossed over Jordan. They are now fulfilling their Canaan land ministry of destroying the "Ites" out of their prophetically destined possessions and position of ruling in life with Christ Jesus (1 Cor. 10:1-13; Deut. 6:2; Josh. 1–6; Rev. 10:7).

5. WARFARE PRAISE AND PROPHETIC INTERCESSORY WARFARE PRAYER: The Prophetic Movement brought forth the revelation and activation of warfare praise and prophetic warfare through intercessory prayer. Every restorational movement has brought new understanding and application of prayer, praise and worship. The scriptures reveal all the purposes of praise. One of those is the use of praise as one of the most powerful weapons of war that the Church has to use against its enemies.

Prophetic Psalmist Robert Gay, in his book *Silencing the Enemy*, gives and explains the numerous scriptural proofs that verify the fact that God intended spiritual praise to be an instrument of warfare. It is in the Church's arsenal of weapons of war. In her book, *Possessing the Gates of the Enemy*, Prophetess Cindy Jacobs reveals the truth of prophetic intercessory prayer being Biblical and a weapon of warfare to tear down the evil principalities and powers that are holding our families, cities and nations captive.

Since the Church has crossed Jordan and entered its promised land, it has gone on the offensive. God's prophetic marines have activated the Church out of its cold-war status against the forces of evil into a hot war by taking the offensive in aggressive warfare praise and prayer to destroy all the evil "isms" that are now dwelling in their promised land (2 Chron. 20; Ps. 8:2; 149:6-9; 2 Cor. 10:3-6; Eph. 6:18).

6. TEAM MINISTRY: The restoration of the office of the prophet and the coming forth of the great company of prophets activated their ministry of leveling out a path for the Second Coming of Christ. God prophetically declared in Isaiah 40:3-5 that the ministry of the prophets was to "make straight in the desert a highway for our God. Every valley shall be exalted, and every mountain and hill shall be made low: and the crooked shall be made straight, and the rough places plain: and the glory of the Lord shall be revealed, and all flesh shall see it together: for the mouth of the Lord hath spoken it."

Immediately after the birth of the Prophetic Movement a multitude of prophets began prophesying in the nations. As a result the Berlin wall was torn down, the Iron Curtain ripped apart and the mountain of communism was leveled. Many dictators throughout the world were dethroned. While God was shaking the dictatorial "one man rule" in the nations, He was also working in the Church. The day of the "one great man" ministry started coming to an end. God began to emphasize the "team ministry" principle as never before since the 1st-century Church. The apostle-prophet teams were restored. The husband and wife teams were activated so that the wife, instead of just serving as a helper to her husband, became a co-laboring minister. We at Christian International Network of Churches ordain the husband and wife equally. If one of the mates does not know his or her fivefold calling, then we believe for it to be made known in the prophetic presbytery that we give with each ordination. This is the day and hour when God is bringing forth His women to be the ministers that God ordained them to be. Husband and wife teams are one of the highest orders of team ministries.

A Truly Prophetic Church is one that is preparing every member to be in a ministry team. There are prophetic teams, apostolic teams, healing teams, administrative teams, pastoral teams and visitation teams, just to mention a few. In fact, all church members need to be on a team that fits their calling and anointed ability to minister to people. As an example, the human body has many members, but they do not work independently. All major parts of the body have their own team members who are especially equipped to make the eye, ear, hand or heart fulfill its purpose. The activation of "team ministry" is definitely a work of the Holy Spirit for this day and hour (Rom. 12:3-8; 1 Cor. 12:12-31; Lev. 26:8; Deut. 32:30).

7. PROPHETS TO THE NATIONS: Prophets function differently from evangelists or missionaries when they go to a nation. They do not go just to have great evangelistic campaigns or build a mission station in a small village. God sends His prophets not only to churches but to nations to fulfill the Prophet Jeremiah's commission of rooting out, pulling down and destroying the ruling evil principalities over that church or nation. They then fulfill the other half of that commission by planting the word of the Lord in them and then building and establishing them in those prophetic present-truth words from the Lord. In the Old Testament nations rose and fell, succeeded or failed, because of their response to God's personal word to them. About ninety-nine percent of the time God had His personal word delivered to a nation through the mouth of one of His prophets. Even to His special chosen nation, Israel, God communicated through His prophets.

God's holy prophets are going to the nations of the world and giving them a "Thus saith the Lord" and their destiny is being determined by their response to God's word to them. I believe the generation is alive that will see the consummation of this Age of the Mortal Church. The prophets of God are aligning the nations to the place where Christ Jesus can fulfill His judging and separating ministry with justice and righteousness.

*All the **nations** will be gathered before Him, and He will separate them one from another, as a shepherd divides his sheep from the goats. And He will set the sheep on His right hand, but the goats on the left. Then the King will say to those on His right hand, "Come, you blessed of My Father, inherit the kingdom prepared for you from the foundation of the world"* (Matt. 25:32-34, NKJV).

Notice that Jesus is not speaking of individuals here but of nations. There will be sheep nations who will be blessed and continue into God's kingdom on earth. But there will also be goat nations whom He will place to His left hand and pronounce to them His judgments. "Then He will also say to those on the left hand, 'Depart from Me, you cursed, into the everlasting fire prepared for the devil and his angels' " (Matt. 25:41, NKJV). How the nations respond to God's word that the prophets speak to them will determine whether they go to the right or left hand of Christ Jesus on that judgment day.

Just through our group of a few hundred prophets, more than forty nations have been given the specific word of the Lord. In most of the nations the prophets were able to speak to the president or whoever was head of the nation. "Prophets to the nations" is something new that God is doing. God is fulfilling many of His end-time purposes through His company of prophets that has arisen during the Prophetic Movement (Jer. 1:5,10; 1 John 3:8; 2 Chron. 20:20; 36:15-16; 2 Cor. 10:4-6; 2 Pet. 1:12).

8. PERSONAL PROPHETIC EVANGELISM: All new truth that is truly Holy Spirit revealed is built upon past restorational movements. The Evangelical Movement of the 1600's activated the truth of personal evangelism. The Divine Healing Movement of the 1880's added physical healings to the evangelistic ministry. The Pentecostal Movement of the 1900's added the gift of the Holy Spirit and His supernatural works in their evangelistic campaigns. The deliverance evangelism that was birthed in 1947 added mass evangelism with convincing miracles.

Now the prophetic ministry is adding a new dimension to personal evangelism. The ultimate goal of activating and training saints in manifesting spiritual gifts is to take the prophetic to the streets, highways, and byways and compel people to turn to Christ by the supernatural gifts of the Holy Spirit. Military leaders train their soldiers in their own military bases before they send them to the front lines. They practice on one another for months, even years, before going out to face the enemy. All the numerous reasons that generals train soldiers are the same reasons that generals in the Church train saints in their weapons of warfare before sending them out to face live ammunition coming from the enemy.

Personal prophetic evangelism is preparing a people to bring in the greatest harvest of souls that has ever been recorded in the history of the Church. The saints must be prepared and made ready to be the main participants in the next move of God after the Apostolic Movement. If church leaders and pastors do not start training their saints now, they will not be prepared to enter God's end-time purpose for His saints. There will be a great company of saints who will minister in personal evangelism with the prophetic and apostolic anointing. They will be the harvesting scythe and sickle in the hand of God for reaping the great end-time harvest of souls. They will be the instruments in the hand of God that fulfill Joel 2:13 and Revelation 14:14-19.

9. PURIFYING AND MATURING THE SAINTS: The Prophetic Movement restored the ministry of the prophet into the Church as God originally ordained it to be. The Prophet is one of the fivefold ministers that Jesus gave to the Church for the perfecting of the saints. The prophets and apostles have to be fully restored, for it takes all five to perfect the saints and bring the Church to the maturity and fullness of Christ, not just three of them. They also must be active in the Church for Christ to fulfill His purpose of having a glorious Church without spot or wrinkle. All movements have been working on this process of bringing the Church from infancy to manhood, spotted to spotless, immature to mature, from unrighteous to the imputed and accumulated righteousness of Christ.

However, the prophets have a special anointing for purifying and perfecting that the others do not have. Christ is coming to His Church in this day and hour through His prophet-messengers who are instruments of His purging fire. "…He is like a refiner's fire and like launderers' soap. He will sit as a refiner and a purifier of silver; He will purify the sons of Levi, and purge them as gold and silver, that they may offer to the Lord an offering in righteousness" (Mal. 3:2-3, NKJV).

When the Prophetic Movement was birthed in 1988, God prophetically declared that He was no longer putting up with unrighteousness in His Church. We would no longer be able to get by with the way we lived our personal lives in the Charismatic Movement. He was laying righteousness to the plumb line. God began to make public examples of big television ministries who were not maintaining a righteous standard in their lives and ministries. They were only the tip of the iceberg, for God was doing the same thing throughout all the ranks of Christendom. God is doing a quick work in this day and cutting it short in righteousness. The prophets are instruments of God's fire and righteousness.

Prophet John the Baptist, of whom the present-day prophets are an extension, said, "And even now the ax is laid to the root of the trees" (Matt. 3:10a, NKJV). Jesus said that unless our righteousness exceeds that of the Pharisees, we would not enter into His kingdom (Matt. 5:20). They did righteous acts but did not have God's righteousness within them as their inward life, character and motivation. Outward acts of Biblical living will no longer be acceptable unless the nature and character of Christ has been integrated into the inner man. I have established the ten M's for evaluating ministers, and for maintaining and maturing in one's life and ministry. They are the M's of Manhood, Ministry, Message, Maturity, Marriage, Methods, Manners, Money, Morality and Motive. The Prophetic Movement activated the prophets so that they could do their part in purifying and maturing the members of Christ's Church (Mal. 3:1-5; Eph. 4:11-16; 5:27; Matt. 5:20; Hos. 10:12; Isa. 28:17; Rom. 9:28; Matt. 24:22).

10. PREPARING THE WAY FOR RESTORATION OF APOSTLES: It has mostly been the leaders in the Prophetic Movement who have proclaimed the restoration of prophets and apostles. Since 1983 when I started writing my first book on prophets, *Prophets and Personal Prophecy*, declarations were made again and again that there will soon come a move of God for the full restoration of God's prophets. The Prophetic Movement was birthed into the Church in 1988. Prophetic declarations were made also that after the Prophetic Movement there would come a move of God to restore the apostles. Then, after the Apostolic, there will come three more movements before the literal coming of Christ.

At the age of eighteen, I was birthed in the restoration teaching that there are still present-day apostles and prophets in the Church. I was ordained and started pastoring when I was nineteen. I turned sixty-two in 1996, which means for the whole forty-three years of ministry my belief has been that apostles and prophets are alive in the Church. Romans 12:6 says we prophesy according to our revelation and faith. Because of this faith and by revelation from God, during the forty-three years of my ministry I have prophesied to more than two thousand individuals that they were called to be apostles or were apostles. Of the more than twenty-five thousand people to whom I have given personal prophecies, more than twenty-five percent had to do with being a prophet or prophetess, or that the person had a prophetic anointing, prophetic ministry or something similar.

I believe with all my heart that God showed me there would be ten thousand prophets on the North American continent and one hundred thousand throughout the rest of the nations. This is coming to pass faster than was anticipated. The company of prophets was not only to prepare the way and make ready a people for Christ's return to earth in His glorified human body, but also for Christ to come to the Church as the Apostle.

One of the divine commissions of the Prophetic Movement was to point the way to the full restoration of Christ's holy apostles. The restoration of apostles is no threat or intimidation to the prophets, for they know they are to make ready a people to receive the ministry of the apostles. There will be no competition between God's true prophets and His new breed and generation of apostles. They will know how vital they are to each other. No superiority or inferiority will be in their hearts but a submitting and drawing from one another's ministry. Those who have this understanding will co-labor and network together to fulfill their mutual ministry of preparing the saints for the next move of God, which I presently call the Saints Movement. This movement, coming after the Apostolic Movement, will be discussed further in the section covering the Coming Moves of God.

SIXTEEN TRANSITIONS
THAT HAPPEN WHEN A CHRISTIAN RESTORATIONALLY LEAVES THE WILDERNESS, CROSSES JORDAN AND ENTERS THEIR CANAAN LAND.

(For more detailed information, read Chapters 4-6 in *Prophets and the Prophetic Movement*.)

THE CHARISMATIC MOVEMENT compared to THE PROPHETIC MOVEMENT
(Restorational Journeys in the Wilderness)   *(Across Jordan & conquering Canaan)*

1. Wilderness Journeying - Deut. 2:7 . . . . . . Conquering Canaan - Josh. 1:1-6; Deut. 7:22

2. Uncircumcised in Wilderness - Jos. 5:5 . . . Circumcision before Commissioning
   Ex. 4:24; Rom. 2:29; 4:11; Col. 2:11.

3. Gift of the Holy Ghost . . . . Gifts of the Holy Spirit -1 Cor. 12:7-11

4. Freedom, Rights, Independent - Judg.17:6 Righteousness, Relationship, Accountability

5. Blood of Lamb and Testimony - Rev. 12:11 Love not own life unto death - Rev. 17:14

6. Miracles for Preservation - Deut. 6:24. . . . Miracles for Possessing - Josh. 10:8-14

7. Manna in Wilderness - Ex. 16:35. . . . . Canaan Food - Josh. 5:12; Deut.8:7-10

8. Praise for His Presence - Ps. 22:3 . . . . Powerful Warfare Praise - 2 Chron. 20:19-23

9. Updating and Maintaining - Num. 20 . . . . Crossing & Conquering - Josh. 3:1-17

10. Generation Enduring till Death - Num. 14:33 New Joshua Generation - Num. 14:28-31

11. Fire by Night/Cloud by Day - Num. 9:16-22 Prophets and Apostles - Eph. 3:3-5

12. Revelation of Prophets - Eph. 4:11 . . . . . . Restoration of Prophets - Luke 11:49

13. Occasional Defensive Battles . . . . Constant Offensive Warfare - Rev. 11:15

14. Mild, Melodious & Merciful . . . . Militant, Miraculous, No Mercy on "ites"
    Ps. 78:9-54; 1 Cor. 10:7; Deut. 7:1-2;
    20:16-17

15. The Bleating of the Lamb . . . . The Roar of the Lion of Judah - Isa. 40:1-2;
    Song 2:4; Amos 1:2; 3:8; Prov. 28:1;
    Rev. 5:5; 10:3-7

16. One-Man Platform Ministry . . . . Team Ministry & Apostle/Prophet Teams

—••●◖◗●••—

9

THE SPECIAL MINISTRIES
OF APOSTLES AND PROPHETS

—••●◖◗●••—

The original Greek and Hebrew meanings of prophet and apostle have a different emphasis than the evangelist, pastor and teacher. The prophet means one who speaks for God and has a divine specific message for those to whom he ministers. Prophets can teach the Logos word, preach the gospel, shepherd saints and do just about anything the other four can do, but not with the same anointing and success of those who are especially called to their particular office and ministry. Prophets excel when they are functioning in their special calling and anointing. I have fully covered all the functions and ministries of the prophet in my trilogy of books on prophets. I will not take the space to repeat many of those things, since this book is majoring on the apostle and minoring on the prophet.

PROPHETS: The specialty of prophets is their God-given ability to speak for God, not just teach and preach the Bible truths about God and His Son, Jesus Christ. They have the special calling to speak a "thus saith the Lord." The prophet has rights and authority in his prophesying that others do not have, such as those with the gift of prophecy or those who function on the saints' level of prophetic ministry. Those who are truly commissioned prophets have the right to prophesy direction, correction, guidance and new revelation to a person, church or nation. Some are used to pronounce God's judgments and reveal the calling and purposes of God to whomsoever God wants to speak. In fact, the prophets are to be God's mouthpieces to speak whenever and wherever and to whomsoever God wants to personally express His thoughts, purposes and specific will.

APOSTLES: In other chapters of this book we discuss the original Greek language root meaning and the unique ministry of the apostle as portrayed in the New Testament. I have done a thorough study and research of "APOSTLE" in the following areas: etymologically—to determine proper word usage; theologically—to evaluate the thinking of other theologians; exegetically—to derive the original Greek meaning; topically—to be sure the interpretation given is in agreement with the teaching of the whole Word of God. The conclusion is that the basic root meaning is "one sent as representative of another," with the power and authority of the representative coming from the one who sent him. They are like ambassadors who represent a country. The continuing ministry of an apostle/ambassador is based on how well he conveys the heart and message of the king.

PROPHETS AND APOSTLES: When we study all fivefold ministers using the same studying methods previously mentioned, we find that apostles and prophets have the special ministry and commission of speaking directly from God. They speak His "rhema" word and REVELATIONS of the MYSTERIES OF CHRIST. They also reveal His will and purpose, which establishes the Church on God's foundation and aligns the whole Church with Jesus Christ, the chief cornerstone of the building.

The same study of pastors, evangelists and teachers reveals that they do not have the same type of commissioning and anointing that the apostles and prophets have. It shows that they have the anointing to teach the written Word of God [Logos] and proclaim the revelations that apostles and prophets have brought forth with each restorational movement within the Church. The pastor, evangelist and teacher are extensions of Jesus Christ, as are the apostles and prophets. The main difference is that the apostles and prophets have been given a unique anointing that carries with it a greater responsibility and accountability before God.

Martin Luther is referred to as a prophet by some historians. I believe all the fathers of the restorational movements were either apostles or prophets. This does not make them greater or lesser than the other three, but it is a Biblically demonstrated fact that God invested these anointings and ministries in His prophets and apostles.

Remember that prophets wrote the majority of the thirty-nine books of the Old Testament. Apostles wrote most of the twenty-seven books of the New Testament, with Apostle Paul authoring fourteen of them. This gives further evidence of their special equal ministry of revelation from God and laying the foundation of the New Testament Church and every restorational truth and ministry. The scriptures throughout the Bible reveal this truth. Some have said that the apostles of the Church took the place of the prophets of Israel. This is an inaccurate assumption. The scriptures do not state or suggest such a thing. It is possible that, if the ministry of the apostle had been in existence in the Old Testament, several men who were called prophets might have been called apostles, such as Moses, Abraham and David. The Bible declares that these great leaders were prophets. We today might call them apostolic prophets or prophetic apostles. The apostles do not take away the ministry of the prophets. As we have discussed in other areas of the book, the "apostle" is a new ministry that Christ brought forth for His own purpose. Apostles are only found in the Old Testament by symbolically evaluating in relation to patriarchs, judges and kings. Apostles and prophets are two distinct ministries that Christ set in the Church. They have more similar anointings and similar ministries than any other two ministries in the Bible.

> *Surely the Lord God does nothing, unless HE RE-VEALS HIS SECRET to His servants the PROPHETS* (Amos 3:7, NKJV).

> *How that by REVELATION He made known to me the MYSTERY (as I have briefly written already, by which, when you read, you may understand my knowledge in the MYSTERY OF CHRIST), which in other ages was not made known to the sons of men, as it has now BEEN REVEALED by the Spirit to His holy APOS-TLES and PROPHETS* (Eph. 3:3-5, NKJV).

> *Now, therefore, you are no longer strangers and foreigners, but fellow citizens with the saints and members of the household of God, having been built on the FOUNDATION of the APOSTLES and PROPHETS, Jesus Christ Himself being the chief cornerstone* (Eph. 2:19-20, NKJV).

> *But in the days of the sounding of the seventh angel, when he is about to sound, the MYSTERY OF GOD would be finished, as He declared to His servants the PROPHETS* (Rev. 10:7, NKJV).

> *Rejoice over her, O heaven, and you holy APOSTLES and PROPHETS, for God has avenged you on her!* (Rev. 18:20, NKJV)

The various ministries of the prophets were fully demonstrated in their ministry to God's chosen people, Israel. The ministries of the apostles were fully demonstrated in their ministry to God's chosen people, the Church. God did not change into a different God when the Church and the Dispensation of Grace were established. He just demonstrated His loving, forgiving, redeeming and saving grace nature and character through Jesus Christ, His Son. God didn't change. He just changed His covenant with new ways for His people to relate to Him. God is the same God in the New Testament as He was in the Old Testament. "For I am the Lord, I change not" (Mal. 3:6a). If the eternal God does not change, and Jesus Christ is the same yesterday, today and forever (Heb. 13:8), and Jesus Christ and His Father are one (John 10:1), then there is not a God of the Old and a God of the New Testament, but one eternal unchangeable LORD God. It was God the Father who so LOVED the world that He gave His only begotten Son (John 3:16). The Bible talks about the LOVE of God and the fact that God is LOVE. The whole plan of love, mercy and grace for the New Testament came from the heart and nature of God. Jesus was the manifestation of the God of love and the instrument to implement all the blessings that we have in the Church.

The Old Testament prophets were an extension and expression of the heart and mind of God. The New Testament prophets are an extension and expression of Jesus Christ, the Son of God who is the same as His Father. Jesus, the Son of God, and God the Father are not two separate Gods with different traits, attributes, attitudes and character. Jesus said that He and His Father are one, which means They are identical in every area of Their being. So why do some teachers declare that the New Testament prophets are different from the Old Testament prophets? The prophets are the same as the one eternal God whom they represent. Jesus was declared to be the Prophet of God; that is, the expression of the heart and mind of God. The prophet is one of the fivefold ministers who are an extension and expression of the heart and mind of Jesus Christ, who was God "manifest in the flesh" (1 Tim. 3:16).

God already had several thousand years of the ministries of His prophets recorded to be canonized in the Bible. Therefore, in the records of the New Testament Church He minimized illustrations of the prophet and maximized the ministry of the apostle. Because apostles were unknown ministries, they had to be established as permanent, important and vital ministries in building Christ's Church according to His preordained pattern and ultimate purpose.

All That the Prophets Did for God's Old Testament People, the Apostles Did for Christ's New Testament People.
Present-day prophets have the same anointing, authority and ministry they had in the Old Testament. Apostles and prophets are coequal ministers with many similar anointings, abilities, authorities and ministries. Apostles are nearly always mentioned first because of all the reasons previously mentioned and because of the preeminence of the twelve Jesus chose and called "apostles." He did not call them priests, high priests, kings, prophets, pastors, evangelists or teachers. None of the New Testament books were written by any other acknowledged fivefold ministry other than that of the apostle. It's the same as most of the books of the Old Testament being written by men whom God called, "prophets," like Moses, Samuel, David and the five major and twelve minor prophets who have books of the Bible called by their name, such as Daniel, Isaiah, Jeremiah, Joel and Malachi. Luke, the physician, wrote the only Biblical history of the Church in action, called "The Acts of the Apostles." Throughout history "the book has been called by a variety of names besides the one it currently holds: *The Acts of the Ascended and Glorified Lord, The Book—The Demonstration of the Resurrection, The Acts of the Holy Spirit, The Gospel of the Holy Spirit,* and sometimes called the *Fifth Gospel*" (Adam Clarke, *Clarke's Commentary*, Volume 5, New York, NY: Abington Press, 1967, p. 679). The main reason they settled on "Acts of the Apostles" is because the book

majors on the ministries of two apostles, Peter in the first part, and Paul for the remainder of the book.

The name for the book was not finalized for several centuries after the Church was established. By that time the title of bishop had become synonymous with apostle. Bishop Calixtus in AD 220 was the first to proclaim himself as bishop of bishops and apostle of apostles. He based his authority on Matthew 16:18, claiming that he was in a direct apostolic succession from Apostle Peter. The church world made another transition in the fourth century.

> "By the end of the fourth century the Bishops were replaced with the title of Patriarch. They were of equal authority, each having full control of his own province. The five Patriarchs who dominated Christendom were headquartered in Rome, Constantinople, Antioch, Jerusalem, and Alexandria. After the division of the Roman Empire into East and West, the struggle for the leadership of Christendom was between Rome and Constantinople" (Bill Hamon, *The Eternal Church*, Santa Rosa Beach, FL: Christian International Publishers, 1981, p. 94).

The Church World Was Later Divided Into Two Great Religious Organizations. The Eastern Greek Orthodox Church headquartered in Constantinople, and the western world of Christendom under the dominion of the Roman Catholic Church. The Orthodox retained the titles of patriarchs but the Catholics used the titles of fathers, priests and bishops, gradually developed other titles, such as cardinals, to describe the positions in their pyramid of authority. After many years the title of pope was chosen to identify the man who was the father of fathers and apostle of apostles. He took the claim of apostolic succession all the way back to Apostle Peter. My wife and I were in Rome and visited St. Peter's Cathedral. On one great wall they have listed all the names of the apostles from Jesus Christ, with Apostle Peter, and then a succession of hundreds of names to the last apostle, the current pope at Rome. They say their rights and authority come from being in a direct succession of apostles from Apostle Peter to the present apostle-pope of the Roman Catholic Church. When their sovereign headship was established, he was proclaimed "The Apostle-Father-Pope" with claims of headship over all Christendom, just under Christ Jesus. He was proclaimed to be the only one on earth who could receive direct revelation from God and make apostolic-papal decrees that were as binding as Scripture. So we can see why these Christian leaders preferred the title "Acts of the Apostles" over the other titles that had been used to describe the activity of the Church during its first decades of existence.

Church leaders from many nations are concerned about this area and how it will develop in the Apostolic Movement. Some are already teaching and writing books stating the following about apostles: that every minister and local church should be under an apostle; and if not, they are out of divine order and improperly covered. This statement is idealistic but not realistic. It has some merit of truth, but not enough to be dogmatic. Why? First, there is no scripture rightly interpreted that supports this concept. Second, it will lead to abuses and extremism.

It is the same thinking and reasoning from Scripture that the extremists in the Discipleship Movement used to declare that every woman, married or single, must have a man to be her covering or she would be out of order and without proper covering. It created great bondage, confusion and a pyramid authority structure that God had to dissipate. They did, at least, have Biblical statements: "The head of every man is Christ; and the head of the woman is the man," and "Neither was the man created for the woman; but the woman for the man" (1 Cor. 11:3b,9). But there are no Biblical statements that the apostle is the head of every minister and local church. The apostles were not created for the other fivefold ministers and local churches, nor were the ministers and churches created for the apostles to have the dominion over and to always be in supreme headship. Such teaching, when taken to the extreme, could produce the same results that took place in the deterioration of the Church and that produced the papal system.

Though I am an apostle, I would rather have as my headship a mature pastor who has years of experience and has attained great wisdom and counsel, than a novice who has been prophetically "called to be" an apostle but has no years of experience, maturity, wisdom and apostolic commissioning. Read again Chapter 6 on "Calling vs. Commissioning." Remember that one's calling to a fivefold ministry does not automatically give one the ability to immediately be that minister with all the authority and anointing the office carries.

We who are destined and chosen to be leaders in the Apostolic Movement must not jump in and start making emphatic statements concerning who apostles are and what they can and cannot do. At this time there has not been an official Apostolic Movement that meets all the seven principles of a God-ordained, Holy Spirit-directed sovereign move of God. As an illustration, we had four apostles and four prophets as speakers at our 1992 sixth annual CI International Gathering of the Prophets Conference. Most of them were not CINC ministers. They all witnessed and prophesied that conception of the Apostolic had taken place for us in that conference. Several other ministries have testified to similar things happening over the last few years.

In 1994 at CI's eighth annual IGOP Conference I accepted God's "commissioning" as one of His new breed of restored last-days apostles. This was in fulfillment of more than twenty prophecies during the last twenty-five years that contained statements such as, "called to be an apostle," "apostolic anointing and mantle," "an apostle to the prophets and a prophet to the apostles," "an apostle that would bring forth a company of apostles'' (as I had fathered and brought forth a company of prophets). Those prophetic statements had been spoken by mature apostles and prophets from many places in the United States and in several nations of the world. But I did not propagate these things until God's preparation process had brought me to His divine timing and commissioning for the fulfillment of that part of my calling and destiny.

CI has not, nor has any other place I know of, had a sovereign restorational move of God that could be called the birthing of the Apostolic Movement. Nevertheless, God could do a new thing and allow the apostles to evolve and come up alongside the prophets and co-labor together with them in fulfilling God's divine purpose for the full restoration of prophets and apostles. One of the ten major things God brought forth in the Prophetic Movement was to prepare the way and make ready a people to receive the ministry of the apostles. However, that would be different from the normal way God has restored truths and ministries to His Church. Regardless of whether it has happened, or how, when and where it may take place, the fact is that the revelation that apostles are in the Church is being propagated by ministers and churches who are walking in the present truth. Many leading ministers are in agreement that the Holy Spirit is bringing forth an Apostolic Movement that will not cease until apostles are fully restored and fulfill their ministry to the Church as God predestined and ordained for them.

Examples of the Co-laboring Ministries of Apostles and Prophets: In chapter 16 of Matthew, Peter receives the revelation that Jesus is the Son of God. In chapter 17 Jesus takes Peter, James and John with Him to the top of what has become known as the Mount of Transfiguration. He wanted to clarify the revelation to Peter and the rest of the apostles that He was not just a great prophet like Elijah or just a great leader and deliverer like Moses. **JESUS is the Son of God.** He is the only begotten Son of God. He was not just a great and wonderful man, but He was the Man who would become the one and only Mediator between God and mankind. When Peter saw Moses and Elijah standing with Jesus in His glory he said something that revealed he did not have the complete revelation of Jesus Christ.

> *Then Peter answered and said to Jesus, "Lord, it is good for us to be here; if You wish, let us make here three tabernacles: one for You, one for Moses, and one for Elijah." While he was still speaking, behold, a bright cloud overshadowed them; and suddenly a voice came out of the cloud, saying, "This is My beloved Son in whom I am well pleased. Hear Him!"* (Matt. 17:4-5, NKJV)

After that, Elijah and Moses disappeared and Jesus alone stood before them.

Though Peter had received a revelation that Jesus was the Son of God, he had not received the full implication of it. He was ready to make three tabernacles of equal significance, which would reduce Jesus to being just one among the great representatives of God. Many groups named among Christendom describe Jesus thus, as does the Islam religion. This Biblical account reveals that we can have a revelation of a coming Apostolic Movement and the restoration of apostles, but not have the complete implications and accurate applications of that revelation. There is only one supreme Apostle and one all-knowing Prophet, Jesus Christ, the Great Shepherd and Apostle of our souls, and the Mighty Prophet, who not only points the way but is the Way, the Truth and the Life. In no way must we convey that the last-days apostles and prophets have some high position and authority over the Church such as the Apostle-Pope of Rome claims. They are just two of the five-fold expressions of Jesus Christ. Their position is beneath the building of the Church, not on the top. Their God-given place was not to be the pinnacle and roof of the Church, but the foundation of the Church. They are not exalted ministries, but undergirding supernatural ministries of the Church.

There Was Another Purpose for the Transfiguration.
Apostle Paul stated to the Jews that Moses and the prophets testify of Jesus being the promised Messiah and God's only Son. He was referring to the Pentateuch (the first five books of the Bible) that Moses wrote, which included the Law and the Tabernacle of God. The "prophets" made reference to all the Old Testament books that were written by the prophets. The books that Moses wrote and the writings of the prophets were the only Bible the first-century Church had, other than the letters/epistles that had been written by recognized men of divine authority within the Church. It was several centuries before the writings of the New Testament authors were compiled together and joined with the Old Testament writings to make one Bible of sixty-six books. There are several applications of past, present and future truths that the transfiguration of Jesus with Moses and Elijah portrays other than its merely being a witness to Jesus' Messiahship. I believe there is also an application for the restoration of apostles and prophets.

MOSES and ELIJAH PORTRAYAL

<u>MOSES</u>	<u>ELIJAH</u>
A. Pentateuch, Law and Tabernacle.........	A. Writings of the Prophets
B. Witness of the Law	B. Witness of the Prophets
C. New Testament Apostles	C. New Testament Prophets
1. Olive tree on right of Lampstand	1. Olive tree on left of Lampstand
2. One olive branch ministering oil.......	2. Other olive branch giving oil
3. One of the two witnesses	3. The other witness
4. Right hand and eye of the Body	4. Left hand and eye of the Body

Prophet Zechariah saw a vision of a lampstand with a bowl on top of it. There were two olive trees by it, one on the left and one on the right. He also saw olive branches dripping oil into the receptacles of the two gold pipes from which the golden oil drained out. Then the angel asked him if he knew what all this was and he said, "No, my lord." The angel then told him, "These are the two appointed ones, who stand beside the Lord of the whole earth." (See Zechariah 4.) Theologians have interpreted these two to be Moses and Elijah, Israel and the Church, and Archangel Michael and Archangel Gabriel. Any one of the two or possibly all three sets in different ways, times and purposes of God could possibly represent these two olive trees. I would like to present another possibility of the two olive trees being the end-time apostles and prophets. They could be a company of prophets and a company of apostles standing at Christ's right hand and left hand to co-labor with Him in bringing about the consummation of the Age of the Mortal Church of Jesus Christ and helping to establish God's kingdom on earth. Let us first consider several things in determining the validity of this as a real possibility.

The apostle and prophet are the two that have the anointing to pour the oil of revelation into the bowl of the other fivefold ministers and leaders who are the pipes from which the golden oil of truth pours out to the whole Church. Listen to what this prophetic passage has to say: "Who is she [the Church/Bride of Christ] that looketh forth as the morning, fair as the moon, clear as the sun, and terrible as an ARMY with banners? ... Return, return, O Shulamite [Church]; return, return [be restored, be fully restored], that we may look upon thee. What will ye see in the Shulamite? As it were the **company** of **two armies**" (Song 6:10,13). This could apply to the two companies of apostles and prophets who shall bring revelation, application and timing for the Army of the Lord saints to arise and take the kingdom for God (Dan. 7:18,27). But the cry of the Bridegroom is for the apostles and prophets of God to be fully restored within the Church and bring it to the full beauty and stature that God has predestined for the Bride of Christ.

The book of Revelation, which talks much about the Church's end-time ministry and eternal destiny, makes the following statements: It declares that a great angel came down from heaven and put his right foot on the sea and his left foot on the land. He then roared like a lion as he declared that there should no longer be any delay in the executing and finalizing of all of God's prophetic purposes. He then declared that "the mystery of God would be finished, as He declared to His servants the prophets" (Rev. 10:7, NKJV). The prophets who reveal the last mysteries of God would begin with the first note played at the sounding of the seventh trumpet. The DAYS of the sounding of the seventh trumpet would continue until all mysteries were revealed, scriptures fulfilled and everything prepared, so that when the seventh angel sounded the last note, a climactic, victorious transition could take place in Christ's Church and this world that belongs to God. "Then the seventh angel sounded: And there were loud voices in heaven, saying, 'The kingdoms of this world have become the kingdoms of our Lord and of His Christ, and He shall reign forever and ever!' " (Rev. 11:15, NKJV)

However, many things happen between Revelation 10:7 and Revelation 11:15. Apostle John, who was seeing the vision and communicating with the angel, ate the little book that the angel gave him. Then the angel said to him, "You must **prophesy** again about many peoples, nations, tongues, and kings" (Rev. 10:11b, NKJV). He handed Apostle John a measuring rod and said to him, "Rise and measure the temple of God, the altar, and those who worship there" (Rev. 11:1b, NKJV). This means that the prophetic apostles and apostolic prophets are going to measure the Church from top to bottom, discovering where it is lacking and then bring the Church to the full measure of the stature of Christ Jesus.

God then declares:

I will give power to My two witnesses, and they will prophesy.... These are the two olive trees and the two lampstands standing before the God of the earth. ...fire proceeds from their mouth and devours their enemies. And if anyone wants to harm them, he must be killed in this manner. These [two witnesses] *have power to shut heaven, so that no rain falls in the days of their prophecy; and they have power over waters to turn them to blood, and to strike the earth with all plagues, as often as they desire* (Rev. 11:3-6, NKJV).

This sounds like the same things Moses and Prophet Elijah did. Moses struck Egypt with ten plagues, including turning water into blood, causing the weather and elements of nature to bring forth plagues of flies, hailstones, diseases and death to their animals, and finally bringing death to all the firstborn in Egypt. Elijah prophesied and called for a three-year famine in Israel. Prophet Elijah called down fire on two groups of fifty soldiers who came to harm him. The fire fell and burned them to cinders. Apostle Peter spoke judgment upon Ananias and Sapphira for lying to the Holy Spirit, causing them to die immediately. Apostle Paul spoke a judgment of blindness to a man who was trying to hinder the gospel. Prophet Agabus prophesied about famine and world conditions. The prophetic decrees of the prophets of old and the signs, wonders and miracles of Moses are the same things that apostles and prophets do in the New Testament. Apostles bring forth signs, wonders and miracles, and prophets prophesy divine decrees that affect the natural elements, nations and peoples. There are many similarities that Prophets Moses and Elijah have with God's Church apostles and prophets. They have the same ministry and attributes of the two powerfully prophesying, miracle-working witnesses in chapter 11 of the book of Revelation. Therefore, I believe this correlation and application of all of these sets of two meet enough of the rules of Biblical interpretation and dualistic prophecies to be God's fully restored end-time apostles and prophets. They are the generals of a company of apostolic ministers and saints and a company of prophets, prophetic ministers and prophetic saints.

The Persecution and Power of Apostles and Prophets
(Luke 11:49; Rev. 18:20). God, in His wisdom, said that Jesus
would send APOSTLES and PROPHETS during the Age of
His Church and some of them they would PERSECUTE and
KILL (Matt. 23:24). Revelation chapters 16–18 contain the
description of Babylon the Great, the Mother of Harlots. It describes a "Babylon" religious system and a secular Babylonian Empire. These chapters describe the judgments God puts
upon Babylon. They are similar to the judgments God poured
upon Egypt through Moses. "And great Babylon was remembered before God, to give her the cup of the wine of the fierceness of His wrath" (Rev. 16:19b, NKJV).

God declared that His judgments and plagues were being
poured out on Babylon. "For they have shed the blood of
saints and prophets, and You have given them blood to
drink. For it is their just due" (Rev. 16:6, NKJV). In the midst
of these plagues coming upon Babylon and the saints being
greatly persecuted, the Lord Jesus gives a word of comfort to
His Church: "Behold, I am coming as a thief. Blessed is he
who watches, and keeps his garments, lest he walk naked and
they see his shame" (Rev. 16:15, NKJV).

John the revelator said he saw the woman (Babylon) drunk
with the **blood of the saints** and with the **blood of the martyrs of Jesus**. "And those who dwell on the earth will marvel,
whose names are not written in the Book of Life" (Rev. 17:8b,
NKJV). During this time there will be saints on earth whose
names are written in God's Book of Life. Another angel
"cried mightily with a loud voice, saying, 'Babylon the great
is fallen, is fallen, and has become a dwelling place of demons, a prison for every foul spirit, and a cage for every unclean and hated bird!' " (Rev. 18:2, NKJV) "And I heard
another voice from heaven saying, 'Come out of her, **My people**, lest you share in her sins, and lest you receive of her
plagues' " (Rev. 18:4, NKJV).

Then a voice from heaven said, "Rejoice over her, O heaven, and you **HOLY APOSTLES** and **PROPHETS**, for God has avenged you on her!" (Rev. 18:20, NKJV) Like the two witnesses who were martyred but supernaturally raised back to life, many of the apostles and prophets who minister during that time will be persecuted and killed. The reason Babylon becomes so incensed against God's holy apostles and prophets is because they are God's instruments on earth speaking these plagues into existence. **What the angels trumpet forth in heaven the prophets and apostles echo on earth.** They are the ministers on earth who proclaim what the angels are decreeing in heaven, the same as Moses spoke the judgments and plagues on Egypt that the angels were sounding forth in heaven.

God's holy Church apostles and prophets have a co-laboring ministry of bringing about the mighty fall of Babylon the Great. Their authority will be beyond anything we have seen in our day. They also will receive the greatest persecution from the religious Babylon system and the worldly Babylonian empire. Like Moses and Elijah, God's apostles and prophets will prevail over all their enemies unto the end.

The Mutual Ministries of Apostles and Prophets.

The ethical meaning of mutualism is interdependence opposed to individualism. Mutual means that two people have so many things in common in their abilities, vision and ministries that they are interdependent on each other rather than independent of each other. There is no competitiveness, but a complementing of each other. Their callings, ministries and destinies are linked together. They give each other their mutual respect and honor with each having acceptance and appreciation of the other. The mutual ministries of apostles and prophets could be likened unto twins who have so much in common, but each has his or her own unique personality and abilities. But their methods and approaches seem to come from opposite directions, like the right and left hand, in fulfilling goals for their personal life and ministry.

Both of Them Are Given the Revelation Ministry for the Church (Eph. 3:5). Paul declared that his understanding of the Church being the many-membered corporate Body of Christ was obtained by the divine revelation anointing that God had given him as an apostle. He received his revelation of the Church direct from the heart and mind of God. The revelation was the fact that Jews and Gentiles, male and female, bond and free, could become direct members of the Body of Christ without the Law of Moses, circumcision or becoming a proselyte Jew first. In his epistles to the church at Rome, Galatia and Ephesus, he laid the foundation for this revolutionary truth. He also reveals that this anointing for divine revelation was not just given to the prophets of old but has now been equally given to Christ's HOLY APOSTLES and PROPHETS in His Church.

Their Mutual Foundation-Laying Ministry (Eph. 2:20). Paul emphasized that Jesus Christ is the cornerstone of the Church, which is called a building that grows until it is able to be a habitation of God through His Holy Spirit. By the spirit of revelation in Christ Jesus he declared that the apostles and prophets were the foundation upon which God's Church/Building was to be built. They were not only to lay the foundation for the Church Age but were also to be ongoing foundation-laying ministries in the Church. They have co-equal ministries for laying foundations in churches. But like the right hand and left hand feeding the mouth, their approach is from opposite directions.

The apostle and prophet function differently in their mutual foundation-laying ministry. For years I functioned in this ministry as a prophet and also co-labored with apostles in establishing churches on a firm foundation. Now for a few years, I have been functioning as an apostle and have been divinely invested in both ministries. I can tell when I am moving in the prophetic or the apostolic and when I am ministering with both.

Let me try to explain the approach of the prophet on one hand and the apostle on the other. About twelve years ago God started challenging me to give a prophetic word of what Christ Jesus would say to a particular local church if He was there personally. This would help found them on a foundation of confidence concerning where they were in their progressive journey in fulfilling God's purpose for their existence.

Christ Jesus dictated to John seven letters to seven different churches in Asia. He followed the same outline for each church but had a specific revelation, commendation, condemnation and overcoming reward for each local church. Jesus works in a similar way with me when I go to different churches and nations. He has always given me a scriptural setting with special application to the pastor and his local church. God will sometimes reveal one of the seven letters as being applicable to that church. The Holy Spirit may reveal where they are in their personal journey from coming out of Egypt to being in their promised Canaan land where they are fighting for and possessing their inheritance. At other times He uses a Biblical setting in one of the books of the prophets or historical books. This type of prophetic word is not delivered the same way as personal prophecy. I explain to them that I am speaking to them this Sunday morning not as a preacher with his favorite message or as a teacher teaching established Biblical truth, but as a prophet with a prophetic word that the Holy Spirit wants to personally apply to their church.

Wisdom for Prophesying to Leadership. The leadership in the majority of places where I minister have confidence that the word spoken will be accurate, seasoned with salt and delivered in love with wisdom and discretion. I make it a policy to always check first with pastors who are not familiar with this type of prophetic ministry. If they feel uncomfortable or say they would rather not receive that type of ministry, then I seek the Lord for the Logos truth He wants me to preach or I just preach whatever I feel the most comfortable with in my spirit. However, if God declares that I must deliver it whether the pastor wants it or not, then I either speak it to the pastor in private or write it out and give it to him there or mail it to him later. This is based on the prophetic principles found in Jeremiah and Ezekiel.

If there are major things in the prophetic word that could suggest a change of direction or personnel changes for the local leadership, then I share these first with the pastor in detail and make a general application for the congregation to hear. I teach all our prophets and apostles who travel to other churches to respect and honor the pastoral headship of the local church. He is the gatekeeper of that flock of sheep. The pastor has the responsibility before God as to what he does with that word. If he knows it is of God then he must get the wisdom of God concerning when, where and how to deliver that prophetic word to the church.

Prophets and **apostles** have no more right to go into a church and try to rearrange everything than a father of a married son with several children has a right to go into the son's home and rearrange everything. Nor does a true pastor go into the home of one of his members and rearrange everything in that home. If a family gives the pastor the right or a pastor gives his apostolic oversight the right and authority, then they have liberty to go in and relay a proper foundation for that family or church. If gross sin is going on in the local church, then their apostolic or prophetic overseer has a right to step in to bring correction and adjustment to the situation. The independent churches, pastors and traveling ministers, who are not seriously committed in covenant relationship with a mature overseer, will have no one to turn to in their hour of need. Friends will give sympathy and help where they can, but no one can bring wisdom and resolution to the situation like those who have been given and have been accepted as God's delegated overseeing authority in one's life and ministry. The worst position anyone can be in this day and hour is one of a "lone ranger" minister or saint who is his own covering and is not submitted to anyone. Next to this, the worst position to be in is being committed to the wrong group, under immature leadership, who is neither anointed nor walking in present truth. It is just like there is something worse for a young woman than being single—being married out of the will of God to the wrong man.

Prophets help lay foundations in churches by prophetically clarifying their vision, giving prophetic direction and order for certain areas of the church, and revealing where they are in their journey of fulfilling God's progressive purpose for their local church. Prophets can reveal what is going on in the demonic spirit realm concerning demons who have been assigned by the devil to stop and destroy that work of God. Prophets can supernaturally reveal and give clarity and application to what the leadership is sensing, as Prophet Daniel did for the king of Babylon and Joseph did for the Pharaoh of Egypt. I have given such words to hundreds of churches over the last decade.

Discovering and Establishing Foundations. Discovery has been made by the Spirit that some churches and ministries were established by someone who just wanted to make a place for their ministry. Other churches were actually born of God and are being raised up to fulfill Christ's own purpose. Some pastors become the pastor of a church that has already been established for years. They may know their own vision but may not know whether God or man planted that church. If it was a church birthed and established by the will of God, the new pastor may not know what God's original purpose was for establishing that type of church in that particular area. Sometimes the original foundational purpose has to be prophetically uncovered or a new foundation laid that fulfills God's current purpose for that church. All churches preaching and practicing the truth are good. However, some are ordained of God and He especially directed that church or ministry to be established for His sake, and not just for the sake of the pastor or congregation. Such prophetic revelation lays a foundation that cannot be shaken when the pastor knows in his heart and then has it confirmed and amplified by a "Thus saith the Lord."

The Power of Prophetic Revelation. Many churches have been saved from splits and destruction when a prophet came in not knowing anything about the pastor or congregation and prophetically revealed what was going on in the spirit realm. It changes the saints from fighting one another and the leadership to being united in fighting the evil principalities and powers that are arrayed against them. It especially helps when the prophetic word can confirm that the pastor was not denominationally or self-appointed, but is God's choice and is in that position and place by divine appointment. When the congregation and pastor realize that it is not flesh and blood humans they are fighting but certain evil spirit forces, it destroys confusion and lays the foundation of unity. It causes the congregation to join together with each other and the leadership by laying down their own individual visions and becoming committed to fulfilling God's one vision and main purpose for their local church.

Apostles lay foundations by divine revelation, presenting the truth with apostolic authority and wisdom. Apostles usually like to hear both sides of the situation and then give wise counsel that corrects and adjusts with the voice of wisdom, maturity and divine authority. If it is a new foundation being laid for church planting, then they teach, preach and demonstrate the doctrines of God and lay the foundation with the fundamentals of the Christian faith. The true apostles who are God-anointed and walking in present truth do this with more than words and arguments that convince the mind. They lay foundations with a supernatural spiritual authority that changes hearts and activates the spiritual gifts of eternal life, the Holy Spirit and membership ministries. They do not establish people by enticing words of man's wisdom but in the power and demonstration of the Holy Spirit with signs, wonders and miracles (see 1 Cor. 1–16).

Apostles and Prophets Equip and Mature the Saints. They are co-laborers along with Christ's evangelists, pastors and teachers to spiritually equip the saints in their particular membership ministry in the Body of Christ (Eph. 4:11-16). When every member in the Body is in its proper place and fully functioning as it should, then the whole Body of Christ functions and fulfills its purpose as it is motivated by love. **This scripture is the only place in the Bible where all fivefold ministers are listed together** (verse 11). The five, including apostles and prophets, are to continue functioning until Christ's Church "come[s] in the unity of the faith, and of the knowledge of the Son of God, unto a perfect man, unto the measure of the stature of the fulness of Christ" (verse 13). Now that is a big commission from Christ Jesus. The word "stature" means age or maturity. This means that God's destiny for the Church is for it to be conformed to Christ's likeness and manifest the fullness of His maturity and ministry before the Second Coming of Jesus. The Bible declares that every scripture will be fulfilled. The heavens and the earth may fail and pass away but God's word will never fail or pass away (Matt. 24:35). It is settled forever in heaven as well as on earth (Ps. 119:89).

There Are Some Christian Ministers Who Do Not Believe in the Full Restoration of the Church. They believe that there will be just a few walking in the faith. They declare that the purpose of the Second Coming of Christ (rapture) is to snatch the Church off the earth before the anti-Christ arises and completely destroys them.

What will motivate Jesus to return for His Bride/Church? Jesus was not motivated to remove the Church from earth when multimillions were being martyred during its first three centuries. He was not motivated to return during the great falling away of the Church. It was in an apostate condition for more than a thousand years during the Dark Ages. If Jesus was waiting for the great falling away of the Church before He came, then He could have come during that time, but He didn't. However, He did come by His Holy Spirit to begin the great restoration of the Church, which has been progressively growing since the 1500's to the present.

The Bible reveals only one thing that will motivate Jesus to return and that is the fulfilling of all prophetic scriptures written by the prophets and apostles. One of those prophetic scriptures is the one we're discussing, which states that all fivefold ministers must function until Christ's Church is a fully restored Church, a glorious spotless Church, an overcoming-all-things Church, which subdues all Christ's enemies and places them under His feet. If the rapture of the Church takes place before this is accomplished, then declaration would have to be made that these scriptures failed to come to pass, or the apostles, prophets and other fivefold ministers will have to continue their ministry after the rapture until these scriptures are fulfilled.

Apostles and Prophets have a coequal ministry of bringing Christ's Church to full maturity and ministry. God established five, not three, to fulfill this ministry. Therefore, the full restoration of prophets and apostles is essential to God's purpose being fulfilled. The cry needs to arise within all saints and leadership for God's holy apostles and prophets to be reestablished in their rightful position and powerful ministry within the Church.

In Conclusion: Sufficient scriptural evidence has been presented that apostles and prophets are kindred ministries. They can both do the same things but approach them from opposite directions. They both lay foundations in the Church and have the ministry of revealing the new things that God is doing upon the earth. They both minister with a similar anointing, but have different concerns and methods of accomplishing their mutual objectives. They both prophesy, activate gifts and ministries, perform miracles and have supernatural signs and wonders in their ministries. However, apostles have more anointing for planting churches and pastoring successfully. Prophets have a greater anointing for spiritually activating saints and ministers in their gifts and ministries.

Prophets produce most of their miracles while prophesying and receiving a word of knowledge of a certain situation, and then prophetically decreeing God's miracle-working power. I would say over ninety percent of the hundreds of miracles that have transpired in my prophet ministry happened while prophesying. There have been cancers healed, hearts and blood systems restored and numerous couples who could not bear children were healed and enabled to conceive and bear children.

Apostles Work Their Signs, Wonders, and Miracles With the Power Gifts of Working of Miracles and the Gift of Faith. They have more of the outward miracles such as cripples walking, the blind seeing and the deaf hearing. (In another section we cover the differences between the miracle ministry of the evangelist and that of the apostle.) These divine abilities are standard equipment that come with the commissioning to the office of an apostle. Just as joy and peace come with the gift of eternal life, and a new spiritual language comes with the gift of the Holy Spirit, so does prophesying come with the ascension gift of prophet and the miraculous with the apostle. It might take volumes of books and hours of teaching and demonstration by the apostle before he is fully known within the Church. Apostles were the first to be activated in the Church and are now the last to be restored. However, at this time we want to establish the Biblical reality that there are prophets and apostles present in the Church.

Apostles and prophets have mutual ministries in all they do in the Body of Christ. Like twins, they are separate and unique in their own ministries but have more things in common than any other ministries mentioned. They are powerful and effective in their own ministry but when they join together they are multiplied many times over. One can put a thousand to flight, but when they co-labor together, two can put ten thousand to flight. The devil, old order religion and independent pseudo-apostles and prophets will do all in their power to keep the apostles and prophets separated into two different camps. They will try to bring competition and conflict between these two anointed ministries. But God's will in this area is already preordained to be done, for it is His will for prophets and apostles to work together.

Apostles and prophets are like a team of two horses harnessed together and pulling one wagon load of anointed ministry. They are like Moses and Elijah, the two witnesses, the two olive trees and branches standing before the God of the whole earth. They have been joined together by almighty God, and what God has joined together, let no man put asunder.

—◦◦●◉◉◉●◦◦—

10

THE CALLING AND MINISTRIES
OF FIVEFOLD MINISTERS

—◦◦●◉◉◉●◦◦—

In the latter years of the 1990's and early years of the 21st century, further illumination and understanding will come from the Holy Spirit to help fivefold ministers properly interrelate during the restoration of apostles. There will also be revelation and divine application for the co-laboring of prophets and apostles.

In Paul's writings to Timothy and Titus he gave directives concerning qualifications and standards for bishops, elders and deacons (1 Tim. 3:1-13; Titus 1:5-9). These are general instructions and requirements for those who will be in leadership within Christ's Church. But there are no statements in the New Testament that make a distinction between fivefold ministers in relation to qualifying standards of character or supernatural experiences, nor are any distinctions or directives given concerning what positions can be held within the structure of the Church.

Five important insights must be considered and understood concerning fivefold ministers:

1. They are all headship ministries. That is, they are an extension of the headship ministry of Jesus Christ, the

Head of the Church. They are not "Body" ministries such as the gifts and ministries that the Holy Spirit gives to members of Christ's corporate Body. Technically speaking, they are not gifts of the Holy Spirit, but ascension gifts of Jesus Christ Himself.

2.   All fivefold ministers are called to govern, guide, gather, ground and guard God's people. However, each has been given special grace and gifted ability in one area more than the others. These one-word explanations should not be seen as limitations on each minister's activities, but rather as a one-word description of each one's major anointing and divinely given ability.

3.   It is unscriptural and unwise to put an apostle, prophet, evangelist, pastor or teacher into a box of limited anointings and activities. There are no scriptures that even suggest that fivefold ministers are limited to certain ministerial activities or leadership positions. The fivefold ascension gifts of Christ overlap and integrate just as the nine gifts of the Holy Spirit do. Fivefold ministers are not independent ministries separated from one another but rather interdependent ministries vitally related to each other in Christ. They are the fivefold ministry of the one Christ. They are five parts of one whole. It takes all five working together to make the fullness of Christ's ministry to the Body of Christ. None are inferior or superior but all are anointed and appointed of God for a specific purpose.

4.   It is detrimental to the function of fivefold ministers for them to be categorized with details concerning personalities, performances and positions. The Holy Spirit is also grieved when people formulate methods for evaluating and determining a fivefold ministry office by some psychoanalysis technique or personality profile. God will not allow anything to take His place in this area.

5. Each fivefold minister knows best his own calling and ministry. It is not the prerogative of the prophet to give guidelines, directions and restrictions on the ministry of the apostle. Likewise the apostle has not been granted authority from Father God to be daddy and director over the prophet. Only a prophet really knows the ministry and function of a prophet. And even one prophet should not try to box another prophet into his prophetic role, personality or performance. However, we all must receive from one another and be subject to correction and adjustment in methodology and interrelationships.

The Mighty Hand of God.

The fivefold ministry can be illustrated by the human hand.

The Apostle = Thumb: The thumb more properly represents the ministry of the apostle. Notice that the thumb can touch and minister to all four of the fingers. As the hand functions, sometimes it is flat and all are side by side. When taking hold of something the thumb goes to one side of the object and the fingers encircle from the opposite side. This motion of coming from opposite directions gives power to the hand. The thumb is not in opposition or over the fingers but is designed to complete the hand for its full function and power. The hand of God of the five-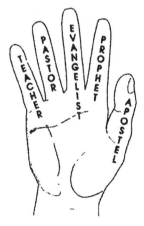fold ministry has been greatly restricted in its powerful purposes. The hand of God has had to function with only four fingers. The power and function is limited greatly by the lack of a thumb. Now the apostle-thumb of the hand of God is being restored to proper placement and power. Since all elements of the hand of God are being restored fully, the hand of God will be extended in full power and demonstration.

The Prophet = Forefinger: The forefinger is referred to as the one that points. The prophet has the ministry of revelation and anointing that points the way for the Body of Christ. The forefinger is also the one most closely related to the thumb. Though they approach their grip on something from opposite directions, it is this opposite approach that gives the hand the power to take a powerful grip on things. The prophet and apostle have the closest working relationship in their hand ministry to the Body of Christ.

The Evangelist = Middle Finger: The middle finger extends the furthest on the hand. It is the outreach ministry extended to the evangelization of the world. It is in the middle of all activity of the hand. It is usually the largest of the fingers. The evangelist usually has the largest meetings in evangelistic campaigns. The evangelist is a vital part of the ministry of the hand.

The Pastor = Ring Finger: This is the finger that the wedding rings goes on. The pastor is married to the saints. He is with them twenty-four hours a day. Prophets and evangelists come and go but the pastor is bound to the local saints by the ring of their shepherding relationship.

The Teacher = Little Finger: Though the little finger is the smallest, it provides balance to the hand. The teaching of the Word of God line upon line, precept upon precept, is desperately needed within the Church. The teacher is a vital member of the hand ministry of Christ to His Church.

There are many more applicable illustrations that can be made to the fingers and thumb representing the fivefold ministry of Christ. Some have tried to say that the pastor and teacher are one ministry and therefore there are only four ascension gifts. But there are several Biblical illustrations that portray the fivefold ministry: the hand, the five bars on the sides of the tabernacle, the five pillars at the entrance to the Holy Place, the five senses and five being the number of grace and redemption. The fivefold ministry is God's main group of ministers for ministering God's grace and redemption.

The hand is the only outward member of the body that can minister to all parts of the body from back to front and from head to toe. In First Peter 5:5-6, it says for the saints to humble themselves under the mighty hand of God and they will be exalted in due time. The fivefold ministry represents the hand of God. It is almost impossible for individuals to humble themselves under God without humbling themselves in submission and relationship to Christ's delegated representatives of Him to His Church.

Artificial Methods of Determining Ministry. Some ministers, teachers and theologians like to have every ministry organized and categorized in detail according to personality, performance and position. But such charts and designations cause those who teach them to put every ministry in a separate box. This may help some ministers to better understand their calling, but at the same time, it will cause other ministers to think they are boxed in by those things designated on the chart for their area.

It may also cause novices to assume that they have a certain ascension gift and fivefold ministry calling simply because they seem to meet those descriptions. This results in determining a person's divine gifts or fivefold calling by some analysis chart instead of a Holy Spirit revelation and conviction. This is not to say that some forms of personality, skill or purpose analysis are not useful at all. Such tests and charts can be helpful in understanding individual temperaments, strengths and weaknesses. But that is not the same thing as identifying a person's divine calling.

Divine Calling Comes by Holy Spirit Revelation. God sovereignly chooses to call whom He will for whichever purpose He wills. And He often does so in spite of an individual's temperament, strengths or weaknesses. The proof of that call is evidenced by a minister's submission to God's progressive training over a period of years. Afterwards, the ministry is recognized by the rest of the Body of Christ because of the years of fruitful and consistent ministry, not by an analysis chart.

Man-Made Tests Cannot Determine Divine Calling. We once had someone come to our campus to teach on knowing and recognizing ministry. He had researched some scientific medical studies on right and left brain functions. According to the results of the study, right brain people are more artistic, imaginative, intuitive and visionary. The left brain people are more analytical, mathematical, logical and practical.

All of this was useful information. But then the teacher went further to say that prophets would typically fit into the right brain group. So ten of our prophets on the campus took the test to check his conclusion.

On a scale of 0 to 10, below 5 shows that the person functions more from the left brain and above 5, the right brain. The teacher was shocked and puzzled to discover that all of our prophets except our prophetic worship leader scored below 5. My own score was 3.9. My wife took the test not as one of the ten prophets but out of curiosity. Her score was 5.0.

Whether these same results would hold for the majority of prophets is hard to say. But the point is that only one out of ten of our prophets who took the test scored as a right brain person. The natural man wants to have a formula for everything rather than depend on the leading of the Spirit and revelation knowledge from Christ Jesus. Therefore God will never allow us to come up with methods to take the place of Himself and the workings of His Holy Spirit.

Human-Made Analysis Charts Cannot Determine Divine Ministry. In all the prophetic pronouncements over me, confirmation of my calling to the ascension gift and ministry of prophet has been repeated over fifty times and of the apostle twenty times by numerous prophetic ministers through the years. I have also demonstrated more than forty-three years of proven, fruitful ministry as a prophet, and the last five years as an apostle. But when I took the "motivational gifts" test, it concluded that my main motivational gifts were mercy and exhortation, not prophet or administration.

Which should I believe: the prophecies that have gone over me along with inner revelations and convictions and years of proven ministry, or some human-made chart for determining a person's gift? You cannot determine a divine, God-ordained calling by some human analysis, even though it may use a few scriptures as a basis for its formulas and tests.

The motivational gifts test is good for insight into the human temperament that a person is born with. Dividing people into "four temperaments" or testing them to determine motivational gifts or their unique human nature helps to understand why people act and react certain ways. It has other psychological benefits for understanding ourselves and counseling others. But none of those human-made systems can help a person determine his or her divine calling as a fivefold minister, or tell them his or her membership ministry in the spiritual Body of Christ. In our CI Ministry Training College, we declare that we will help the students to know their God, know themselves, and know their calling, gifts and ministries.

We use every chart and analysis available to help them to know and understand themselves, but this does not reveal divine gifts of the Holy Spirit, fivefold ministry calling or any other Biblical ministry that requires the Holy Spirit's divine impartation and enablement.

The divine seed of a spiritual gift or call must be planted by God, then incubated in the womb of prayer, obedience and spiritual growth until God's appointed time for birthing. After the ministry is birthed, it must be nurtured, protected, exercised and progressively matured until all the person's potential reaches fullness of manhood or womanhood and ministry. There is a difference between the time of one's initial ministry "calling" and the time of one's full "commissioning" to that ministry position in the Body of Christ.

Human-Made Limitations vs. Abiding in Our Own Calling. Never swing to the extreme of limiting yourself or anyone else where Scripture does not impose a limitation or restriction. Only God knows the fullness of what He has called a person to be and become.

Nor should you swing to the other extreme of trying to be and do everything that other ministers are being and doing. Pastors, teachers and evangelists who read this book should not get a feeling of lesser importance than the apostle or prophet. We are not emphasizing them because they are more important than, or superior to, the others, but simply because they are less understood and recognized than are the pastors, teachers and evangelists. The fivefold ministers should never be compared as greater or lesser, more essential or less essential, for they are all equal parts of the one Christ. We cannot say one part of Christ's nature and performance is more valuable than some other part of Christ. Read First Corinthians 12 and Romans 12 and you will find that the Holy Spirit is very emphatic about this. Apostle Paul declared that they who compare themselves among themselves are not wise (2 Cor. 10:12). Each calling and ministry has its own special purpose and performance. Be content in your calling, while at the same time pressing toward the mark of apprehending all of that for which Christ has apprehended you (Phil. 3:12-14; 1 Cor. 7:20).

The Biblical principle concerning divine gifts and talents is that if you faithfully use what you have been given, then God will give you more (Matt. 25:14-30). In fact, according to Biblical principle, if you become a faithful and profitable servant, God will even take the talents from those unprofitable servants who are afraid to use what they have, and give them to you to bless His Church (verses 28-29). This truth and divine principle of God's doubling one's gifts and ministries is what was used to help me accept the anointing to be an apostle. I had pioneered and fought for the restoration of the prophets and their rights to their ministry for several decades. I did not want it to appear that I was forsaking the prophets or had graduated to a higher level when I accepted my role as apostle. I definitely do not believe that there is superiority or a hierarchal line of authority and importance among the fivefold ministers. God assured me this was not what He wanted me to do, but rather, I should take the apostleship He was giving me to help pioneer and bring forth a great host of apostles, and then to join the two together as equal, co-laboring representatives of Christ's apostolic and prophetic ministry to His Church. Because I had faithfully used the talent of prophet, and had reproduced and brought forth hundreds of other prophets, Christ Jesus was going to double my talents by adding the talent of the apostle to my anointed ability. It would be like a double-barreled shotgun; one barrel would be that of the prophet and the other would be the apostle. The Holy Spirit would teach me what trigger to pull to meet what needs, as well as show me when I needed to pull both triggers at the same time to release the power in the barrels of the apostle and prophet. All things are possible for those who accept, believe and faithfully use what they have divinely received.

No One Person But Jesus Is All Five. Never allow your faith to become a presumptuous belief that you can have the calling and abilities of all fivefold ministers. Only Jesus had the fullness of all five ministries in one human body (Col. 2:9). No other human can have the fullness of all five—not even the Pope, or an apostle over hundreds of ministers, or a pastor of a congregation of thousands.

Christ never did, and never will, give all five gifts and anointings to any one person. But when He ascended on high He did give His ministry to men and women (Eph. 4:8). He took His whole ministry mantle and distributed it into five parts, dividing His wisdom, ability and performance into five categories. He designated them with certain titles that reveal these special gifts and ministries that He gave to His corporate Body. To some He gave His apostle ministry, to others His prophet mantle, to others His pastoral anointing, to others His evangelistic zeal and to still others His master teacher ability.

The Pastor Cannot Do It All Alone. I have seen some pastors who rarely have outside speakers in, as though they assume that they can perfect and properly equip the saints all by themselves. But there is no way a local congregation can reach proper Biblical maturity and ministry without receiving mature ministry from the other fivefold ministers. There are no scriptures that even suggest that one senior shepherd of a local flock has been given all the truth and ministry needed to perfect his saints.

However, I do believe 21st-century churches who are walking in present truth will have all fivefold ministers within the local church. Here at CI Family Church, we have about fifteen ordained ministers who are heads of the various organizations and ministries and are also ministering elders in the church. My son and daughter-in-law, Tom and Jane Hamon, are the "pastors" of the local church. Many have tried having all fivefold ministers as coequal heads of a local church. But anything with more than one head is not according to God's order in natural creation and it is the same spiritually in the local church. There must be a set-man, the vision-holder whom God has called and commissioned to fulfill His purpose for that church. He could be any of the fivefold ministers. If the vision-holder has the gift and calling of "pastor," that does not mean that the apostles and prophets in that local church have authority or preeminence over the pastor. But we could have five departments in the church overseen by fivefold ministers.

The ones called to be apostles would oversee the **apostolic department**. Their ministry would be to develop apostolic teams for miracle ministries and to send apostolic teams to other churches to impart, activate and demonstrate the apostolic anointing. These would go to other areas and nations to establish new churches and help the local pastors to restore order and unity in existing congregations.

The **pastoral department** would oversee all the home group leaders, help the senior pastor fulfill pastoral ministries of conducting weddings, funerals, visitations, praying and ministering to the needs of people by counseling, as well as other pastoral ministries. In our church the **teaching department** is over all educational and training ministries such as our distance education college with eight thousand students, the resident Ministry Training College students and other training programs within the local church. The **evangelistic department** oversees all evangelism outreach and the evangelistic teams, maintains the enthusiasm and vision for winning more souls to Jesus and trains prophetic evangelists to conduct ministry like Philip's evangelistic campaign in Samaria.

The prophetic department would oversee the prophetic department, developing prophetic teams to be able to give an accurate and timely prophetic word in personal prophecy and in forming prophetic presbyteries or teams consisting of two or three qualified members.

At our last annual CI conference more than a thousand people were in attendance, as were thirty from our Board of Governors. These are mature ministers who are pastors of churches, traveling ministers or heads of organizations. There were also two hundred fifty of our four hundred fifty CINC ministers in attendance. We formed fifty prophetic teams with hand-held tape recorders and prophesied to one thousand people in one afternoon. We have been training prophetic ministers for twelve years, and we only allow proven ministers to prophesy to the people.

When we started prophetic seminars in 1983, I was the only seasoned prophet, so I did all the preaching, teaching and prophesying. You can see the power of the reproducing anointing. For instance, I did it all at the beginning, but at this last conference I did not even participate in the prophetic teams. We believe God will help us do the same with those called to be apostles and other ministers who want to minister with an apostolic anointing. The seed principle in Genesis is that every seed is to reproduce after its kind. Based on this principle all fivefold ministers who are ministering to people should reproduce like kind, not just one or two but many. As an example, one grain of corn will reproduce about two thousand grains on one large stalk of corn. Wouldn't it be wonderful if all great evangelists and successful pastors, who have been in the ministry for several years, had all reproduced thousands of ministers who could do the same works and ministry that they are doing?

A pastor may conform his congregation to his doctrines, ways and ministries—but not into Christ's fullness. The Scripture emphatically declares that it takes all five, including apostles, prophets, evangelists, pastors and teachers to do the job. All five are needed to perfect, mature and equip the saints for entering into the work of their membership ministries in the Body of Christ so that it is continually built up, "till we all come in the unity of the faith, and of the knowledge of the Son of God, unto a perfect man, unto the measure of the stature of the fulness of Christ" (Eph. 4:13).

Same Ascension Gift, Different Performance. Not only does each of the five have their own unique calling and special gifting, but each of those called to the same office do not have the same personality, commissioning or performance. "Now there are diversities of gifts, but the same Spirit. And there are differences of administrations, but the same Lord. And there are diversities of operations, but it is the same God which worketh all in all" (1 Cor. 12:4-6). There are as many diversities of operations as there are people with ascension gifts.

Apostles Used as Examples of All. Of all the fivefold ministries, we have the most life examples of the apostle in the New Testament with information relating to their calling, training and ministry. So we will use them to portray this truth, which applies to all five. Each of the original Twelve Apostles plus the thirteen others mentioned—including the Apostle Paul— had their own particular calling and commissioning from the Lord Jesus Christ. God's different methods of calling and His special commissions for Apostle Paul and Apostle Peter demonstrate that people can have the same ascension gift, while each manifests a unique personality and performance.

Peter and Paul are the only two apostles of whom the Bible gives examples of their apostolic ministry. Peter had no supernatural experience in his calling to be an apostle. He simply made his contact with Christ through his brother Andrew's effort to bring him to the Lord. After he had followed the Lord for a while, Christ commissioned him as one of the Twelve at the same time as the others.

Paul was not one of the original Twelve, but came to know the Lord after Christ was resurrected and appeared to him in a supernatural blinding light on the road to Damascus. Paul's conversion and calling to be a servant of Jesus Christ came through this supernatural encounter with Jesus. His calling to bear the name of Jesus to the Gentiles came through personal prophecy (Acts 9:15). His commissioning to his apostleship came through the prophetic presbytery at Antioch some seventeen years later.

Peter had a limited education and no theological schooling. Paul was highly educated and probably had what would be equivalent today to a Doctor of Theology degree.

While at Cornelius' house, Peter was the first to receive the revelation that Gentiles could become Christians without first becoming proselyte Jews. But it was Paul who received the commission from Christ to become the apostle to the Gentiles.

According to human logic, it would seem that Paul should have been the apostle to the Jews and Peter the apostle to the Gentiles. But God does things His way, not ours. Apostle Peter was called and commissioned to be an apostle to the Jews while Paul received the commissioning from Christ to be an apostle to the Gentiles (2 Tim. 1:11; Gal. 2:7-9).

Both Peter and Paul were apostles. But each had a special calling and commission from God, according to His sovereign choice.

Apostle James spent all of his life's ministry in the position of senior pastor of the church in Jerusalem. Seemingly, he never ministered outside of Jerusalem. But Apostle Paul traveled continually during his thirty-plus years of ministry. His longest stay at any local church was two years in Ephesus where he established the first New Testament church apart from being connected with a Jewish synagogue. So we can't say all apostles will be pastors of large churches, or that they just travel and establish churches. For the rest of the twelve and most of the church apostles, there is no Biblical record of what they did and for how long. Let us not put apostles in a box and say all apostles will always do this or that, or be in a position of oversight in the Church.

Personality Profiles for Prophets and Apostles. I was once asked, "After more than three decades as a prophet, can you give us the personality profile of a prophet?" I sought the Lord about it, and this was His answer: "Take the Twelve Apostles and evaluate each of their personalities. If you can find that there is a consistent personality pattern for an apostle, then you can give a personality profile for prophets." This is also true of pastors, evangelists and teachers.

Needless to say, a study of the Twelve Apostles shows clearly that they were different in personality, natural motivation and character. There is no personality profile for apostles, prophets, evangelists, pastors or teachers. There are no consistent human character traits that are unique to any one of the five.

I have prophesied to thousands of people their fivefold ministry calling. Notice was made that most of those with the calling of an apostle were usually stockier built, spoke slower, had more of an easy-going mannerism and were more concerned about the practical side of Christianity than the spiritual gifts and ministries. Most prophets were built more slender, talked much faster and had an intense personality with more concern for the Church being spiritual, visionary and on purpose. However, I would never set that as a way to determine whether one is an apostle or a prophet. I have seen proven apostles who were tall and slender and had more of the temperament of the typical prophet. I have also worked with proven prophets who were very large in body and had more of the temperament and motivation of the typical apostle.

Sometimes I jokingly tell people, "For thirty years of my ministry I was tall, slender, talked fast and was an impatient visionary, but during the last twelve years I have slowed down in my preaching, become stockier built and more patient and easy-going. I was the prophet type but now the apostle type. I am now adjusting my size and balancing out so that I can be both!" While prophesying to a husband and wife team where the husband has the calling of an apostle and the woman of a prophetess, I have often heard the Holy Spirit use the example of the apostle being like a Clydesdale workhorse and the prophetess as a race horse. God had joined them together and they must learn to understand and appreciate each other and pull together. These observations are interesting but not worthy of being a determining factor in knowing one's fivefold ministry.

The original Twelve Apostles were privileged to walk and talk with Christ for over three years, but the other apostles mentioned were not. Only three of the twelve wrote material that became books in the Bible. Yet Apostle Paul's writings produced fourteen New Testament books, more than that of all the Twelve Apostles together. For some of the apostles, we have no record of them ever writing anything at all. (I am, of course, using the apostle as an example of standards and principles that apply to all fivefold ministers.)

Know Them by Their Fruit. The Bible offers no standards of personality, style of ministry, supernatural experiences, mode of ministry or any formula by which we can classify a person as a fivefold minister.

The only way a fivefold minister's calling can be determined is by receiving a revelation from God, training for that ministry and then evidencing the fruit of that ministry. Jesus does the calling and gifting, and He declares that it is by their fruit that you shall know them (Matt. 7:16).

We can illustrate this further. Some are saying today that all apostles will be pastors of large successful churches and have several ministers and churches who look to them as their apostle-pastor. But Apostle Paul during some thirty years of ministry never stayed as pastor of any one church for more than two or three years. He was mainly an itinerant minister who traveled all over the nations as what we would call today an apostolic missionary. Paul won new converts to Christ and left them in the local synagogue or established a New Testament church with them.

He returned to these churches on other ministry trips and established leadership in these congregations. He formed prophetic presbyteries and laid hands upon the candidates and prophesied to them their gifts and callings. Those he prophetically sensed had the calling and qualifications he set in as the eldership ministry over that congregation (1 Tim. 4:14; 1:18; Acts 14:23).

As we previously mentioned, Apostle James pastored the church in Jerusalem all the days of his ministry. As far as we know, he never traveled beyond his local area.

Anyone who forms a psychological chart or establishes standards of personality, positions and performances to determine whether someone is an apostle will do injustice to the callings and purposes of God for His fivefold ministers. Using analysis charts to determine one's fivefold ministry will do more harm than good. It requires only a little thinking along this line to see that each minister is as unique in personality, power, performance, position and commission as five natural sons of one father would be different in these areas.

Two Prideful Extremes to Be Avoided. Already I am hearing from some quarters two teachings that are not Biblically based and that unduly limit the function of ascension gift ministers.

The first is that only apostles can govern and be head administrators. The **second is** that only prophets can prophesy guidance, gifts and ministry. The seedbed from which these plants of extremism have sprouted is the alliterated list of one-word descriptions some have given for identifying the main ministry of each of the fivefold ministers. This list insists that apostles govern, prophets guide, evangelists gather, pastors guard and teachers ground. Because of these two words—"govern" for the apostle and "guide" for the prophet—the teaching has begun to be spread among certain circles of influential church leaders that prophets are not supposed to be in any headship ministry such as a pastor of a church, a president of a ministry organization or a bishop/overseer of an international fellowship of ministers. I have diligently searched and could find no scriptures that put such limitations on any of the fivefold ministers. There are no directives concerning when, where, how or what some can or cannot minister. There are no Biblical examples or scriptures that state that some of the fivefold ministers can hold certain positions in the Church and others cannot.

Can Prophets Govern and Be Heads of Ministry? If the one-word descriptions of the fivefold ministers' roles cited previously were allowed to become literal limitations (rather than suggestive descriptions), then pastors could guard the church but not be senior ministers in headship to govern the church. Pastors could guard the sheep but not ground them in the Word of God and church life, for that would have to be turned over to the teachers. Apostles could govern but not until the prophets guided them in what to govern and how to govern it. We can thus easily see the unscriptural and impractical nature of such limiting notions of fivefold ministries.

One divine principle in Biblical interpretation is that whatever was established in the Old Testament remains proper as a principle or practice unless the New Testament does away with it. For instance, tithing was established in the Old Testament, and since nothing is stated in the New that abolishes it, then it is still a proper practice for Christians. The same is true of worship and singing praises accompanied with all kinds of musical instruments, as was done in David's Tabernacle. And the same is also true concerning the ministry of the prophet.

Jesus came and fulfilled all things pertaining to the ceremonial law of sacrifices and offerings. By the sacrifice of Himself upon the cross, He fulfilled the Old Covenant for humanity's relationship to God and established a New Covenant. In the New, Jesus is the only way for humankind to be forgiven of its sins and to have fellowship with God. For by one sacrifice He has made perfect forever those who are sanctified (Heb. 10:14), and has become the end of the law for righteousness for all believers (Rom. 10:4).

One God Who Does Not Change. Nevertheless, we do not serve one God of the Old Testament and another God of the New Testament. There is only one eternal God. He remains the same and shall never, ever change. Jesus Christ is the same yesterday, today and forever (Heb. 13:8). God the Father, Son, and Holy Spirit are One in nature, motivation and performance (John 5:7; Mark 12:29; Mal. 3:6; Deut. 4:35; Isa. 45:5; 47:8).

God has changed the ways for humanity to relate to Himself down through the ages and dispensations. But the God that has spoken through His prophets since the beginning is the same God that speaks through His prophets in the New Testament Church. The privileges, ministries and authority that the prophets had in the Old were not deleted in the New. Therefore, Old Testament prophets can properly be used as examples concerning what Church prophets can be and do (Heb. 1:1; Luke 11:49; 1 Cor. 12:28).

Old Testament Prophets Prove That New Testament Prophets Can Govern. With these principles in mind, we can now answer the question that arose in the Prophetic Movement and is arising again in the Apostolic Movement. That is whether apostles can prophesy and prophets can govern, administrate and be heads of ministries. We can find examples of prophets who founded a group of people, exercised senior headship, made final decisions for a great multitude and served as administrators of the material matters of a whole kingdom.

Abraham was a prophet (Gen. 20:7) and he pioneered and fathered the Hebrew/Jewish people. He had the foundational ministry of establishing the borders of the land of Canaan. He received the revelation, call and commissioning from God for establishing the Jewish people. He was the head of hundreds of servants born and raised under his ministry. He was able to accumulate great wealth in material possessions.

Moses was a prophet (Deut. 34:10; Acts 3:22; Hos. 12:13). He received divine revelation from God concerning His purpose for His people. He did not receive that divine guidance and then turn it over to an apostle to govern and administrate. He demonstrated God's miraculous power and led over three million people out of bondage—then was senior pastor over them for forty years. He made the final decisions and administrated the affairs of God over His people.

Samuel was a prophet (1 Sam. 3:20). He did more than prophesy and give guidance. He was judge over the whole nation of Israel (1 Sam. 7:15-17). He founded the schools of the prophets and established them in cities throughout Israel. He had his home and headquarters in Ramah, but traveled throughout the nation. He was head of his own ministerial association. He anointed and ordained other prophets to the ministry. He also ordained priests, Levites, porters and two kings over all Israel (1 Chron. 9:22; 1 Sam. 9:16-17; 10:1). He was bishop-overseer of the company of prophets that he established during his day (1 Sam. 19:20).

David was a prophet (Acts 2:29-30) and he was king and administrator of all the affairs of the nation of Israel. Both Prophet Moses and Prophet David received revelation knowledge for the building of God's house. Moses received the pattern for the Tabernacle and David received the blueprint for the Temple that Solomon built (1 Chron. 28:11-12). Joseph was probably a prophet, for he had dreams, interpreted dreams and eventually was appointed overseer of the nation of Egypt.

Daniel was a prophet (Matt. 24:15) who received and interpreted many dreams. He was made president and overseer of all the princes in the great Babylonian Empire.

Jesus Christ was a prophet (Luke 24:19; Acts 3:22-23; John 4:19,44; 6:14; 7:40; 9:17) and He established the New Testament Church. He continues to give headship directives and to administer the affairs of the Church. Jesus was the first New Testament Church prophet, and He set the pattern for all of His Church prophets.

These examples of just a few Biblical prophets should be sufficient to show that God has invested much more ability within His prophets than just enough to make them a mouthpiece for guidance. We will not take space to speak in detail of other prophets and prophetesses who had similar responsibilities such as Isaiah, Deborah and others.

Apostles and Prophets: the Foundation. In the New Testament Church, Paul declares that prophets along with the apostles are foundational ministries upon which the Church is built: "And [you] are built upon the foundation of the apostles and prophets, Jesus Christ Himself being the chief corner stone" (Eph. 2:20). Nowhere in the Scripture does it say that the apostle has any more wisdom or authority from Christ for building churches on a proper foundation than the prophet, nor the prophet more than the apostle.

God's true apostles and prophets are not in competition with each other. They were designed by Christ to complement each other. They are the only two of the five that are paired together in ministry and that have similar anointed abilities. Paul declares that they are the two fivefold ministers who have the anointing to receive revelation from Christ concerning the new truths that God wants to bring forth:

> *How that by revelation He made known unto me the mystery; (...when ye read, ye may understand my knowledge in the mystery of Christ) which in other ages was not made known unto the sons of men, as it is now revealed unto His holy apostles and prophets by the Spirit* (Eph. 3:3-5).

Apostles and prophets were the first two ministries that God set in the Church: "And God hath set some in the church, first apostles, secondarily prophets..." (1 Cor. 12:28). They are the two ministries sent by Jesus that He said would be persecuted and rejected the most by the old religious order: "...I will send them prophets and apostles, and some of them they shall slay and persecute" (Luke 11:49). In fact, it is shedding the blood of the prophets that brings the wrath of God upon the Babylonian harlot system described in Revelation: "Rejoice over her, thou heaven, and ye holy apostles and prophets; for God hath avenged you on her. ... And in her was found the blood of prophets, and of saints..." (Rev. 18:20,24).

Prophets and apostles are thus co-laboring ministries with a kindred spirit that will be alive and functioning as long as mortal human beings are alive on planet Earth.

Apostles Can Prophesy Guidance, Gifts and Ministries.
Just as prophets can govern and be heads of ministry, the Bible
records that apostles can prophesy guidance, gifts and ministries. Apostle Paul laid hands upon Timothy and prophesied
his gifts and ministry (1 Tim. 4:14). And he longed to see the
Roman Christians that he might lay hands on them and impart
to them some spiritual gifts (Rom. 1:11). Apostle Paul and
Prophet Silas co-labored equally together in establishing the
first New Testament Church in Ephesus. Even so, present-day
apostles and prophets must be diligent to keep out the divisive
teaching and extreme statements that limit, or any practices
that would hinder, the close working relationship between
prophets and apostles. The new breed generation of apostles
and prophets, those that are truly brought forth of God, will
not have all these hang-ups and attitudes that the old order
apostles and prophets now have.

Apostolic-Prophets and Prophetic-Apostles. Some people
called to be prophets have progressed and matured in manhood and ministry over many years. The fruit of their years of
ministry has proven that they have been commissioned by
Christ to fulfill a senior leadership and fatherhood ministry to
other leaders in the Body of Christ. They are prophets to
whom many other fivefold ministers look to as a prophetic
father in the faith. Such prophets have become what I call an
apostolic-prophet.

Others are called to the ascension gift of apostle and also to
fulfill a greater role of leading and directing others in the
Body of Christ. They have matured in manhood and ministry
over several decades until many other ministers begin to look
to them for fatherhood covering, relationship and accountability. They have exercised their spiritual senses, sharpened
their prophetic perspective and developed their apostolic revelation anointing. They are not depending on their own organizational ability, wisdom or senior leadership position, but are

moving in revelation anointing plus manifesting the super-natural signs and wonders ministry of an apostle. This type of apostle is what I believe to be a prophetic-apostle. In the Church today certain men of God are alive who are truly prophetic and apostolic fathers of the faith. It is these true apostolic-prophets and prophetic-apostles whom God wants to use to es-tablish His restorational movements being brought forth in these last days. They are also the few to whom God has granted the dual ministry of the apostle and the prophet. I believe there is a special purpose and dispensation of grace given to those who mature to the place to be a prophet-apostle minister.

Same Calling, But Not the Same Capability. All who are called to the office of prophet or apostle do not have the same commission to fulfill in the Body of Christ. Some are local church prophets or apostles whom God has not enabled to pas-tor a church, head up their own ministry or write books. Some are called, as Agabus was, just to give the word of the Lord to key people now and then. Some are called, like Daniel, to be in the business world and never have a pulpit position.

The Scripture establishes no precedent declaring that a person must have a pulpit position to be a fivefold minister. (I personally believe, however, that all fivefold ministers should be ordained ministers.) If having your own pulpit was neces-sary evidence of the calling to a fivefold ministry, then the only ministers called to fivefold offices would be senior pas-tors of their own churches. However, I have discovered, over the last forty-three years of traveling to hundreds of churches and prophesying to the "pastors" of the local churches, that many of those ministering in the senior pastoral role do not have the ascension gift of pastor.

Everyone called to be an apostle is not given the commis-sion to be a head over other ministers, to be the senior pastor of a large church or to pioneer into unevangelized areas for es-tablishing new churches. This is important to remember when someone receives a prophecy of a calling to the prophetic or apostolic office.

Prophesying Fivefold Callings Can Cause Confusion. Problems sometimes arise when a prophet or apostle, a prophetic presbytery, a prophetic team member or a loner doing his own thing, prophesies a fivefold ministry calling to a person. When the person's experience does not seem to match up with the prophecy, the problem may lie in one of several areas. Sometimes those prophesying may be missing God. But the majority of the time it is the improper response of the one receiving the prophecy that creates the confusion. This is especially true when the calling of apostle or prophet is prophesied.

Often people receiving the prophetic word may have a wrong concept of the ministry prophesied. They may immediately try to enter into that ministry and fulfill it before God's timing. They may not understand the process and years of preparatory experiences God takes people through before commissioning them to that ascension gift calling. So anyone who has received a divine calling of apostle or prophet should not immediately make name cards with an apostle or prophet title, no more than one who receives the calling of pastor should take on that title until he or she is officially functioning in that capacity.

Modern-Day Apostolic-Prophets and Prophetic-Apostles. Some Christian teachers and theologians have described the ministry of the apostle as being that of an administrator and spiritual overseer of ministers and churches—similar to the ministry of a pastor as the overseer of church members, deacons and other leadership ministries within the local church. We can better evaluate this idea if we provide a historical context for the office of overseer in the Church.

The Historical Development of the Title "Bishop." After an initial three hundred years of rejection and persecution by

Judaism and the nations of the world, Christianity became an accepted religion within the Roman Empire. This change was made law by the Roman Emperor Constantine, who issued an "Edict of Toleration" in AD 313 allowing Christianity to function publicly the same as any other religion or secular society. Christian churches moved from being underground to government recognized. Christians were allowed citizenship and the right to hold political offices. Within a few years hundreds of churches were built throughout the Roman Empire and other parts of the world. Local congregations began to relate to certain translocal leaders, and some leaders began to press for position and control.

Centralization of Control. At the close of what fundamentalist church historians call the Apostolic Age, churches were independent of each other, shepherded by fivefold ministers who were generally called pastors or elders. The main leader or senior pastor came to be called "bishop," which means "overseer." Gradually, the jurisdiction of the bishop came to include neighboring churches in other towns.

Bishop Calixtus (a bishop of Rome, AD 217-222) was the first to base his claim to authority on Matthew 16:18. The great theologian Tertullian of Carthage called Calixtus a usurper in speaking as if he were the "bishop of bishops." When Constantine called the council of Nicea in AD 325 and presided over the first worldwide council of churches, he accorded the bishops of Alexandria and Antioch full jurisdiction over their provinces, as the Roman bishop had over his.

By the end of the 4th century, the eastern bishops had come to be called "patriarchs." They were of equal authority, each having full control of his own province. The five bishops/patriarchs who dominated Christendom at the time were headquartered in Rome, Constantinople, Antioch, Jerusalem and Alexandria. After the division of the Roman Empire into

East and West, the struggle for the leadership of Christendom was between Rome (Roman Catholics) and Constantinople (Eastern Orthodox).

Development of the One-Man Rule Papal Religious Structure. In the earlier centuries of the Church the bishops came to be affectionately addressed as "papa" (father), which gave rise to the word "Pope." About the year AD 500, "papa" began to be restricted in its use by the local bishops, and the title was eventually reserved exclusively for the bishop of Rome.

Over the centuries the word came to mean "universal bishop." The idea that the bishop of Rome should have authority over the whole Church grew slowly and was bitterly contested. By the middle of the Dark Ages, the papal reign of one-man rule had reached a position of supreme power and international jurisdiction.

Prophets and Apostles Need Restored, Not Bishops. Religious people have a way of taking what is scriptural, sacred and workable and converting it into a lifeless religious form and a pyramid hierarchal structure that restricts God's purpose and brings bondage to His people. When the Church becomes more structural than spiritual, it becomes petrified wood instead of a fruitful growing tree with the sap flowing. When it becomes more spiritual than structural, it becomes like dissipating and destructive floodwaters without any control or order.

For this reason, both apostles and prophets must be prominent and coequal in laying the foundation for the Church. No church will have a balanced and proper foundation and function without the ministry of both apostles and prophets.

If a church is built with the ministry of the apostle alone, without the prophet ministry, it may become so doctrinally structured and ordered that it becomes lifeless and formal without the fiery flow of praise and power.

If it is built by the prophet alone, without the ministry of the apostle, the people may become so spiritually activated that everyone is a law unto him or herself, and it could lead to fanaticism. But with the ministry of both the apostle and prophet the Church of Jesus Christ will maintain a balance between structure and spirituality, doctrine and demonstration, prophetic perspective and apostolic order.

Who Can Be a Bishop? The word "bishop" is a scriptural term (1 Tim. 3:1; Titus 1:7; 1 Pet. 2:25). It can rightly be used as a title that designates a fivefold minister who oversees other people and ministries. Apostle Peter referred to Jesus as the "Shepherd" and "Bishop" of our souls. Some other translations use "overseer" instead of "bishop," for they both come from the same root word. Some have made an issue of Charismatic or Prophetic ministers using the title of "bishop." I will also make an issue of it when ministers teach that the term "bishop" can only be used by those who wear religious garments that were developed during the Dark Ages of the Church. I have no problem with some ministers wearing robes and clerical collars as long as they don't portray that the religious garments give them the recognition and authority of a bishop.

This religious protocol was developed from a combination of the Jewish priestly garments and the elaborate robes and ceremonies of kings at that time. Jesus did not wear priestly garments for He was of the tribe of Judah, not Levi. The Jews would have stoned Him if He had worn the attire of the high priest, even though in God His position was higher than that of any high priest. None of the Twelve Apostles wore special garments to distinguish them as apostles. None of them had been trained and ordained as Levitical priests, nor were they of the tribe of Levi or descendants of Aaron. Paul never mentions or implies that he continued to wear the robes he wore as a pharisaic doctor of the Law of Moses. The early Christian Church did not wear special religious garments as the Israeli Aaronic priesthood wore. It had no elaborate hierarchal authority structure, nor complicated ceremonial services. The services were conducted with simplicity in the power and demonstration of the Holy Spirit. Paul told one church that he was very concerned about them because they were getting away from the simplicity of Christianity.

A Title for a Leader of Others. I accepted the title of bishop for no religious significance, but for several practical reasons. First, because it is a scriptural title given to ministers who are in a position of overseeing the work of God. We established our own ministerial fellowship and Network of Prophetic Ministries. Some started calling me, "Papa Prophet," "Senior Prophet," and other such terms. I did not want any title attached to the office of prophet that would sound like there were levels of rank and authority among those called to be prophets. I knew that when the apostolic came along, some would want to call the apostle that was head of the ministry, "chief apostle," "major apostle" or something of that nature. The same problems would occur in the Apostolic Movement as would have in the Prophetic Movement if these things were allowed. After several years of prayer, I accepted the commissioning and title of bishop, because it simply means an "overseer" and does not indicate any particular fivefold ministry. It met the need of identifying my position as overseer of a network of churches and ministers. I accepted it knowing that I would receive some persecution from my Pentecostal and Faith brethren. In fact, I have received more verbal persecution for using the title of Bishop than I have for taking the title of prophet. The title of bishop gave me an overseer identity without polluting the ministries of prophets and apostles. I give any minister the right to reject or accept the title of bishop as being a proper term. I give them the right to not use it or feel good about it. I hope others will give me the same rights without any party condemning the other or refusing to fellowship because of the "bishop" issue.

A bishop may be the senior pastor of a local church, or the apostolic-prophet or prophetic-apostle over several ministers and churches. It is not necessarily a fivefold calling, but an administrative office that is given by others and not by oneself. I am scripturally convinced that the use of the title "bishop" is not wrong if the person bearing the title meets its qualifications and if the motive and purpose for its usage are according to Biblical principles. But if the office of bishop develops into a pyramid papal system as it did during the deterioration of the Church, then it becomes wrong.

May all those who become leaders in the Apostolic Movement do all in their power and wisdom to keep it unpolluted and balanced. I have dedicated the remaining years of my life and ministry to help bring about the full restoration of God's prophets and apostles, linking them together to complement each other's ministry, then joining all fivefold ministers in unity with mutual respect for each other. My higher calling and destiny is to be instrumental in helping to bring about the full restoration of God's Church in Christ's character with the maturity and ministry that God predestined for His eternal Church.

—•••◍◉◍•••—

11

DIVINE PROGRESSIVE PREPARATION
FOR THE APOSTOLIC MOVEMENT

—•••◍◉◍•••—

Everything that God has had the Holy Spirit doing restorationally in the Church has been preparatory for the presently emerging Apostolic Movement. In First Corinthians 14:40 it says, "Let all things be done decently and in order." The cry of the younger generation is, "Let all things be done." The cry of the older generation is for "decency and order." At the beginning of a new restoration movement the Holy Spirit urges the participants to let every new thing come forth to be known and manifested. A few years afterwards the Holy Spirit starts urging the participants to bring balance without destroying the original fire, anointing and supernatural manifestations.

It's like the story Jesus used about casting the fishing net and drawing all the fish into the boat. After the fish are in the boat where they can be seen and examined, the bad fish are separated from the good fish. The boat then continues on without all the nonprofitable fish aboard. Jesus also stated that tares should be allowed to grow with the wheat until harvesttime and then the tares would be separated from the wheat and burned. Every restoration of truth goes through its sprouting forth time and then matures to the place where the movement leaders can properly separate the "tare" manifestations, teachings and practices from the true ones that the Holy Spirit birthed and brought forth. I have been going through that process as a pioneer and participant in the birthing and maturing of the Prophetic Movement. I am just as committed to doing the same in the present move of God to restore God's apostles.

A Cry for Balance, Integrity and Divine Order. The Prophetic Movement was birthed in 1988 but by the end of the following year church leaders were crying out for wisdom, integrity and balance to be maintained by its leaders.

The September 1989 issue of *Charisma* magazine featured a cover story surveying the Prophetic Movement. An accompanying editorial by the publisher, Stephen Strang, made an earnest appeal to prophetic leaders to make sure the movement is maintained with integrity and balance. He discussed some legitimate concerns about the potential for extreme teaching and practices in this movement, and I am in full agreement with his concerns. Strang said, "If abuses begin springing up in this new prophecy movement (and sadly, we are beginning to hear of some isolated instances where this is the case), then the danger of abuse goes far beyond what we ever saw in the Discipleship movement."

Strang continued, "We call on Bill Hamon, Paul Cain and some of the others emerging as leaders in this movement to see that this gift is not abused. We are happy that Hamon has, for example, instituted a policy of checking out the ministry of those submitted to him. The use of tape recordings of prophecies helps cut down on potential abuse. But even more needs to be done. There needs to be a great deal of teaching in the area."

This goal was already my own heart's desire and determination. By the grace of God and the wisdom He granted, I have done and will continue to do all that is within my power and resources to maintain integrity and balance. Until the present, we have maintained the original fire, anointing and supernatural manifestations. We have also received and embraced the anointing and dimensions of the Apostolic.

Update on the Prophetic Movement. The Prophetic Movement has gone to all the continents and most of the nations of the earth. It has penetrated into most areas of the church world. However, the Prophetic Movement has not peaked but is still gaining in momentum. It will not die out or fade away but the prophets and prophetic ministries will continue to play more active roles as the Second Coming of Christ draws near.

I am glad to report that within the seven years since the cry came forth for more teaching, the leadership at Christian International Network of Prophetic Ministries (CI-NPM) has worked diligently to make sure we did our part in this area. We have conducted more than seventy-five seminars for the purpose of teaching and establishing the proper truths and practices for prophetic ministry. I have written four major books on the prophetic, entitled *Prophets and Personal Prophecy*, *Prophets and the Prophetic Movement*, *Prophets, Principles and Pitfalls* and *The Eternal Church*. Each of these books has a teaching manual and a student workbook. A three hundred-page leadership training tool called "A Manual for Ministering Spiritual Gifts" has been produced. More than three thousand leaders in thirteen nations have been trained in how to teach, train, activate, mentor and mature their people in prophetic ministry and the gifts of the Holy Spirit. More than fifteen thousand saints have been taught, activated and established into prophetic teams with the ability to minister to others as they have been ministered to. These materials have been translated into Spanish, Dutch, Korean, Japanese and French with additional translations being prepared in several other languages.

Christian International started Schools of the Holy Spirit in 1979. These schools are places where the prophetic ministry is taught and ministered every Friday night. Christian International Network of Churches (CINC) presently has four hundred forty-nine ordained ministers. There are one hundred forty CINC churches throughout the United States and many foreign nations. Most of these churches conduct a Friday Night School of the Holy Spirit. Christian International School of Theology (CIST) has added to its curriculum a major in the prophets and prophetic ministry. A person can now earn a theological degree with a major in prophetic ministry. In the fall of 1995 Christian International started its residential Ministry Training College (CI-MTC) with the first semester majoring in teaching and the second semester majoring in mentoring and activating the students into experiencing and ministering in the prophetic.

Since 1986 Christian International has been conducting an International Gathering of the Prophets Conference (CI-GOPC). In 1987 at the CI-GOPC a sovereign move of prophetic intercessory prayer for God to raise up a company of prophets gripped the leaders and audience for over an hour. In 1988 during the conference there was another sovereign move of God that birthed the Prophetic Movement.

In 1992 at the annual CI-GOPC, there were eight international speakers, four prophets and four apostles. They were from Uganda, Mexico, Australia, Malaysia and Canada. There was a prophetic-apostolic consensus from all these ministers that there was a marriage that took place between the apostles and the prophets within CI at that time. In the 1995 conference, which was conducted in January of 1996 because of hurricane Opal, Cindy Jacobs was one of the main speakers. There was a divinely orchestrated integrating of intercessory prayer and the prophets and prophetic ministry. A CI-COPG regularly has one thousand in attendance, including three hundred ministers representing many nations.

Prophets to the Nations: Just in the last five years prophets and apostles from CI's network of prophets and prophetic ministries have gone to forty-five nations of the world. In many of these nations they had the opportunity to have an audience with the president and give him the word of the Lord for his nation. For instance, in 1992 my wife and I ministered in twelve nations on six continents of the world. We conducted a national prophetic conference in each of these nations. Different teams of prophetic ministers joined us in each of those nations. In the Philippines there were ten team members. We filled the conference center in Manila with more than four thousand registered attendees and ministered to forty thousand in the open air meetings.

Prophetic warfare was made against the ruling principalities over the nation and the Prophetic Movement was released into that country. Pastor Eddie Villanueva opened the door to the Presidency. The Lord granted us an audience with President Fidel Ramos. We gave him a prophecy with eight major points concerning him and his nation. He and I joined hands and I prophetically commissioned him to fulfill his destiny as president of the Philippines.

The Prophetic Movement has become worldwide and is recognized as a genuine restorational move of God. There is a specially unique indicator to that fact. Fuller Theological Seminary allowed graduate student Daniel Kim to write his thesis for his Master of Theology degree on, "A Review of Literature in the Contemporary Prophetic Movement." There were plenty of sources available since Christian International is only one of many centers that are propagating the prophetic truths and ministries. The Prophetic Movement is growing and here to stay, but it is going through the same process that every movement has gone through over the last five hundred years.

In every restorational movement all participants are not all in one group and some are not under the original pioneers of the movement. Some groups go to extremes either to the right or left. Others maintain more of a middle-of-the-road ministry. Since the beginning of the period of the Restoration of the Church starting with justification by faith, all presently restored truths have gone through the same process.

Understanding the Process. Others must understand the process that every restorational movement has gone through since the beginning of the great restoration of the Church. The leaders and people who are being used by God to restore the new Biblical truths and spiritual experiences are initially rejected, persecuted and made total outcasts from the established Christian denominations and past movement groups. They become the subject of the greatest controversy within the Church; they are accused of being fanatics, heretics, false prophets or teachers—even cult leaders (Matt. 23:29-39).

The old order is like Saul's army who was afraid to go against Goliath. When a fresh move of God came through David, they held back and did not participate until David proved he had a true revelation and faith by killing the giant. Also, it is like Gideon and his three hundred men who had to prove what they had was from God by putting the enemy to flight before the other tribes would start participating. It is time for Saul's army to start aggressively pursuing the enemy with those who have proven that offensive warfare praise and prayer are scriptural and workable. It is time for those who have been secret disciples of the prophetic and apostolic to openly take their stand with the new David and Gideon army. Join the Joshua Generation who has crossed the Jordan River and is attacking the enemy in aggressive warfare. Remember that Jonathan was neutral too long, not taking a stand with David, which resulted in him dying with the old order of Saul.

Only as the movement grows and gradually establishes hundreds of churches throughout the world that propagate and practice the same things will the old order church leaders finally grant them a tolerable status, allowing them to exist without constant harassment. (The Charismatic Movement churches have only recently evolved to that status.) The new movement churches are then finally allowed to join the rest of the Christian community after the fire of the movement has leveled off into an organized structure and some kind of predictable performance.

Hot War and Cold War. Thus a divine restoration of truth first brings about a "hot war" between those who accept it and those who reject it. After the battle is over and almost everyone has either stayed with the old or gone with the new, the two groups evolve into a "cold war" relationship, practicing mutual tolerance without fully accepting one another as fellow members of the Body of Christ worthy of their love and fellowship.

Extreme Swings in the Pendulum of Restored Truth. When truth is in the process of being restored to the Church, it usually swings extremely to the right, then to the left, and finally hangs straight with a balanced message, like the pendulum of a grandfather clock, in the middle of the two extremes. Those who get stuck out on the extreme left become cultic in their doctrines and practices. Those who don't make it back from the extreme right become an exclusive group who separate themselves from the rest of the Body of Christ. Then there is the group who brings themselves together from both extremes to maintain a balance in proper Biblical doctrine and practice as God originally intended it to be restored within the Church.

A restoration movement may also be compared to the times when heavy rains come and cause a river to flood over its banks. Some of the water gets stuck out on the right side of the river and forms little ponds where a few fish stay. Some of the water on the left never makes it back to the river but forms bayous and swamps where all kinds of slimy and poisonous creatures dwell. As the floodwaters recede, the main body of water flows between the river banks of wisdom and maturity in ministering the restored truths and spiritual experiences.

The "Balanced" Group May Lose the Anointing. Nevertheless, the "balanced" group may become so protective of the truth and so reactionary toward the extremists that they keep the original form yet lose the flow of the Holy Spirit. They may keep the purity of the doctrine yet lose the fresh anointing that restored those truths. They may maintain the proper preaching and practices yet lose God's mighty presence and power that originally accompanied their ministry. Sad to say, church history reveals that it is this balanced group that usually becomes the main persecutors of the next restorational movement of the Holy Spirit. They establish wineskins of doctrinal limitations with regard to what, when, where, who and how the truth can be ministered. Their wineskins become dry and set with such limitations that they cannot receive the new wine of restored truth that adds new truth and spiritual ministries to the Church. Those who understand the principles of restoration should never miss a new move of God. Restorational moves of God will continue coming until everything is prepared for the Second Coming of Christ Jesus. The last move of God will be when Jesus comes and sets up His kingdom over all the earth.

Be Established in the Present Truth. For that reason, we must keep our wineskins flexible so that we can go from movement to movement of the Holy Spirit, incorporating into our personal lives and our churches all that God wants to restore to His Church (2 Cor. 3:18). At the same time, we must not become vulnerable to extremism and fanaticism. As Apostle

Peter declared, we must continually "be established in the present truth" without forsaking any of the truths and practices that have already been restored (2 Pet. 1:12). Jesus said that a wise scribe is one who brings out of his treasure chest treasure both old and new. The Church is not a water tank or salty dead sea, but a river of fresh flowing, life-giving water (Matt. 13:52; Ezek. 47:1-12; John 7:38). Let us stay in the middle of God's stream of ongoing restoration.

12

EXTREMES IN THE RESTORATION OF TRUTH

Abuses Cannot Be Totally Prevented. The true apostles and prophets who are called to pioneer this present Prophetic Movement and the emerging Apostolic Movement will do all they can to maintain balance and to keep prophetic and apostolic ministers from doing foolish things that bring disgrace and reproach upon the movement. But none of the past restorational movements were able to prevent abuses and extremes totally, and neither will we be able to do so.

The fact remains that until Christ returns there will always be those who are Biblically uneducated and who never will become birthed in the present truth. There will always be those who are emotionally unstable and spiritually immature who cannot handle the truth, so they start doing weird things that are out of order concerning the present truth. And there will always be charlatans, false ministers and those who are wrongly motivated, who look for an opportunity to promote themselves and to profit from the movement.

These three groups could be called the fanatical right, the extreme left and the middle hangers, balanced between the two extremes. A brief resumé of the major truths restored over the last five centuries will reveal that every movement has had these three groups.

The 1500's—Justification by Faith. This pendulum of truth swung from the one extreme of salvation by works with no faith, to the other extreme of all faith and no works of righteousness with their faith. Those who walked on in the truth came to a balance in the middle. They were justified by faith, demonstrating their faith by works of obedience to righteous living. There were also the theological extremes of Calvinism and Arminianism, along with those who took a balanced position between the two extremes.

The 1600's—Water Baptism. There were the two extremes of those who preached that a person was not saved until he or she was water baptized by immersion versus those who put little value on water baptism. There were those who taught that a baby could receive all the blessings of Christianity through water baptism and there were those who taught that a child could receive nothing from the Lord until the age of twelve. Those who walked on in truth developed a balance between these extremes.

The 1700's—Holiness, Sanctification and Perfectionism. With regard to holiness teaching, there were the two extremes of legalism and libertinism. The legalists believed all sports, amusements and current fashions were sinful for Christians. The liberty extremists declared that grace gave license for all things, proclaiming that "to the pure all things are pure." With regard to teaching on sanctification, one extreme insisted that Christians have only one eternally sanctifying experience, while the other extreme said we need to be sanctified daily. Perfectionism had its two extremes of those who made no allowance for a Christian ever sinning, and those who believed a Christian cannot avoid sinning a little every day. Thank God there is a balance between these extremes of a divine truth. Those who pressed on in present truth maintained a balance between these extreme positions in the teachings and practices of the restored truth.

The 1800's—The Second Coming of Jesus. There were the two extremes of those who proclaimed Christ's imminent return and set dates for His coming, using every world event and calamity as proof, and those who did not believe in a literal return of Christ at all. The great theological controversies were over eschatological viewpoints: premillennialism, postmillennialism and amillennialism. Those who were premillennialist went to extremes in their eschatological preaching about whether there would be a pretribulation, midtribulation, or posttribulation rapture of the Church.

The 1880's— Divine Faith Healing. The theological controversy was whether the stripes Jesus received provided healing for the physical body just as His death on the cross provided forgiveness of sins. In other words, was there physical healing in the atonement of Christ Jesus?

Those who did accept the teaching of healing in the atonement developed different extreme beliefs: Some believed that divine faith was the only acceptable remedy for the physical healing of Christians (with the use of medical care forbidden); those on the opposite side exhausted all natural means before turning to Jesus for supernatural divine healing. Those who maintained the restoration truth of divine healing did so with a balance between those extreme swings to the right and to the left.

The 1900's—Holy Spirit Baptism and Other Tongues. The theological problem was whether "unknown tongues" is the only valid scriptural evidence of having received the gift of the Holy Spirit. Among the Pentecostals who accepted tongues talking there were two extreme groups: those who believed a person was not saved until he or she spoke in tongues, and those who believed there were several different divine proofs (such as the Holiness Movement proclaimed) of the baptism of the Holy Spirit.

The Pentecostals also went to extremes in concepts of the Godhead, with some teaching a form of unitarianism (the doctrine that there is no Trinity, known as the "Jesus Only" doctrine), and some, tritheism (the doctrine that denies the unity of the three Persons of the Godhead). These groups also developed hard religious attitudes concerning water baptism formulas.

There were differences of opinion concerning the proper terminology for describing this "other tongues" experience. Some called it "Spirit baptized" and some, "Spirit filled." Some argued over whether we should say it is the baptism with, in, into, by or of the Holy Spirit.

The terminology used did not hinder the Holy Spirit from baptizing believers. But some groups went into such fanaticism that they eventually destroyed themselves. Others segregated themselves from the rest of the Body of Christ by declaring that all church groups were wrong except themselves. They felt they were the only Pentecostal group who had true salvation and the proper teaching and ministries of the restored truth.

Consequently, scores of Pentecostal denominations and independent groups were established. Most of them still do not grant each other the right hand of fellowship. But there were some major Pentecostal denominations who maintained the original form, doctrines and spiritual ministries of the truth that the Holy Spirit wanted to restore at that time.

The 1940's—Laying On of Hands and Personal Prophecy.
The controversial truth being restored was what has come to be known as "prophetic presbytery." The issue was whether

or not Holy Spirit filled ministers had the Biblical right and spiritual power to prophetically reveal to ministers their five-fold ascension gift calling and to prophesy to saints their membership ministry within the Body of Christ. Also they taught that by prophecy and the laying on of hands Holy Spirit gifts could be revealed and activated within saints (1 Tim. 4:14; 1:18).

This pendulum of truth had its far swings to the right and left before becoming balanced in the middle. Some Latter Rain ministers relegated prophecy to certain appointed apostles and prophets. Others allowed anyone, at any time, without proper supervision, to prophesy to anyone else.

As in every movement, those who maintained the truth in balance established guidelines for teaching and ministering the truth restored. The extremist groups have self-destructed and the pressing on, balanced groups have preserved the truth in the purity of preaching and practice.

The 1950's— Praise Singing, Body Ministry, Praise Dancing. The difference in scriptural emphasis was between those who believed saints could melodiously sing praises and those who thought praise should only be with the Pentecostal shout. Others debated whether spiritual ministry should be released among the body of believers in the congregation or be totally directed and ministered from the pulpit.

In one extreme, whole church services were given to praise and prophecies with very little value put on preaching, while many others continued to view worship only as a preliminary to the total preeminence of the preaching of the Word. Another extreme group established what they called the heavenly hierarchy of twelve apostles and twenty-four elders. They dressed themselves in religious attire like the Old Testament high priests.

Some churches had only slow melodious worship, while others had praise with dancing and shouting for hours. Some argued over whether "dancing before the Lord" was a willful act of faith in praise expression or an uncontrollable "dancing in the Spirit." There were those who believed that church services were mainly for worship and perfecting each other in Christ while others believed the whole role of the Church was to evangelize the world. Those who walked on in the restored truth and ministries on all these issues brought a balance between the extremes and maintained the truth in purity of practice.

The Latter 1940's till the End of the 1950's—Deliverance Evangelism. Hundreds of evangelists arose during this time and won millions of souls to Jesus by supernatural deliverance and miraculous healings. Oral Roberts came forth to demonstrate laying on of hands for divine healing. T.L. Osborne launched mass evangelism in many foreign nations. He would challenge audiences of tens of thousands by saying, "If Jesus heals this deaf or crippled man, will you believe that Jesus is the Son of God and only Savior of all mankind?" Thousands would be converted when they saw the miracles take place.

There were prophets who came forth with great prophetic insight, words of knowledge and miracles, such as William Branham and Paul Cain. Women were also used mightily, such as Kathryn Kuhlman. There were two streams flowing side by side but never flowing together—The Latter Rain Restoration Movement and Deliverance Evangelism. Most of the leaders of the Faith Movement, such as Kenneth Hagin, were never involved in the restoration camp. Their heritage and progression were from Pentecostal churches to Deliverance Evangelism to the Faith Movement. That is the reason their concept of prophets and prophetic ministry is after the order of prophets that were in their camp. My heritage and progression were from an American heathen to Pentecostal to Restoration, to

Charismatic, to Prophetic and now Prophetic/Apostolic. Deliverance was used to clarify and magnify the office of the evangelist. They had their own extremes similar to the Divine Healing Movement.

The 1960's—Demonology: Oppression, Obsession or Possession? The "unknown tongues" issue had been a controversy within the Church since the Pentecostal Movement, so it was not a new issue to them in the 1960's. But some of the Charismatic Movement leaders caused a further controversy to arise concerning the activity of demons. This issue was whether a born-again, Holy Spirit baptized Christian could have demon activity within his or her life to the extent that the demons needed to be cast out.

The controversy developed between those who taught that every negative thought, action and physical affliction was a demon that had to be exorcised before the Christian could change or be healed, and those who believed that the blood of Jesus gave immunity to all who had been cleansed from their sins, because the demons could not "cross the blood line." By the mid 1970's most Charismatics had developed a balanced doctrine and practice concerning demonology.

The 1970's—Discipleship, Family Life, Church Growth and Structure. The Holy Spirit was preparing the Church for great numerical growth in the 1970's. Many churches in South America and Korea especially developed the concept of one large church congregation with numerous cell groups meeting in homes of the church members. The Holy Spirit was seeking to bring mutual respect between the ministers and willing recognition and submission to each other.

Theocratic government was being restored in the Church and the family with the proper chain of command. There was a restoration of proper order of personal priorities, especially for those in leadership and ministry: God first, wife and family second, then ministry. However, the inevitable extremes appeared. Some taught and developed a Christian leadership pyramid. The pastor became almost a papal leader to those under him. All single adult women had to have a male "covering" to be in divine order. All decisions had to be made by leadership, even concerning the daily and personal activities of members. Leaders became domineering and made those under them totally dependent on them.

Some groups went to the other extreme of doing away with church leadership structure by changing from pastorship to co-eldership. Some disbanded the weekly united meeting of a large congregation, breaking it up into small house meeting cell groups only. Some did away with the Sunday night service to make it a home family night.

The "Jesus Movement" came out of the worldly young people's rebellion (the hippie movement) against society. They were more inclined to be opposed to church structure. Nevertheless, they helped deliver the Church from some of its ritualistic traditions. By the end of the decade most non-denominational, present-truth Charismatic churches had developed a balance in doctrine and practice concerning discipleship, shepherding, family life and church structure. When there is a flooding of truth and ministry, the river of the Church overflows its banks. Some water does not make it back into the mainstream, but becomes ponds and bayous. Thus some extreme left and right groups became bayous while God's restoring Church settled into the banks of the river and flowed on in order and balance.

The 1970's—Faith Message, Prosperity and Word Teaching. For centuries the Church had taught that spirituality and poverty were synonymous. The practices of monasticism and asceticism that developed during the Dark Ages were still influencing the Church. Those from the Holiness, Pentecostal and Latter Rain Movements were still under the impression that it was worldly and carnal to have wealth or modern conveniences, or to wear and drive the latest and best.

Oral Roberts was one of the first to propagate the idea that God is a good God and desires Christians to be in health and to prosper, even as their soul prospers (3 John 1:2). But it was not until the 1970's that the truth started being practiced enough to become a worldwide controversy.

Three Camps. The teaching of victorious, prosperous, healthy living in the natural and spiritual came from three different camps: (1) Oral Roberts' ministry of teaching the seed-faith principle of sowing and reaping, of sowing finances to reap finances; (2) Robert Schuller's ministry of positive living and success principles; (3) the group of ministers who became known as "prosperity preachers," "the faith message teachers" or the "Word people." A few of the well-known leaders were Kenneth Hagin, Kenneth Copeland, Hobart Freeman and Fred Price.

The Holy Spirit was striving to bring the Body of Christ to a new faith level and a greater revelation of truth so that the material things needed could be brought in and utilized to communicate the gospel and prosper the Church. Nevertheless, as in the activation and restoration of every truth, different groups became "stuck" in the extreme swings of the pendulum of truth restoration.

The Extremes. Some of the groups that developed in this movement taught and cultivated the attitude that any Christian who was not wealthy and healthy was either an unbeliever or out of fellowship with God. They taught that God does not try the righteous. If you did not have a miracle every day and prosperity all the way, you were not a faith person.

Others became selfish and mammon motivated ministers who took the truth about prosperity and turned it into an opportunity to take inordinate offerings for themselves. Some tried to use the teaching as the basis for "get rich" schemes that ended in bankruptcy—hurting many people along the way.

Still others went to extremes on confession and positive declarations until their teaching approximated the doctrines of Christian Science. Still others swung to the opposite side, declaring that believers have no control over their lives; that they must simply accept whatever comes their way as the will of God; that poverty and sickness are used by God to perfect the saints; and that sickness and poverty must therefore be suffered gracefully. Thank God there is a balance between these extremes.

The old controversy that arose during the Divine Healing Movement of the 1880's arose again among the Faith people. Anyone who used medicine, consulted a physician or had surgery was looked down upon by one group of extremists. Regardless of the differences in the various camps, these ministers were instrumental in establishing the Church on the Biblical principles of overcoming faith, prosperity, faith healing, the power of the Word and the necessity of a continual positive confession. They wrote hundreds of books and made thousands of audiocassette tapes giving scriptural principles for prosperity, health and happiness. By the mid 1980's the movement had fulfilled its restoration mission, and those who had avoided the extremes were pressing on in the restoration truth and ministry.

The 1980's—Kingdom Now, Dominion Theology and Reconstructionism. The Holy Spirit wanted to bring the Church to a dominion attitude and to become more concerned about God's kingdom coming than the Church leaving. He wanted the Church to come out from under its bushel and let its light shine upon the whole world, not just in the church building.

God desires to demonstrate to the world that His Church really is the salt of the earth, and that Christians should be involved in every legitimate activity of humankind to be a witness and influence for the kingdom of God. Separation of church and state does not mean the separation of Christians from the roles of lawyers, senators, corporate managers and even the president of a nation.

Controversy Over the Kingdom. The kingdom message emphasized the Biblical truth that the saints have been made kings and priests to God and shall rule and reign on the earth. The great controversy was over whom, when, where and how God's literal kingdom will be established over planet Earth. The basic conflict came between reformed theology and evangelical theology, and the different views of pre-, post- and amillennialists concerning the timing and strategy of the establishment of God's kingdom on earth as it is in heaven.

The teaching that acted as a catalyst to make the issue controversial within the Church was that of Bishop Earl Paulk of Chapel Hill Harvester Church in Atlanta, Georgia. His emphasis was on a view of the rapture that, to most Evangelicals and Pentecostals, was a denial of the rapture bordering on heresy. He taught that the departed saints would be resurrected and the living saints would be translated in the twinkling of an eye, but this was not for the purpose of leaving the earth. Rather, it was for establishing God's divine order for the human race and Christ's rulership over all the earth.

Some Extremes. As with every movement, different groups arose that laid hold of what God was trying to do and took it to extremes. Some propagated a Christian revolutionary political takeover by natural means without operating in the supernatural power of God. Others pulled back and said that there is nothing the Church can do but pray and hope for the best while the world gets worse until Jesus finally returns to take the Church off to heaven.

Some went into choreographed dancing in ballet fashion to express the music and lyrics of Christian songs. Others went to the extreme of declaring that any worship that was planned and practiced for presentation was unscriptural, and that only the old Pentecostal "dancing in the Spirit" was acceptable to God.

By the end of the 1980's those who propagated the kingdom message had come to a basic Biblical position that the Church is a kingdom witness to all society and that we must demonstrate the kingdom not only in practical ways but also by the supernatural power of God.

The 1980's and 90's—Prophets, the Prophetic Movement and a Prophetic People. This brings us to the latest restorational movement with its wave of restoration truths and ministries. The Prophetic Movement is still the cutting edge move of the Holy Spirit and it will continue with that status until the Apostolic Movement is fully launched. It is restorationally activating into workable reality, vital Biblical truths and ministries within the 20th-century Church of Jesus Christ.

Like every other movement, the Prophetic Movement has had those among it who have taken it to the extremes of right and left. Some prophetic ministers have been unethical and wrongly motivated, attempting to use prophecy to manipulate others for their own purposes. Many of those have fallen and God has moved them out of a public ministry. In the process they have brought reproach upon the truth and offended others who were investigating the Prophetic. But thanks be to God, there are those true prophetic ministers who are establishing and maintaining a proper balance in the middle.

Abuses and Extremes in the Use of Personal Prophecy. As with every move of God, the Prophetic Movement is producing its share of abuses in the sense of people carrying it too far or totally misapplying the truths God is restoring. God's Spirit is pure and restores unadulterated truth and ministry, but unfortunately it is poured into earthen vessels that can be faulty.

We have seen some abuses on a small scale already. So I want to raise a warning against perverting or using the truths being restored for personal gain or for other ungodly purposes. Specific things that we as honest Christians can make sure we avoid are the following:

An Overemphasis on Personal Prophecy. Some Christians think they need a "word from the Lord" to make every major and minor decision. They no longer depend on their personal convictions and the Holy Spirit's leadings (or pastoral counsel and wisdom) to walk daily before the Lord. In some lives personal prophecy replaces personal prayer and hearing from God for oneself.

This is **not** of the Lord. Personal prophecy has a valid place in the Church and the lives of individual Christians, but it was never intended to be a "quick fix" or replacement for seeking God. Another form this abuse has taken is an elevation of prophecy to the same level of authority and inspiration as the written Word of God, causing cultic groups who esteem prophetic utterance as Scripture. However, all mainline Christians believe that the Scriptures are complete and sufficient, and will reject all extra-Biblical revelation claiming authority equal to the Bible.

Ministering Out From Under Authority. Some Christians prophesy to individuals in places other than those the leadership has sanctioned as appropriate. At our seminars we call these "parking lot prophecies," in which people draw others outside of meetings and prophesy strange things to them. We have a list of guidelines we've developed that we require our local church and seminar attendees to read and abide by.

We believe it is vitally important that all prophecies be given only under spiritual oversight, and also that they be tape recorded. This allows the local eldership to adjust or correct any words that are false, wrongly applied or untimely, saving the person who is receiving the prophecy from confusion or misunderstanding. However, some who are new to this movement may prophesy helter skelter as they are "led of the Spirit" without allowing their words to be weighed and evaluated (1 Cor. 14:31; 1 Thess. 5:21). The prophetic ministry has the power to either bless or curse, so all words must be witnessed to and judged by those who are spiritually mature and are in oversight in the local assembly.

Using Prophecy to Justify Rebellion and Sin. The Charismatic Movement caused many prayer groups and unstructured meetings to break themselves off from the Church. Some were of God, as the Holy Spirit poured out new wine that old wineskins couldn't contain, causing inevitable splits. However, many others were just rebellious groups who wanted to do their own thing without any oversight.

The Prophetic Movement is seeing a continuation of this trend, with personal prophecy used as a tool to justify rebellious factions and groups. When confronted by spiritual authority they always say, "God told me" and produce as evidence several prophecies they gave themselves or others gave them that endorse their group or ministry. God never intended prophecy to judge doctrinal or disciplinary matters, and He certainly has not appointed certain saints in the Church to straighten everybody else out through their spiritual ministry.

Controlling or Manipulating Others Through Prophetic Ministry. Some ministers or leaders who already have a problem with being controlling use the gift of prophecy to dictate "orders from God" to those under them. The abuses of the

Discipleship Movement may pale in comparison to this type of abuse of personal prophecy. There are some egotistical, immature and undisciplined Ministers who always try to be sensational in all their prophecies. God's true and mature prophets have the authority to prophesy into any area of human life and activity. But some prophets and saints major in prophesying about world events and setting dates for them to happen, though very few ever come to pass just as they prophesied. These egotistical prophesiers seem to appeal to the speculative and curious nature of mankind. This type of prophesying has disillusioned many about prophets and prophetic ministries. They do all of these things in the name of "spiritual revelation," saying, "God showed me."

Scores of ignorant and immature saints will follow their spiritual leaders because they seem to prophesy the word of the Lord and have signs following their ministry. So Christians must understand the difference between obeying the word of the Lord and getting confirmations on major moves and life decisions. Study Deuteronomy 13:1-5 to understand the reasons why God allows things like this to take place.

Using the Prophetic Gifting for Personal Gain. This abuse takes two forms of deceit as certain ministers see people flocking to the prophetic because God's anointing is upon it. Some ministers who are opportunists are conducting "prophetic conferences" that are prophetic in name only. They are more interested in drawing people in to pay large seminar fees and large offerings for themselves or to bolster the finances of their church than to minister prophetically to the people.

We are now beginning to hear the word "prophetic" hung like a tag on nearly everything in the Church to try to carnally manipulate people to come and be a part of ministries that are not at all prophetic.

The second form of this abuse is as ancient as Balaam, who tried to prophesy for his own personal gain. Even in this decade certain ones have prophesied in every service and on every television program, "Thus saith the Lord, if you will support His servant with a one-time gift of $1,000, He will surely bless you."

Thousands of gullible Christians have sent their money, thinking the man is speaking for God. In the end, however, these false prophets are exposed as charlatans and judged for making merchandise of the gift of God. Many have already been removed during the last few years. God is jealous of His prophetic ministry and will not tolerate abuse very long before He lays the axe to the root of that ministry.

Trying to Fulfill Personal Prophecy Out of Proper Timing. Many Christians who receive true personal prophecies about some great ministry or life situation misunderstand God's dealing over a period of time and run out to try to fulfill their prophecy in their own strength. If God tells them prophetically they are going to be raised up as a great pastor, prophet or apostle, they sometimes run out and print business cards with titles and proclaim themselves as God's wonder worker. They do not allow God to take them through the process from called to be to being able to fulfill their ministry with maturity and wisdom. Remember leaders like Saul, Solomon and Jeroboam, who failed in their ministries and personal lives because of insufficient years of preparation.

Others who are called to be financial stewards for the kingdom of God have rushed into business situations based on a personal prophecy because they think one prophecy will cause them to prosper in all their endeavors. The results are usually broken contracts, bankruptcy and ruined lives. When a true prophecy is spoken to an individual, God intends to accomplish that prophecy at some point in that person's life, not necessarily in the next week or month. Christians will have to learn to wait on the timing of the Lord. (Please see Chapters 16 and 17 in *Prophets and Personal Prophecy* to determine the proper response to a personal prophecy, and Chapter 10 to learn about "Personal Prophecy and Business Endeavors.")

Presumptuous, Critical and Judgmental Prophesying. One of the greatest dangers and abuses in the Prophetic Movement is people prophesying presumptuously or critically. For some reason, a few people with a critical and negative spirit seem to flock to prophetic ministry, feeling that congregational or personal prophecy is their platform to blast everyone else for living in sin (and indirectly implying that they themselves are the true standard for righteousness). I've seen and heard many who felt they were God's lone prophet in the wilderness proclaiming righteousness while the rest of the church was wicked and sinful (Deut. 18:20-22). I've found, however, that the result of such prophesying is bitterness, fruitlessness and condemnation. People who always prophesy in this manner are usually prophesying out of hurts and wounds that have never been healed. They may at times even receive an accurate word of prophecy but as the flow of prophecy comes out of their spirit, it is tainted by the negative areas of their soul.

Everyone needs to know that God has not anointed any **sheriffs** in the kingdom of God to judge and condemn others. I have found God will rarely, if ever, use immature saints and ministers to give a true word of rebuke and correction. This will be left to the mature person whom God can trust with hard words that need to be delivered in the spirit of humility and healing.

These are just a few of the areas that can move us out of balance in prophetic ministry. No one should become guilty of the old saying of "throwing the baby out with the bath water." Don't reject a true ministry and move of God simply because you have seen some bad examples or manifestations. From my personal experience I have found that for every bad example there are a hundred good ones. For every false prophecy or improper use of prophesying there are thousands of true prophecies and proper use of prophecy and the Prophetic Movement truths.

Not Just a Fad. The Prophetic Movement contains vital truths and ministries that Christ wants established within His Church. It is not a religious fad or just a temporary renewal of a previously restored truth or ministry. Ten major things have been restored with new revelation, application and emphasis. Also, sixteen new things have been introduced through what God is doing in the Prophetic Movement that were not present in the Charismatic Movement. The restoration of prophets and the prophetic ministry is absolutely essential for the fulfillment of Christ's progressive purpose for His Church and His ultimate purpose for planet Earth.

The decade of the 1980's was the season for the conception, birthing and development of the Prophetic Movement. Now this last decade of the 20th century is being used to spread it to the ends of the world and to establish the truth and ministries the Holy Spirit was commissioned to restore in this movement.

The Restoration Cycle of History. Every true restoration movement has gone through the same historic process and cycle: First, the truth is injected into the hearts of key ministers God plans to use. Then in His timing it is projected into the Church.

Initially it is rejected by the majority of church leaders. This causes much persecution for a period of time until the movement has ministers and churches established around the world. Then they are passively endured for years until they are finally considered Biblical enough to be accepted into the

Christian community of churches and are no longer branded a cult.

More Transitions and Adjustments Ahead. The Prophetic Movement has gone through the stages of injection, projection, rejection and some persecution. It has now received enough prominence that it is being accepted by some Pentecostal denominational churches and Charismatics. Those ministers and churches who are propagating the prophetic will continue on until the rest of the church world either passively endures them or accepts them. Those who accept and believe that this is something that Christ wants established in His corporate Body will allow the truths and ministries to be incorporated into their teachings, practices and ways of worship.

Our enemy, the devil, hates God's prophets and the prophetic ministry. He is bringing forth whatever will help bring rejection and persecution. Already, as in other movements, the charlatans, the novices, the ignorant, the immature and the wrongly motivated people who are normally on the outer fringes and not in the main flow are beginning to use the product of the prophetic improperly for their own profit.

Such wrongly motivated actions and presumptuous prophesying will cause those non-prophetic church leaders with righteous integrity and moral Biblical standards to reject such religious nonsense. But this is not the true "baby" movement; it is the dirty "bath water" —and we must not throw the baby out with the bath water. The "fathers" who were used to birth the movement have the true spirit and purpose of the movement and are normally not the ones who make merchandise of the restorational truths and ministries.

Misuse and Abuse Is Still Happening. It greatly grieves my spirit, saddens my heart and even at times stirs a righteous indignation in me when I see and hear how some are still using and abusing the truths and ministries of the prophetic. There have been some and probably will be more with television programs who will use the ministry of prophesying to manipulate people to give them financial support. These Balaam-type prophets will eventually be exposed. If the Lord ever did anoint them to prophesy, then that anointing left when they started using the gift for personal promotion and manipulating for money.

I was shocked and disgusted when I heard another television personality say, "Write to me and I will send you your personal prophecy tape for personal prosperity." I sent for it so I could hear for myself what was said. It was a soulish sham of using the prophetic to manipulate and motivate people to support his ministry.

"There Must Also Be Heresies." I sometimes wish I had the power to cut them off and close their mouths, but then the Lord reminds me of what Paul told the Corinthian church. He said, "For there must be also heresies among you, that they which are approved may be made manifest among you" (1 Cor. 11:19). In relation to the Prophetic Movement this means that there must be the false prophets, the ignorant, the immature and the wrongly motivated prophetic ministers who are improperly using the office of prophet and the ministry of prophesying, so that those who are true and proper may be made manifest as the true prophets within Christ's Church. Jesus said for us to let the tares grow along with the wheat until the time of harvest (Matt. 13:24-30). The emerging Apostolic Movement will go through many of these same processes.

Please understand that all the truly God-ordained fathers within the Prophetic Movement and emerging Apostolic Movement will be doing all in their power to teach, write books and produce teaching manuals giving Biblical guidelines as fast as they can, for the proper administration of these truths and ministries. This is my main purpose for writing this book. The ideal is to keep proper structure, order and practice while the truths and ministries are being restored with nothing ever done to bring reproach upon the ministry. This is the ideal that a few will fulfill. The reality is that it has never fully worked this way in any movement.

The preacher of old declared that the only way to constantly have a clean stall was to not have a live ox in it (Prov. 14:4).

The Extremist vs. the Chosen and Faithful. The ones who do not manifest the truth as God intended are the ones who do not make it back to the middle from the extreme swings of the pendulum of restored truth. Those who have the heart of God and mind of Christ for this movement are proceeding on with proper prophetic procedures and practices. This is an update on the present Prophetic Movement but we want to discover some of the potential extremes that will probably come forth during the Apostolic Movement. What an exciting day to live— sovereign restorational moves are escalating as we rush to the glorious climax in the Age of the mortal Church. We dare not miss out on anything that God is doing in this day and hour.

—••••@@@@••—

13

APOSTOLIC MOVEMENT
AND ITS POTENTIAL EXTREMES

—••••@@@@••—

Many wonderful life-giving things will be restored in the coming Apostolic Movement. The main thing will be the complete restoration of apostles to their full recognition, acceptance, powerful ministry, place and position within the Body of Christ. The new generation of apostles will not be sterile hybrids who cannot reproduce like kind. They will have the Genesis principle declaring that every seed shall produce after its own kind. The restoration movement of the late 40's brought the revelation that there are still prophets and apostles in the Church. But they did not receive the revelation and anointing for reproducing other apostles and prophets.

Now the Apostolic Movement will bring the anointing for reproducing thousands of apostles just as the Prophetic Movement reproduced thousands of prophets. The biggest criticism I received from my old restoration brethren was over this issue of reproducing like kind. Rumors and false reports were made that "if you go to CI they will make you a prophet." Because we charge registration fees for those who attend prophetic conferences, a few from a couple of camps started saying, "Go there and they will ordain you as a prophet for two hundred dollars." Of course these were all rumors made up by those who had never attended one of our Prophets Seminars or Prophetic Conferences.

Anyone with basic knowledge of God's gifts and ministries knows that one human being cannot give another person a divine gift or ministry. The gifts of the Holy Spirit are given, imparted and activated by the Holy Spirit Himself. The fivefold ministry ascension gifts are only given by Christ Jesus. We all know that nobody can make saints into fivefold ministers if God has not called them to one of those offices.

Nevertheless, those who have a divine calling to be a prophet or a prophetic saint can be taught, activated, trained, mentored and matured in their calling and gifts. We have proven this a thousand times over by raising up hundreds of prophets and thousands of prophetic people. This revelation and reproducing anointing can do the same in producing the great company of apostles that God wants raised up—not just a few in America but tens of thousands in all the nations of the world.

God's true apostles will come forth, but there will arise false apostles, the immature, the wrongly motivated and the pseudo apostles who will bring reproach and make an improper, unbalanced presentation during the Apostolic Movement. And like all restoration movements, there will be those in the Apostolic Movement who will take some things to the extreme left and right. Let us now consider some of these potential extremes.

Making the Apostle Something God Never Intended. There is one teaching that has the greatest potential for throwing the restoration of apostles out of balance. It stirs up too many attributes of our old nature. In fact, if this can be negated now and in the early stages of the movement, then eighty percent of the problems of making the apostle something God never intended can be avoided.

The main thing is the overemphasis and misapplication of the "First-mentioned principle." This principle states that whatever is mentioned first is the greatest and always has the preeminence. The fundamentalist theologians, who do not believe in the supernatural experience of speaking in other tongues, used it to belittle the value of tongues. They said it is mentioned last in Paul's list in First Corinthians 12:28; therefore, it is the very least important.

The same would be true for Ephesians 4:11. Since apostles are mentioned first in both of these scriptures it is concluded that the apostle is the greatest ministry and should always have the preeminence over all other ministers and ministries.

Hermeneutics is the science of proper Biblical interpretation. One of its rules states that when proper interpretation and application are given to a scripture, then it will not contradict another scripture. That makes applying the first-mentioned principle to these two scriptures improper, for they do not meet this rule of Biblical interpretation.

If Ephesians 4:11 is interpreted as the first mentioned being the greatest in authority and the last mentioned being the lowest in the chain of command, then there is a hermeneutical problem. It would make apostles the first in authority, prophets second, evangelists third, pastors fourth and **teachers fifth**. But in First Corinthians 12:28, Paul, who wrote the letter to the Ephesians, states that God set in the Church first apostles, second prophets, and **third teachers**. So, where are **teachers** in the chain of command—**third or fifth**?

Do the Holy Spirit and Scripture contradict themselves? Was Paul confused about what he was writing? Yes, **if** the Holy Spirit who inspired Paul to write both of these scriptures had the "first-mentioned principle" in mind. But they do not contradict themselves when proper application is given to these scriptures. In the one scripture Paul is simply giving a sampling of fivefold ministries and in the other he is listing in one place all the fivefold ministries of Jesus Christ to His Church.

In First Corinthians, he is giving the chronological order in which they were placed in the Church. In Ephesians, he is not giving a pyramid structure or chain of command order from the greatest to the least. Therefore it would be hermeneutically improper to use these two scriptures as proof texts in trying to prove that the apostle is always the greatest and first in authority over all the other ministries. Insistence on using the "first-mentioned principle" as the correct interpretation of these scriptures will lead to many extremes in the Apostolic Movement.

There are many other problems caused by this concept if the title "apostle" carries with it the necessity for that person to always be first. How are apostles going to reproduce more apostles under them if each one must be the greatest? What does a pastor do with several in his church who have the calling of an apostle? Must every apostle be the head of his own ministry to fulfill his calling? Is there such a thing as an apostle of apostles? If so, then who was the apostle of the Twelve Apostles? The Catholic theologians say that Peter was, but the Bible does not say so. Some who do not want to take the title of apostle call themselves the pastor of pastors. One may truly be a pastor who has matured to the place that younger pastors look to him as their pastor. But if there has been no inner conviction or prophetic revelation that he is an apostle, then he should not take the title of apostle just because other ministers look to him as a father figure. It does not necessarily mean that one is an apostle.

The Dangers of the Old Order Concept. Those who have not been around the old order teaching about apostles do not realize the seriousness of this situation. For instance, there is one group who is teaching that only apostles can minister to apostles. It would be improper for a lower ranked minister to prophesy to, counsel or teach them. This would make the apostles a law unto themselves and a higher elite society in the Body of Christ. Let me give you a personal living example of how this concept can affect the minds of ministers.

Several years ago another ministerial association joined with Cl Network of Churches. My main reputation was that of being a prophet at that time. The head of the other ministerial association was known as an apostle. The merger was presented that I would be the vision-holder and head of the ministry. The apostle-pastor of the church where we conducted the conference listened to our proceedings. As a courtesy to his hospitality he was allowed to speak. The old order concept of the apostle was ingrained within him. In his time behind the pulpit he made this statement: "I saw an atrocity today, an apostle submitting to a prophet."

Biblically or Traditionally Oriented? Where are the scriptural examples that support such an inflated idea of the supremacy of the apostle? Was that the reason Paul and Barnabas parted company, or was it simply because they could not agree on taking John Mark with them? Does the concept of greatest and least and highest and lowest in rank follow the teachings of Apostle Paul or the kingdom principles that Jesus taught in the Gospels? If we could put this old concept concerning apostles to rest then there could be greater unity between the fivefold ministers. It would make it easier for the Church to accept the thousands of apostles that will come forth during the Apostolic Movement. It would also allow those who are truly God's commissioned apostles to be properly identified as such without everyone feeling they are putting themselves in the highest position in the Church. The new generation of God-ordained apostles arising today will not have that old order attitude or concept.

Who Then Is the Greatest? Jesus answered this question when His own apostles asked Him, "Who is the greatest in the kingdom of heaven?" (Matt. 18:1b) He also answered it when Apostles James and John came to Jesus requesting to be the greatest among them by having one of them sit on His right hand and the other on His left. This activated great strife among the twelve concerning who would be the greatest. They were curious as to who would be the chief apostle among them or the apostle of apostles.

Jesus answered the apostles and basically told them that they were thinking like the world. Their whole concept of greatest and least was completely wrong, for in the kingdom of heaven no one has those kinds of thoughts and concerns.

> *But Jesus called them to Himself and said to them, "You know that the rulers of the Gentiles lord it over them, and those who are great exercise authority over them. Yet it shall not be so among you; but whoever desires to become great among you, let him be your servant. And whoever desires to be first among you, let him be your slave—just as the Son of Man did not come to be served, but to serve, and to give His life a ransom for many"* (Matt. 20:25-28, NKJV).

> *If anyone desires to be first, he shall be last of all and servant of all* (Mark 9:35b, NKJV).

This forever settles the issue of who is the greatest and least in the Church. The greatest is not the one who has the highest title, position, authority or thousands serving him. The greatest in the Church is the one who is the most humble, serves the most people and doesn't even concern him or herself with thoughts of whether he or she is the greatest or highest in position. This seems to be an apostolic characteristic—a concern about the structure of the Church and who is first, second and so forth. Their strength becomes their weakness if it is not sanctified and saturated with kingdom thinking.

Paul, a Type of the New Breed of Last-Day Apostles: This was never a part of Paul's thinking. In fact, he said he did not feel worthy to be called an apostle. He said that this apostolic ministry was given to him who was less than the least of all the saints (Eph. 3:8). Paul, who planted the Corinthian church, being their apostle and spiritual father, had not been there for quite some time for a particular reason. "Moreover I call God as witness against my soul, that **to spare you** I came no more to Corinth. **Not that we have dominion over your faith**, but are fellow workers for your joy; for by faith you stand" (2 Cor. 1:23-24, NKJV). Paul never thought about apostles being the greatest and always first.

For I think that God has displayed us, the apostles, last, as men condemned to death; for we have been made a spectacle to the world, both to angels and to men. We are fools for Christ's sake, but you are wise in Christ! We are weak, but you are strong! You are distinguished, but we are dishonored! To the present hour we both hunger and thirst, and we are poorly clothed, and beaten, and homeless. And we labor, working with our own hands. Being reviled, we bless; being persecuted, we endure; being defamed, we entreat. We have been made as the filth of the world, the offscouring of all things until now. I do not write these things to shame you, but as my beloved children I warn you. For though you might have ten thousand instructors in Christ, yet you do not have many fathers; for in Christ Jesus I have begotten you through the gospel (1 Cor. 4:9-15, NKJV).

Those who desire the calling and name of apostle because they have some grandiose ideas of power, respect and prestige, need to take a closer look at these scriptures. The last-day apostles that will be raised up in the Apostolic Movement will be after the order of Paul, not the Dark Age religious presentation of the apostle (Pope). If the apostolic ministry-life that is revealed in First and Second Corinthians was presented, there would be fewer ambitious leaders desiring to take the title of apostle.

The Ministry in Which Apostle Paul Boasted. Paul never bragged or boasted about his apostolic ministry. There was only one ministry that he exalted. That was the ministry of going from glory to glory and being continually changed until he was conformed to the image of God's dear Son, Jesus Christ (2 Cor. 3:18–4:1; Rom. 8:29).

A Foolish Time of Boasting. The only time that Paul boasted about his apostolic ministry and life experience was when those superficial, pseudo apostles were promoting themselves as the greatest. They were exercising dominion over the saints in a high-handed way. He felt it necessary to counteract what they were doing though he felt foolish in giving all of his apostolic credentials, including all the things he had suffered to be the type of apostle that God desired. He said, "I consider that I am not at all inferior to the most eminent apostles" (2 Cor. 11:5, NKJV).

He describes how the Corinthian Christians were being so enthusiastic about these super apostles, and were willingly putting up with their carnal ways, while at the same time they were scorning Paul's humble and unselfish apostolic ministry. He told them that they put up with fools gladly. For they put up with it even when those "apostles" brought them into bondage, devoured them, took their finances and resources, exalted themselves by demanding respect and submission to their apostleship, and even slapped them in the face. He then declared what type of apostle those are who act that way.

> *For such are false apostles, deceitful workers, transforming themselves into apostles of Christ. And no wonder! For Satan himself transforms himself into an angel of light. Therefore it is no great thing if his [Satan's] ministers also transform themselves into ministers of righteousness, whose end will be according to their works* (2 Cor. 11:13-15, NKJV).

Please read chapters 10, 11 and 12 of Second Corinthians in several translations, for they give many insights concerning the ministries of true and false apostles. These scriptures alone should be enough to make every true "called to be" apostle want to have the right attitude, attributes and actions that God will require of His last-day apostles.

There will be extremes in the Apostolic Movement. Yes, there will be a few extremes, which are normally caused by immature, ambitious novices and leaders who are wrongly motivated. Those who have made in-depth studies of the human temperament say that about seventy percent love to be followers and the remainder is made up of those who want to lead and a few who want to dominate, having absolute power and authority. The few ministers who fit the latter personality profile, and who have never allowed themselves to be sanctified, will quickly accept the concept that the apostle is the superior minister with absolute authority over all others. Such a person will quickly proclaim himself as "the apostle" of his city or region and egotistically expect all ministers and churches in that area to recognize and submit to him as God's apostle over the area.

Cut the Root and the Bad Fruit Will Disappear. The old self with its self-importance, self-exaltation, self-promotion and self-preservation and concern is the root for all extremes and imbalances. The old apostolic concept is rooted in self rather than in kingdom principles. These few things mentioned will give some insight into what kinds of extremes will arise in the Apostolic Movement. If we can keep human ego and pride out of it, then most of the extremes will be just the general things of the carnal nature that follow every work of God.

Therefore we who are called to be and are now apostles need to concentrate on serving and ministering to the saints, upholding and building them into the building that God wants them to be. Remember, the apostles and prophets are not the roof and pinnacle on top of the building but the foundation at the bottom of the building. We are not to lord it over the saints and other ministers but remain the apostle-prophet foundation that undergirds the Church.

Let us now venture into the next chapter to see what will be the last-day ministry of the apostles and the prophets. There we will talk about the powerful ministry that comes with the calling and commissioning of an apostle.

—••◉◉◉◉••—

14

THE LAST-DAY MINISTRY
OF APOSTLES AND PROPHETS

—••◉◉◉◉••—

When the apostles are restored in their fullness, it will activate many things. It will cause many prophecies concerning the end times to start coming to pass at an accelerated rate. The apostle is the last of the fivefold ministers to be restored. It is like a great machine that needs five things to happen in sequence before it will fully work. It could be compared to a space rocket booster that must have five switches turned on before it can launch the space shuttle—the Church. Each switch or button represents one of the fivefold ministries.

The Evangelist switch was turned on fully in the 1950's and it made progressive preparation for the launching of the Church space shuttle. The restoration of the Pastor in the 1960's to his proper role did the same things. It was the same with the restoration of the Teacher in the 1970's. The booster rockets turned on with all their fiery force in the 1980's with the restoration of the Prophet and God's great company of prophets. With the full restoration of the Apostle and God's great company of apostles, the space shuttle of the Church will be launched to fulfill its end-time ministry and eternal destiny.

The final restoration of apostles will cause all ministers who will receive it to be raised to a higher level of anointing and ministry. It will revolutionize the whole function of the Church. It could be compared to how the world functioned at the beginning of the 20th century in travel, electronics and communication and how it is functioning now at the end of this century.

An Example. Just as the world went from motorized vehicles and began to fly through the air and travel into space, so will the Church advance that much in one generation. People at the turn of the 20th century could not imagine what we would be doing by the beginning of the 21st century. Only a few visionary scientists had some insight into what was coming. The common people and some leaders ridiculed their predictions. Church scientists, called prophets, have had insights and are even now having prophetic visions concerning what will be happening in the 21st-century Church. However, average saints and some church leaders deny such possibilities happening or scorn and make light of such prophetic predictions. Don't be the nearsighted and unbelieving church member, but receive the prophetic and apostolic revelations coming forth in this day and hour.

The Bible declares that natural eyes have not seen and ears have not heard all the things that God has prepared for His people. However, many of those things have already been revealed by the Holy Spirit. Isaiah and the other prophets prophesied them in the Old Testament. Paul and the other apostles wrote the revelation and applications of most of those prophecies in the New Testament. Now those things are being revealed more fully and divine applications given for appropriating and fulfilling them.

There are last-day apostles and prophets who are friends of God like Prophet Abraham. God is now revealing His plans and will continue showing them what He is about to do before He does it. Learn to recognize the true voice of God through His holy apostles and prophets (Isa. 41:8; 64:4; 1 Cor. 2:9-10; Eph. 3:3-5; John 15:14-15; Gen. 18:17; Amos 3:7).

Different Types of Apostles. All the fivefold ministers—apostles, prophets, evangelists, pastors, teachers—vary in their special anointing and ability. In more than four decades of ministering with ministers around the world, I have found that most major in their God-given ascension office and minor in one of the others. For instance, there are those who function as pastors, but each with a different emphasis. There are pastoral pastors, apostolic pastors, prophetic pastors, evangelistic pastors and teaching pastors. It only takes being in a church one or two services to determine what type of ministry is shepherding that flock of sheep. I could give you detailed characteristics and ministry emphasis on each one. However, our purpose in this book is not to explain the pastor, but the apostle. The same is true for all fivefold ministers. We will use this principle to show the different types of apostles.

Apostolic-Apostles: These are the apostles whose whole ministry expression is apostolic. They are more like the Apostle Paul who demonstrated all the things that apostles are capable of being and doing. The scriptures do not reveal that any of the original Twelve Apostles ever pastored a local church. Apostle Paul and Prophet Silas stayed three years establishing the New Testament church in Ephesus. Paul stayed eighteen months in Corinth while establishing the local church. He also stayed a few months here and there establishing churches, but he never became the long-term pastor of any church.

The church world for hundreds of years has substituted the term "missionary" for the apostolic work that has been done in other nations and regions. But a true apostle is more than the typical understanding of a missionary. The Apostolic

Movement will reveal and demonstrate what this type of apostle is to be and do. How he relates to local churches, how he is supported and how he relates to the other fivefold ministers and their ministries will be made known.

Prophetic-Apostles: These are true apostles who have a strong anointing for prophesying to individuals, churches and nations. They may do this as an individual minister or with others in a prophetic presbytery. Paul was a prophetic apostle. He laid hands on Timothy and prophesied to him his calling and gifts. He had the ministry of prophetically revealing things to individuals and imparting spiritual graces and gifts (1 Tim. 4:14; 2 Tim 1:6; Rom. 1:11).

However, as an apostle he fulfilled his ministry with the discerning of spirits, faith and working of miracles. The apostolic prophet does similar things by his prophetic office gift of prophesying, and by the word of knowledge and gifts of healings. The end result is the same for the people but the prophet and apostle minister their anointing and ministry in a little different manner. If King David, Moses and Joseph had been active ministers in the church, they could have been called prophetic-apostles.

Evangelistic-Apostles: These are more the missionary type. Their greatest concern is for world evangelization. If they are in a pastoral position, then their church will be very outreach oriented. They will be taking teams and sending teams to the nations. They will propagate that the greatest responsibility of the apostle is reaping the harvest by mass evangelism meetings and taking the gospel to all nations.

Apostle Miracle Ministry vs. Evangelistic Miracle Ministry. We promised you in another chapter that we would show the differences between the miracle ministry of the true evangelist and that of the apostle. The basic difference is revealed in Acts chapter 8 where an evangelistic campaign was conducted. The evangelist had one main concern: that of winning souls for Jesus Christ. Like Philip, as soon as an evangelist brings thousands to Christ in one campaign, then the Holy Spirit leads him to another evangelistic ministry, whether to one or one hundred thousand.

Apostolic Miracle vs. Evangelistic Miracles. The church at Jerusalem sent Apostles Peter and John to Samaria to follow up with apostolic ministries. They established the new converts in the fundamentals of the faith, laid hands on them to receive the Holy Spirit and established them in the present-truth ministries and spiritual experiences of the New Testament Church Movement. They then gathered the new converts together and established them into a New Testament local church. The evangelist anointing works miracles to get them saved and then baptized in water. The apostles work miracles not only to get people saved, but also to establish them into a progressive, growing local church. These are the main differences between the evangelistic-evangelist and the apostolic-apostle. However, there are evangelistic-apostles and apostolic-evangelists. Some who are really apostles are calling themselves evangelists, and some who are really evangelists are calling themselves apostles. They base this on the fact that they have signs, wonders and miracles following their ministry. The only way to tell the difference is by divine discernment, prophetic insight and evaluating one's concerns and motivational purpose. Then there are those who are apostles with an evangelistic zeal who can properly be called evangelistic-apostles.

Pastoral-Apostles: Apostle James, the natural brother of Jesus, is an example of a pastoral-apostle. He pastored the local church at Jerusalem. Neither the Bible nor history says that he ever traveled beyond Jerusalem. He was the senior pastor of one local church during his entire ministry. He never conducted any apostolic crusades or traveled among the churches as did Peter and Paul. James did write one letter, which became the Epistle of James in the Bible. He addressed it "to the twelve tribes which are scattered abroad." The Twelve Apostles probably made Pastoral-Apostle James's local church in Jerusalem their home church when not itinerating.

Can you imagine what it would be like to have the Twelve Apostles that walked with Jesus for more than three years sitting in your congregation? Especially when you did not accept Christ as your Savior until after His resurrection. I doubt if Senior Pastor-Apostle James turned the pulpit over to one of the twelve every time they were in town.

A Modern-Day Example. My thirty-seven-year-old son, Tom, who pastors our local CI Family Church, has had a similar situation for the last ten years. We have twenty-three ministers who travel full time in ministry, but make CI Family Church their home church. All eleven couples and one single are apostles, prophets, and prophetesses. Two of the men are younger than Tom, four are less than five years older and the rest are in their fifties and sixties. Jim Davis, who is president of the CI Network of Churches, founded a local church and pastored it for twenty years. He is a prophetic-apostle who oversees all the CINC churches and ministers. Most of these ministers have national and international ministries. Several of them have Master's degrees and Doctorates. Pastor Tom has an Associate and Bachelor's degree and is working on his Master's.

One of the ministers who is not counted among the travelers is Tim Hamon. He is Pastor Tom's older brother, president of CI School of Theology and the CI Ministry Training College. He is an ordained minister and functions as a prophetic-teacher. Tim and five of the other ministers serve as Pastor Tom's board of elders. My wife and I, their parents, serve as bishop over the local church, over all five presidents of CI Ministries, and bishop-overseer of all CINC churches and ministries. I am bishop over all these ministries and have three times as much ministry experience as Tom, yet I only speak in the local church three or four times a year.

When we are home, I do not feel I have to do the preaching. I just sit on the platform with Pastors Tom and Jane and most times never say a word, but occasionally give ministry reports or a prophecy. Rarely does one of the traveling ministers have opportunity to speak on Sunday morning. They do not come home to minister but to rest and receive personal ministry. Pastors Tom and Jane can tell you the burdens and blessings that come with pastoring a church of this nature. I'm sure if we could talk to Pastor James, he could really tell us many things about pastoring a church with many apostles, prophets and older elders of the Faith. Normally only prophetic and pastoral-apostles have the personal security, faith, grace and confidence to pastor such a church.

Teacher-Apostles: There are teacher-apostles teaching in Bible colleges, pastoring churches and itinerating among the churches. Their greatest concern is for the establishing of saints in proper doctrine and practical living. They make volumes of outlines, teaching manuals and workbooks to help the saints be established in all truth and Christian experiences. They will make sure they have a K-12 academy for the children, a Bible college and training programs for all groups in the church. They will have their weekly home groups organized and have teaching outlines for each one to follow. They will have follow-up programs for all their converts to make sure they are firmly established in the church. Their weakness is that they have a tendency to depend on their organizational skills and programs more than their apostolic ministry for the supernatural signs, wonders and miracles.

God's supernatural power should be manifest in the apostle's ministry regardless of what type of apostle a minister may be. Apostles have been described for years as administrators, concerned about church structure, practical Christianity and ruling over others. Apostles have been so busy trying to live up to that job description that they have forsaken their greater ministry, the ministry of giving themselves to prayer, study of the Word and manifesting the miraculous. It is time for all of us to make the same decision and dedication as the early church apostles. They realized they had become too involved in the administrative affairs of the church. "...It is not desirable that we should leave the word of God and serve tables. Therefore...we will give ourselves continually to prayer and the ministry of the word" (Acts 6:2-4, NKJV).

Let all fivefold ministers, and especially apostles, take this Biblical principle seriously. Begin now to delegate others to take care of the natural matters and many of the minor counseling and pastoral duties. Then fill up that time, not with more golfing and fishing, but with hours of prayer for spiritual enlightenment while studying the Word. Give yourself to activating the apostolic anointing with its divine enablement to minister with miraculous manifestations confirming the Word preached. The football of obedience is now in our hands. We can either sit on it or arise and run with it toward the goal. Let us be God's type of apostle and not an apostle with some religious job description. If we older apostles do not become the Calebs and Joshuas to help lead this new generation of apostles, then God will leave us in the wilderness and raise up new leaders that are not afraid to be all that God intended for His apostles to be and manifest.

Ministries of the Last-Day Apostles and Prophets. They will be the generals that lead God's fivefold officers and warrior saints into and through the coming moves of God after the Apostolic Movement. Twenty years ago while prophetically writing the fifth division of the book *The Eternal Church*, which deals with the future activities and destiny of the Church, the following declarations were made:

Get Ready for a New Restorational Movement.

"Oh, present generation of the Church, especially you that are young in heart and your eye has caught the vision and your heart has felt the thrill, to the call of the Master, and your heart has said, 'I will get ready for the conflict of the ages,' oh His fury is upon us, is upon us today."

These are more than words to a chorus; they are the cry of the Holy Spirit to this generation. If you have never been a part of a restorational move of God, then get ready and get excited! There is another restorational truth coming to the Church that will bring us into full reality.

"But be assured it will be the same among Christendom during this time as it was when Israel was challenged to go in and possess their promised possessions. Twelve Israeli spies went into the land of Canaan. They all saw the same bountifulness and truthfulness of which God had told them about the land. But ten of them were overwhelmed with the giants, walled cities and fortified areas. Joshua and Caleb saw the impossibilities in the natural, but they believed God's prophetic promises and said, 'We are well able to overcome and possess.' The ten unbelieving spies said, 'We are not able' " (Num. 13:30-31).

Two Family Camps—the "Ables" and the "Not Ables."
This next challenge of the Holy Spirit to the Church will sound just as unreasonable, irrational, impossible and ridiculous to the majority of present-day ministers as it did to the ten natural, humanistic-minded Israelis. If this Old Testament type holds true in the percentages, then it means for every two ministers who are preaching this truth, there will be ten against it. Every minister in Christendom, and even those among the Charismatics, will be faced with a challenging decision. The

Church will be separated into two camps: the "we are able" group, and the "we are not able" group. The majority has never been right. God is not looking for a multitude of leaders, but for a few who are willing to cross their Jordan of death to self, arise in resurrection life and be united with the believers into a mighty army that shall go in and possess their promised possessions.

Like the prophets of old, I prophetically saw something was coming but didn't know how, when and where. I had no idea then that there would be a Prophetic Movement in the 1980's, an Apostolic Movement in the late 1990's and then three more finalizing moves of God before this came to pass in fullness. Even now I am sure there will be refreshing moves and revivals taking place around these restorational moves of God. We see in part and prophesy in part but when the perfect or fullness of revelation comes, then we will see the whole as God sees it from eternity (1 Cor. 13:9-12).

I closed that chapter by declaring, "If I am privileged of the Holy Spirit to be a Joshua or a Caleb to this new generation, then I shall do all in my power to maintain a balance by the grace, wisdom, and maturity of the Head of the Church Himself, Jesus Christ our Lord." Thank God that twenty years later I had my first experience of being at the birthing of a sovereign restorational movement—The Prophetic Movement. As you have read in this book, I fulfilled my commitment by doing all in my power to teach, write and demonstrate God's grace, wisdom and balance without going to extremes to the right and left. When we did make a few swings in our ignorance and enthusiasm, God quickly brought us back to the middle.

Now We Are About to Participate in the Apostolic Movement. If I live to the age of eighty-five to ninety, I will probably have the opportunity to be a part of the coming moves of God. Several prophecies have been given to me by proven prophets and apostles that I would never miss a new move of

God as long as I am alive on earth. If I leave this earth before the translation of the saints, then I know I will still be a part of all that Christ Jesus will ever do throughout eternity. I am an heir of God and joint-heir with Jesus Christ in all that He shall ever be or do in His eternal kingdom and everlasting ministry (Rom. 8:17).

God's purpose is to use the Church to teach all earthly and heavenly creatures the manifold wisdom of God.

> *And to make all see what is the fellowship of the mystery, which from the beginning of the ages has been hidden in God who created all things through Jesus Christ; **to the intent** that **now** the **manifold wisdom of God might be made known by the church** to the principalities and powers in the heavenly places, according to **the eternal purpose** which He accomplished in Christ Jesus our Lord* (Eph. 3:9-11, NKJV).

> *Now to Him who is able to do exceedingly abundantly above all that we ask or think, according to the power that works in us, **to Him be glory in the church** by Christ Jesus to all generations, **forever and ever.** Amen* (Eph. 3:20-21, NKJV).

Jesus was the glory of God manifested on earth. The Church is the glory of Christ Jesus being manifested on earth. That glory will be made known by the Church throughout the endlessness of eternity. "Glory" means the personification of Christ's personality, portrayal of His presence, manifestation of His ministry, revelation of His reality, conveying of His character, performing of His purpose and the revelation of His grace, goodness and greatness. The Church is the glory of the Lord that God shall cause to cover the earth as the waters cover the sea (Eph. 1:12,17; 2 Cor. 3:18; Isa. 11:9; Num. 14:21; Hab. 2:14).

The Church Never Ends. It only escalates and begins on a higher realm of immortality. The corporate Body of Christ is as everlasting in its life and ministry as is Jesus Christ the Head of the Church. Membership ministry in the Body of Christ does not cease at one's death or at the translation and resurrection of the Church. The Church is now and forever will be as timeless and everlasting as its God.

Some Specific Ministries of the End-Time Prophets and Apostles. As mentioned earlier, they will manifest all the miracles and judgment ministries of Moses and Elijah and the two prophetic witnesses in Revelation chapter 11. Ministering by their anointing and the leading of the Holy Spirit, they will pronounce judgments upon the opponents of Christ and His gospel, such as Paul did by proclaiming blindness upon Elymas, the sorcerer. They will prophesy great changes in nature and the nations. They will accurately predict earthquakes, tidal waves and other catastrophes of nature. These prophecies given in the time of Jesus Christ will come to pass exactly as predicted. They will cause the fear of Jehovah God to come upon the people, causing whole nations to turn to God.

New Creative Miracles in Abundance They will produce creative miracles among the maimed and deformed. New limbs will grow back where they had been removed or never developed. Not only will there be creative miracles in the human body, there will also be creative miracles performed in nature. There will be such undeniable miracles taking place that it will shake the nations (Hag. 2:7).

The Gospels and the Book of Acts Reenacted. God will not do these things just to confirm someone's revelation or ministry; to satisfy curiosity or human ego, or just a desire to see the miraculous. As needs arise apostles, prophets and apostolic saints of the restored Church will do the following. They will "walk on water"; be transported by the Spirit from one geographical location to another as Philip the evangelist; multiply the loaves and fishes to feed the multitudes when there are no other resources; supernaturally preach to nationals in their own language; have supernatural preservation during calamities; be miraculously and timely directed. There will be a greater number of incidents of people being raised from the dead and many other things that would be hard now to grasp and believe they really could happen.

The Church Will Reach Its Peak of Performance. Jesus will continue to arise in His true present-truth apostles, prophets, evangelists, pastors and teachers until the saints are perfected and moving in their ministry. Fivefold ministers will continue in their ministry to the saints until they reach Christ's fullness of maturity and ministry. Some are even destined to grow up into the shoulders and headship of Christ where the government of the kingdom of God will be placed upon them. The last day Church-Bride will not be a little girl (immature) or an old woman (fallen away and deteriorated), but a fully developed and grown young woman in her prime and peak of her performance (Isa. 9:6-7; Eph. 4:16).

Prerequisites for Participation in the Last-Generation Church. Those who will be participants in the great apostolic and prophetic companies of overcomers will not be there simply because of their faith, revelation and preaching. They will have to be absolutely Christlike and powerful in ministry. Participants and leaders of past restorational movements were mightily used even though they were immature and carnal in areas of their lives. But those days have come to an end for the last generation that will participate in these coming moves of God. The only Christians who will participate in these last activities of the mortal Church will be those who have fully died the death to sin and self. The declaration of Galatians 2:20

will have become a lifestyle reality to them. Every attitude and action contrary to divine principle will have to be purged. Nothing short of conformity to the image of Jesus Christ will suffice.

First-Century and 21st-Century Ministries. As the ministry of the apostle and prophet founded the Church, so shall the ministry of the apostle and prophet put the finishing touches on the Church. They are being raised up in the Church to purge the ministers and believers. There is a great lack of the reverential fear of God within Christendom. Holy Spirit baptized Christians come to church services with all types of sin in their lives. These range from sexual immorality to gossip, rebellion, selfishness and party spirits. They sing, praise, rejoice, prophesy, testify and preach as though there was nothing out of order in their lives.

Anointed ministers, especially apostles and prophets, will move into a new realm of prophecy, words of knowledge and discerning of spirits. They will openly expose this hypocrisy and cause the reverential fear of God to fall upon the congregation and preachers. The time is coming very soon when Christians will thoroughly examine themselves in prayer and the Word of God before they ever enter the doors of the local church or conference meetings. They will make sure all sin, unforgiveness and all sinfully selfish acts are fully forgiven and under the blood of Jesus. The religiously proud who try to make excuses or justify themselves by lying to the Holy Spirit who is speaking through these ministers will receive the same judgment of God as Ananias and Sapphira did when they lied to the Holy Spirit speaking through Apostle Peter. This will bring great fear and respect for the Church and God's anointed ministers. It will cause many souls to be saved and added to the Church daily. The same judgment ministry of the last-day apostles and prophets will begin the greatest harvest of souls that has ever been seen during any other time of the Church Age.

The Whole Creation Is Waiting for the Last-Generation Church. The earth and all of creation are waiting for the manifestation of God's last-day apostles and prophets and fully restored Church. "For the earnest expectation of the creation eagerly waits for the revealing of the sons of God" (Rom. 8:19, NKJV). When the Church is fully restored, then the saints will receive their final redemption, the immortalization of their mortal bodies. When this happens, then the natural creation of plants and animals will be delivered from their bondage of corruption into the glorious liberty of the children of God.

We the Church have a responsibility and ministry to the rest of God's creation. The whole of creation is groaning and anxiously waiting for the Church to reach full maturity and sonship. When the Church reaches that final stage and its last act of redemption, it will cause a redemptive chain reaction throughout the heavenlies and over all the earth (Rom. 8:18-23).

Another Group Waiting and Cheering Us On. There is one other group waiting for the Church to press on to the finish line. Chapter 11 of Hebrews tells of all the great heroes of the faith. But it concludes by saying, "And all these, having obtained a good testimony through faith, did not receive the promise, God having provided something better for us, **that they should not be made perfect apart from us**" (Heb. 11:39-40, NKJV). All of those who have died in the faith since the beginning of time are cheering us on from the balcony of heaven. They cannot be complete without the full obedience of the last-generation Church.

We have come to Mount Zion, the heavenly Jerusalem and the Church of the Firstborn where the spirits of just saints have been made perfect but are waiting for their final act of redemption at the first resurrection. But they cannot receive it until we, the last-generation Church, fulfill our destiny. This is the reason the first two verses of Hebrews chapter 12 say what we are to do because of this cloud of witnesses. When you see the word "therefore" at the beginning of a chapter, read the previous verses to discover what it is "there for."

Therefore we also, since we are surrounded by so great a cloud of witnesses, let us lay aside every weight, and the sin which so easily ensnares us, and let us run with endurance the race that is set before us, looking unto Jesus, the author and finisher of our faith, who for the joy that was set before Him [His Church-Bride] *endured the cross, despising the shame, and has sat down at the right hand of the throne of God* (Heb. 12:1-2, NKJV).

Father God then said to Jesus, "*Sit at My right hand, till I make Your enemies Your footstool*" (Heb. 1:13b, NKJV).

God is going to make all enemies Christ's footstool and put them under His feet through Christ's corporate Body, the Church (Heb. 1:13; 11:39; 12:1-2,20-22). Now accompany us on the journey to discover the coming moves of God that we must experience before all these things will be accomplished.

15

THE COMING MOVES OF GOD

The Fundamentals of the Coming Moves of God. The main purpose for presenting these coming moves of God is to let the Church know what is coming and why God has ordained them to take place. They are coming and are ordained of God to help fulfill His progressive and ultimate purposes. They will be activated in a timely manner for the purpose of accomplishing certain things that are progressively necessary for the fulfilling of His ultimate purpose. I know by prophetic insight and apostolic revelation that they are coming and the purpose they are to accomplish. But there will be no attempt to give details concerning where, when, who and how. Our revelation only answers two of the six normal questions: what and why. We know what is coming and why. However, all the answers are never fully known until we experience the restoration of truth.

Knowing It's Coming But Lacking Details. Once we know God's purpose for something, then we can go to the scriptures that deal with that subject and surmise what may take place. For instance, Jesus told His apostles, "I will build My church" (Matt. 16:18). They believed Him and accepted the fact that Christ was going to build His Church, whatever that meant. However, they knew very little about the Church Movement that was coming until the Church was birthed on the day of Pentecost. It was several years after that before they worked out its doctrines and the fundamentals of the faith. Likewise, He told them there was coming a movement that would cause them to be baptized with the Holy Spirit and Fire. John baptized with water, but they would be baptized with the Holy Spirit (Acts 1:4-8). They demonstrated they believed Him by going back to the upper room in Jerusalem and tarrying there until the Holy Spirit Movement was brought forth. They knew the general time of its happening and that its purpose was to give them power, but they did not know whether they would have to wait hours, days, weeks or months.

They believed it was coming and that it would do certain things for them. They made preparation by reading the Word, praying, fasting, repenting before God, singing and praising the Lord Jesus. Then suddenly on the day of Pentecost the sovereign visitation they had been believing for came forth like a mighty rushing wind. The one hundred twenty who had persevered and occupied until He came were filled with the Holy Spirit and began to speak in unknown tongues. They had no idea that this would be part of the experiences that would accomplish this Holy Spirit Movement. They spoke in tongues for years before they knew all the ways to appropriate all the benefits of speaking in tongues. We must remember that they immediately began to move in the power and fire of the Holy Spirit and in the miraculous that accompanied the preaching of the gospel. It was ten years later before Peter received the revelation that Gentiles could become Christians without becoming proselyte Jews first. It was approximately twenty years after the New Testament Church Movement began when the first general council of the Church was convened to settle some doctrinal issues.

Telescopic Prophets and Apostles. We can see from these illustrations that we will not know all the experiences that will accompany a restoration movement. It will take several years afterward to work out all the details. Therefore I refuse to try to lay down dogmatic ideas of all that is going to happen, but rather I would try to prove scripturally that it is in the heart and purposes of God. I believe that the anointed ability of restorational prophets is similar to the equipment that astronomers have to look into far distant space. They can see things numerous light years away. They are developing newer and greater ways to see with greater clarity farther distances away. The prophets and apostles are developing new and greater ways to see into the distant future. The prophets spoke of the coming of the Messiah Movement hundreds and thousands of years before it was manifest on earth. They did not know the what, how and when, but they did know that it was coming.

Restorational Specialist. I believe God gave a prophetic insight concerning these coming restorational movements. Prophets and apostles have proclaimed that certain acts of God were going to come forth. Their true prophetic predictions did eventually come to pass. But they never happened when, where and how their natural minds' preconceived ideas imagined. I have personally experienced that reality. I did Biblical and Church history research in every book I could find dealing with special moves of God and great revivals of the Church. These studies were conducted from 1954 until 1978, when I began three years of intensified research while writing the book on the origination, deterioration, restoration and destiny of the Church, which was named, *The Eternal Church*. While writing the book, God revealed to me that before Jesus returned, there would be restoration movements to reestablish the ministries of prophets and apostles to the Church. I did not give the full revelation but I did mention on page 347 that there would be a "last-day ministry of prophets and apostles." I am no longer a novice in the area of prophets, apostles and the history and destiny of the Church. In fact, this has been God's major area of anointing and revelation in my life. All apostles have key anointings and revelations in which they major. The Body of Christ is one, but consists of many members who have their particular calling, purpose and ways of fulfilling their membership ministry. There are no two members exactly alike in every area, just as all members of the human race have their own set of fingerprints and unique individuality of personality and expression. That is why it is so essential that authors and preachers do not use limited and rigid ways to describe in detail how every apostle will function. Every time a divine gift or ministry is integrated into a born-again human being, it brings forth another unique way to minister that gift or calling.

In another chapter we gave the main scriptures on the restoration necessary before Jesus can leave heaven and come back to earth (Acts 3:21). Those who will read this book with their old fundamentalist, dispensational tinted reading glasses on will not relate to or assimilate what Christ is trying to communicate to His Church, unless the Holy Spirit gives divine revelation and application. As Apostle Paul prayed for the Ephesian Christians, I pray for you to have the spirit of revelation and enlightened understanding that you may know, and have spiritually anointed ears to hear, what the Holy Spirit has to say to you, as a member of His Church.

> [I] *do not cease to give thanks for you, making mention of you in my prayers: that the God of our Lord Jesus Christ, the Father of glory, may give to you the spirit of wisdom and revelation in the knowledge of Him, the eyes of your understanding being enlightened; that you*

may know what is the hope of His calling, what are the riches of the glory of His inheritance in the saints, and what is the exceeding greatness of His power toward us who believe, according to the working of His mighty power (Eph. 1:16-19, NKJV).

Our Inheritance in Him—His Inheritance in Us. In verse 11 of Ephesians 1 it talks about our inheritance in Christ and in verse 18 it talks about the riches of the glory of His inheritance in us. I pray that while you are reading this book, you will gain a greater revelation and appreciation of our inheritance in Him and His inheritance in us. In the seven letters to the seven churches Jesus says seven times, "He who has an ear, let him hear what the Spirit says to the churches" (Rev. 2:7,11,17,29; 3:6,13,22).

16

THE SAINTS MOVEMENT

God declares that He will do nothing unless He first reveals it to His servants the prophets (Amos 3:7). The type of prophets who are like the tribe of Issachar know the seasons and times for God's plans and when they are to be implemented (1 Chron. 12:32; Rev. 10:7). The Saints Movement is based on a prophetic insight by a prophet and then an apostolic revelation of certain scriptures.

The Establishment of Saints as Deacons. The Church was birthed on the day of Pentecost. The original apostles retained their "apostles of the Lamb" status while becoming apostles establishing Christ's New Testament Church, by supernatural miracles and apostolic teaching. But like many modern-day ministers, they became overly involved in the daily administration of the church. They realized they had to return to giving themselves "continually to prayer and to the ministry of the word," if they were to continue their apostolic ministry with signs, wonders and miracles. They appointed seven men who were full of the Holy Spirit, faith and wisdom to take care of these special administrative needs. They took the position of deacons (Acts 6:1-6; Phil. 1:1; 1 Tim. 3:8-13).

Deacon Stephen began to be mightily used of God for more than natural things. "And Stephen, full of faith and power, did great wonders and signs among the people" (Acts 6:8, NKJV). The old religious order falsely accused him, brought him before their council and gave him opportunity to speak. He gave that dynamically anointed message as recorded in chapter 7 of Acts. He incensed them with his closing remarks declaring that he was seeing a vision of the heavens being opened, and Jesus, the Son of Man, standing at the right hand of God. This inflamed them with rage. They picked up stones and stoned Stephen to death. This activated great persecution, which helped to activate the Early Church Saints Movement.

"Now Saul [the one converted later to become Apostle Paul] was consenting to his [Stephen's] death. At that time a great persecution arose against the church which was at Jerusalem; and they were **all [the saints] scattered throughout the regions** of Judea and Samaria, **except the apostles**. ... Therefore those who were scattered **went everywhere preaching the word**" (Acts 8:1,4, NKJV).

This Activated the 1st-Century Church Saints Movement. There is another Saints Movement coming in the 21st-century Church. The original apostles stayed at Jerusalem but the saints/believers went everywhere preaching the Word. They not only preached but did what Jesus said believers would do. They healed the sick and cast out devils; "And they went out and preached everywhere, the Lord working with them and confirming the word through the accompanying signs. Amen" (Mark 16:20, NKJV).

Immediately Philip (not Apostle Philip, but one of the seven deacons) "...went down to the city of Samaria and preached Christ to them. And the multitudes with one accord heeded the things spoken by Philip, **hearing** and **seeing** the miracles which he did. For unclean spirits, crying with a loud voice, came out of many who were possessed; and many who were paralyzed were healed. And there was great joy in that city" (Acts 8:5-8, NKJV). This is the follow-up proof text to show what the believers did when they went everywhere preaching. Philip, at this time, was not recognized as a fivefold minister, but as one of the saints who went everywhere preaching.

Stephen and Philip are examples of the type of saints that will be in the Saints Movement. They were full of the Holy Spirit, wisdom and power; were of good reputation and faithfully did whatever the leadership appointed them to do. These two typical New Testament believers spoke boldly with wisdom and power. They were saints who were the type of believer that Jesus described in the last chapter of Mark, and was demonstrated by Philip. They were Holy Spirit filled, as evidenced by speaking in other tongues. They healed the sick, cast out devils, did mass evangelism and personal evangelism, were transported by the Spirit from one place to another [Philip] and were mighty witnesses for Jesus Christ.

The great harvest that will soon take place will not be reaped by just a few great apostles, prophets and evangelists, but by God's prepared and anointed saints. What is the preparation that anoints and enables the saints to fulfill their membership ministry as believers in the Body of Christ?

The full restoration and activation of all fivefold ministers will bring about the teaching, training, activating, mentoring and maturing of the saints, when these ministers start fulfilling God's main purpose for giving them their ascension gift ministries. That purpose is the equipping of the SAINTS for the work of their membership ministries. Then as every member functions, and every joint supplies, the Body of Christ can fulfill its prophesied purpose and destiny (Eph. 4:11-16).

There are still multimillions of unsaved people whom God wants to make members of His Church/Body. God knows the specified number and types of members He has predestined to make the Body of Christ complete. The human body requires thirty trillion cells to be a complete and fully functioning body. Each member of the body contains many cells. The Godhead is the only one that knows how many members are to be in the Body of Christ, the Church. I believe there is a predestined number that is in God's original blueprint and specifications for His corporate Body. The Church was in the womb of the Old Testament, with all of its members in God's mind, until it was birthed in the New Testament (Ps. 139:14-16).

More Members Needed for Christ's Corporate Body. There are still multimillions of people with whom God needs to fill all the places at His banquet table for the wedding of His Son. When the ones who had received the wedding invitation made excuses why they could not come, Father God became very angry and said to His servants (the saints), "…The wedding is ready, but those who were invited were not worthy. Therefore go into the highways, and as many as you find, invite to the wedding" (Matt. 22:8-9, NKJV). In Luke's narrative of this wedding supper, the Lord said, "…'Go out quickly into the streets and lanes of the city, and bring in here the poor and the maimed and the lame and the blind.' And the servant said, 'Master, it is done as you commanded, and still there is room.' Then the master said to the servant, '**Go out into the highways and hedges, and compel them to come in, that My house [Church] may be filled**' " (Luke 14:21-23, NKJV).

The Compelling Ministry. This will be one of the key texts in the Saints Movement. How do the saints compel them to come in? They will use the fundamentals of personal evangelism, giving people an invitation to receive Christ. However, their compelling will be by the supernatural power of God and not by persuasive words. This is what the Prophetic and Apostolic Movements are preparing the saints to do. There will be a company of saints that will be equipped by fivefold ministers to go forth under the prophetic and apostolic anointing to do what Philip prototyped.

Apostolic and Prophetic Evangelism. The saints are being trained now in their military bases of international training centers and their local church armories. The goal is to have them taught, equipped and field trained to be the officers that lead God's army of prophetic evangelist saints during the coming Saints Movement. They will minister under the covering and leadership of the fivefold apostolic and prophetic generals who trained them. These saints will function like God's army prophetically described by Prophet Joel (Joel 2:1-11).

The Saints Movement will fully manifest apostolic-prophetic evangelism with God's consuming fire and miraculous power. Evangelism has always been in the heart of God but during the Saints Movement it will be escalated to a level that has not been seen since the 1st-century Saints Movement.

Personal evangelism was restored in the Evangelical Movement and has taken on new dimensions with each additional move of God. The Prophetic Movement is now adding a new dimension to evangelism. Saints are being instructed and activated in the supernatural gifts of the Holy Spirit. They are being trained within the Church, but the goal is to send teams of them into the highways and byways, compelling the people to come into the kingdom of God with supernatural ministry of the Holy Spirit. I believe the Saints Movement will cause more souls to be saved than have been saved in all the other restoration movements.

That's why it is so essential for the full restoration of apostles and prophets, and for the saints to be taught, trained, activated and fully equipped in their "compelling" tools of the supernatural gifts of the Holy Spirit. The Holy Spirit has been commissioned to bring all these things to pass.

Pastors and People Must Choose. If local pastors do not respond to this commissioning by providing time and place for this training, then the Holy Spirit will cause one of three things to happen. If the pastor has a vision to do it but the congregation will not respond, then the Holy Spirit will give the pastor a new generation congregation by moving out the old passive generation. He may move the pastor to a new pastorate or to start a new church. If the congregation wants it but the pastor doesn't, then God will remove the passive pastor or send the congregation to a pastor who will train and equip them. If God cannot find a pastor or congregation who will receive the vision and run with it, then God will cause a new prophetic-apostolic church to be established in that area. For the pastor and his congregation who will not fulfill Christ's commission of equipping the saints, God may not write "Ichabod" over it (1 Sam. 4:21), but He will decree that they will not cross over their Jordan and possess their promised possession or fulfill God's intended destiny. They will stay on the level they are on with less anointing while they wander in the wilderness till they die or Jesus returns.

They will be like King Saul who failed to properly obey God. He was left in his position of king (pastor) over Israel (his congregational or international ministry), but the anointing was removed from him in his second year. However, he continued his ministry for thirty-eight more years. He even expanded Israel, won many battles and built many new things. But he caused God to cancel his prophetic destiny. There will be many heads of ministries who will stay active in their ministry, but have become old order, the glory has departed, "Sauls." They will also be like the children of Israel who refused to move out of their comfort zone, make the transition and take the challenge to become warriors and drive out the tribes who were squatters on their promised land. God canceled their personal prophecy and destiny of possessing and living in Canaan. God supernaturally fed them with manna and did not forsake them but watched over them until that generation died. We must not allow anything to keep us from going all the way with God, regardless of the changes and challenges.

Lord, do not let us become "old order Sauls" or "wandering wilderness walkers," but soldiers going forth as "Canaan-conquering warriors."

Jesus is very serious about His saints being supernaturally equipped and matured to the level of Christ's maturity. He is going to deal very severely with His fivefold ministers who are not willing to fulfill His original purpose for calling and commissioning them. Resources and know-how methods are now available for equipping the saints. Heads of churches and ministries will stand without an acceptable excuse when Jesus asks, "Why didn't you equip My saints for My Body's sake and prepare them to be reapers in the great harvest by activating them in their supernatural gifts and ministries?"

Now Give Weapons to Those in Armor. Ministers of Christ's Church have worked for hundreds of years to make sure the saints have on their righteous garments, protective and preserving armor and the fruits of the Spirit. But now it is just as essential that they be equipped in their supernatural gifts of the Holy Spirit, which are their weapons of warfare. The front-line, present-truth division of the Church has crossed their Jordan River and entered their Canaan by making the transition into offensive warfare. They have come out of their forts of protectionism and defensivism and entered their inheritance in Canaan. They are moving into offensive aggressive warfare to destroy all the "ites" and "isms" out of their promised land. You, who are reading this book, have now been exposed to the heart and mind of God in this divine purpose. How you respond to this truth could affect your personal prophecies and ultimate ministry destiny. Do not be fearful, passive or unbelieving, but stirred and challenged to be one of God's overcomers and receive the overcomer's rewards. (Read about the overcomers' rewards in Revelation chapters 2 and 3 and become bold, faithful and courageous warriors like the Joshua Generation [Josh. 1:1–11:23].)

17

ARMY OF THE LORD
AND ETERNAL JUDGMENT

God is preparing His Church to become an invincible, unstoppable, unconquerable, overcoming Army of the Lord that subdues everything under Christ's feet. There will be a sovereign restorational move of God to activate all that is needed for His army to be and do what He has eternally purposed. The generals who will lead this army will be those who have progressively been prepared by incorporating every restorational truth into their life and ministry.

The Church has always been God's "Army," but has gone through stages of "active" and "inactive" cold wars and hot wars. It was a defeated and disbanded army during the Dark Ages, except for the few warrior knights of the holy crusades. The Church was reactivated into a militant army at the beginning of the "Period of the Great Restoration of the Church."

God's Great Generals. General Martin Luther led the progressive church members in a war of many battles until they had fully restored and established the truths of the Protestant

Movement. Around every hundred years God has raised up warrior Generals to lead the Church forth to restore another truth. This continued until 1950. Then the battles for restoring truth began to happen about every ten years. Now we have crossed Jordan and entered a war that will not cease until all the enemies of God are destroyed out of the Church's Canaan Land [earth] and Christ and His Church Army have established God's kingdom over all the earth (Heb. 1:13; 10:12-13; Num. 14:21; Isa. 11:9; Eph. 1:12; Rev. 11:15).

"The earth is the Lord's, and the fulness thereof" (Ps. 24:1a). Some translations say that the earth and everything in it belongs to the Lord Jesus. Jesus declared that everything the Father had given Him, He has given to His Church. Jesus said that all power in heaven and earth was given to Him and He has given all that power and authority to His Church. In short, He said, "For as the Father hath sent Me, so send I you with the same commission. Go ye therefore and preach My gospel and demonstrate My kingdom with all that has been given to you" (Matt. 28:18-20; John 17:18; Luke 10:19; 1 John 3:8).

God's great end-time army is being prepared to execute God's written Judgments with Christ's victory and divine judgment decrees that have already been established in heaven. The time is set when they will be administered and executed on earth through God's saintly army. All that is destined and needed will be activated during God's restorational Army of the Lord Movement. Before we say any more, let us examine the scriptures that verify this truth and destiny for the Church. Hear with a believing heart what God has to say to His end-time saints who are preparing to be warriors in His army.

Scriptures That Must Be Fulfilled by the Church.

*Let the saints be joyful in glory; let them sing aloud on their beds. Let the high praises of God be in their mouth, and a two-edged sword in their hand, **to execute***

> *vengeance on the nations, and punishments on the peo-*
> *ples; to bind their kings with chains, and their nobles*
> *with fetters of iron; **to execute upon them the written***
> ***judgment—this honor have all His saints.** Praise the*
> *Lord!* (Ps. 149:5-9, NKJV).

Hear Prophet Daniel's unconditional prophecy.

> *...and **judgment was given to the saints** of the most*
> *High; and the time came that the saints possessed the*
> *kingdom. ... And the kingdom and dominion, and the*
> *greatness of the **kingdom under the whole heaven***
> ***shall be given to** the people of **the saints** of the most*
> *High, whose kingdom is an everlasting kingdom, and*
> *all dominions shall serve and obey Him* (Dan. 7:22,27).

Hear the prophecy of the prophet, who walked perfectly with God, defeated the angel of death for his personal life and prototyped the translation of the Church saints.

> *Now Enoch, the seventh from Adam, prophesied...say-*
> *ing, "Behold the Lord comes with **ten thousands of His***
> ***saints**, to execute judgment upon all, to convict all* [like
> judges convicting and sentencing criminals] *who are*
> *ungodly among them of all their ungodly deeds which*
> *they have committed in an ungodly way, and of all the*
> *harsh things which ungodly sinners have spoken*
> *against Him"* (Jude 14-15, NKJV).

Be an Overcomer Saint. Jesus confirms that the overcoming Church saints are to execute His eternal Judgments and rule.

> *And he who overcomes, and keeps My works until the*
> *end, to him I will give power over the nations—"He*
> [the overcomer] *shall rule them with a rod of iron; they*
> *shall be dashed to pieces like the potter's vessels"—as*
> *I also have received from My Father; and I will give*
> *him* [the overcomer] *the morning star. He who has an*

ear, let him hear what the Spirit says to the churches (Rev. 2:26-29, NKJV).

To him who overcomes I will grant to sit with Me on My throne, as I also overcame and sat down with My Father on His throne. He who has an ear, let him hear what the Spirit says to the churches (Rev. 3:21-22, NKJV).

Apostle Paul in the New Testament **confirms** the **same judgment ministry by** the **Church saints.**

*Do you not know that **the saints will judge the world?** And if the world will be judged by you, are you unworthy to judge the smallest matters? Do you not know that **we shall judge angels?**...* [The angels that fell with lucifer, who became satan] (1 Cor. 6:2-3, NKJV).

Look with your eyes of revelation and see what John saw in the heavenlies and prophetically wrote in his Revelation of Jesus Christ.

*...and behold a white horse: and He that sat on him had a bow; and a crown was given unto Him: and He went forth **conquering, and to conquer*** (Rev. 6:2).

"We are more than conquerors through Him," Paul said in Romans 8:37.

*...And behold a white horse; and He that sat upon him was called Faithful and True, and in righteousness **He doth judge and make war.** ...on His head were many crowns...He was clothed with a vesture dipped in blood.... And the **armies** which were in heaven **followed Him** upon white horses, clothed in fine linen* [the righteousness of the saints], *white and clean. And out of His mouth goeth a **sharp sword,** that with it He should smite the nations: and He shall rule them with a rod of iron: and **He treadeth the winepress of the***

fierceness and wrath of Almighty God. And He hath on His vesture and on His thigh a name written, KING OF KINGS, AND LORD OF LORDS (Rev. 19:11-16).

Prophet Joel prophesied about the invincible, unstoppable Army of the Lord. This is a dualistic and progressive prophecy, like the one Isaiah prophesied and Paul used to prove a Church truth (Isa. 28:11; 1 Cor. 14:21). Isaiah was prophesying about God raising up a nation to bring Judgment upon Israel. They would speak in strange and unknown tongues to Israel. They would speak with stuttering lips when they tried to communicate with Israel. Though that seems to be the setting for the prophecy, Paul uses it to scripturally validate the truth and experience of Church saints speaking with other tongues when they receive the gift of the Holy Spirit. The same hermeneutical principle that Paul used for Isaiah's prophecy can apply to Joel's prophecy being God's army that shall be manifested during the Army of the Lord Movement.

Blow ye the trumpet in Zion, and sound an alarm in My holy mountain [God's Church, Isa. 2:2-3]: *let all the inhabitants of the land tremble: for the **day of the Lord** cometh* [when He comes to be glorified in His saints, 2 Thess. 1:10], *for it is nigh at hand; a day of darkness and of gloominess, a day of clouds and of thick darkness, as the morning spread upon the mountains* [a day of darkness for the world, but the dawning of a new day for the Church].... *A fire devoureth before them...and nothing shall escape them. ...like the noise of a flame of fire that devoureth the stubble, as a strong people set in battle array* [God's fiery warriors who devour the wicked who are stubble, Mal. 4:1]. ... *They shall **run like mighty men**; they shall climb the wall like **men of war**; and they shall march every one on his ways* [know and be faithful in their membership ministry], *and they* *shall not break their ranks* [submissive and consistent in their calling]*: neither shall one thrust another* [unity and love]*; they shall walk every one in his path* [maintaining their position and performance]*: and when they fall upon the sword, they shall not be wounded* [death to self, fullness of life and one with God's Word-sword]*. They shall run to and fro…. The **earth shall quake before them;** the **heavens shall tremble**…and the Lord shall utter His voice before **His army;** for His camp is very great: for **He is strong that executeth His word**…* (Joel 2:1-11).

Proclaim this among the nations: "Prepare for war! *Wake up the mighty men, let all the men of war draw near, let them come up. Beat your plowshares into swords and your pruning hooks into spears* [that which was used to plow and bless with, is now turned into weapons of war]*; let the weak say, 'I am strong.' "As-semble and come, all you nations, and gather together all around. Cause Your mighty ones to go down there, O Lord. "Let the nations be wakened, and come up to the Valley of Jehoshaphat; for there I will sit to judge all the surrounding nations, put in the sickle, for the harvest is ripe. Come, go down; for the winepress is full, the vats overflow—for their wickedness is great." Multitudes, multitudes in the valley of decision! For the day of the Lord is near in the valley of decision.* [The greatest harvest of souls ever is during this time, as well as God's greatest destructive Judgments upon the wicked.] *The sun and moon will grow dark, and the stars will diminish their brightness. The Lord also will roar from Zion, and utter His voice from Jerusalem; the heavens and earth will shake; but the Lord will be a shelter for His people, and the strength of the children of Israel.* [While these scriptures are being fulfilled by and through natural Israel, they will at the same time be fulfilled spiritually by and through Christ's Army of the Lord Church] (Joel 3:9-16, NKJV).

Prophet Isaiah prophesies Babylon's downfall by the Army of the Lord.

The burden against Babylon which Isaiah the son of Amoz saw. "Lift up a banner on the high mountain [the Church]*, raise your voice to them; wave your hand, that they may enter the gates of the nobles. I have commanded My sanctified ones; I have also called My mighty ones for My anger—those who rejoice in My exaltation." The noise of a multitude in the mountains, like that of many people! A tumultuous noise of the kingdoms of nations gathered together! The Lord of hosts musters the army for battle. They come from a far country, from the end of heaven—the Lord and His weapons of indignation, to destroy the whole land. Wail, for the day of the Lord is at hand! It will come as a destruction from the Almighty. ...* **Behold, the day of the Lord comes***, cruel, with both wrath and fierce anger, to lay the land desolate; and He will destroy its sinners from it. ... "I will punish the world for its evil, and the wicked for their iniquity; I will halt the arrogance of the proud, and will lay low the haughtiness of the terrible. I will make a mortal more rare than fine gold, a man more than the golden wedge of Ophir. Therefore I will shake the heavens, and the earth will move out of her place, in the wrath of the Lord of hosts and in the day of His fierce anger"* (Isa. 13:1-13, NKJV).

The Church—God's Weapons
of War Against Spiritual Babylon.

"You are My battle-ax and weapons of war: for with you I will break the nation in pieces; with you I will destroy kingdoms; ... And I will repay Babylon and all the inhabitants of Chaldea for all the evil they have

done in Zion in your sight," says the Lord. ... And the land will tremble and sorrow; for every purpose of the Lord shall be performed against Babylon... (Jer. 51:20, 24,29, NKJV).

I saw the woman [Babylon], *drunk with the blood of the saints and with the blood of the martyrs of Jesus.... "And the woman whom you saw is that great city which reigns over the kings of the earth"* (Rev. 17:6,18, NKJV).

These will make war with the Lamb, and the Lamb will overcome them, for He is Lord of lords and King of kings; and those who are with Him are called, chosen, and faithful (Rev. 17:14, NKJV).

Therefore her [Babylon's] *plagues will come in one day—death and mourning and famine. And she will be utterly burned with fire, for strong is the Lord God who judges her ... Rejoice over her, O heaven, and you holy apostles and prophets, for God has avenged you on her!* (Rev. 18:8,20, NKJV)

After these things I heard a loud voice of a great multitude in heaven, saying, "Alleluia! Salvation and glory and honor and power belong to the Lord our God. For true and righteous are His judgments, because He has judged the great harlot who corrupted the earth with her fornication; and He has avenged on her the blood of His servants shed by her." Again they said, "Alleluia! Her smoke rises up forever and ever!" (Rev. 19:1-3, NKJV)

The Bride of Christ Is a Warrior.

Who is she [Bride of Christ] *that looketh forth as the morning, fair as the moon, clear as the sun, and terrible* [awesome] *as an army with banners?* (Song 6:10)

Return, return, O Shulamite [Church]*; return, return,* [repent, be prepared and fully restored], *that we may*

> *look upon thee. What will ye see in the Shulamite* [fully restored Church]*? As it were the **company of two armies*** (Song 6:13).

Behold the Tremendous Power and Protection That God Gives His Army. We lay hold of these promises somewhat now, but in the Army of the Lord Movement and Eternal Judgment ministry of the Saints these scriptures will be accomplished in their fullness.

> *"**No weapon formed against you shall prosper**, and every tongue which rises against you **in judgment you shall condemn**. This is the heritage of the servants of the Lord, and their righteousness is from Me,"* says the Lord (Isa. 54:17, NKJV).

> *"And I will give **power** to My two witnesses, and they will **prophesy**".... And if anyone wants to harm them, **fire proceeds from their mouth and devours their enemies**. And if anyone wants to harm them, he must be killed in this manner. **These have power to shut heaven**, so that no rain falls in the days of **their prophecy**; and they have power over waters to turn them to blood, and **to strike the earth with all plagues, as often as they desire*** (Rev. 11:3-6, NKJV).

Now that is unlimited power given to His Army. Can you imagine how purified, proven, dead to self and full of Christ's life, perfected in Christ's character, wisdom and maturity, we will have to be before God will entrust us with such power?

God not only gives power and authority to His Army, but also gives them the assurance that they will be protected against all the horrible weapons of the enemy as they engage in this war of wars. It will be a spiritual battle, but executed by the mortal saints who are walking in the first phase of Christ's supernatural resurrection life.

Heaven and Hell Will Meet Face to Face in the Human Race. It will be the redeemed righteous face to face in battle array against the unredeemed wicked. It will be as when righteous David stood face to face against his enemy the wicked giant, Goliath. Before the day was over, either David or Goliath would lay dead upon the battlefield. But the young Prophet David prophesied his enemy's downfall and then followed through by taking that which he had proven and used it to destroy those who wanted to harm him. He prophesied a divine decree of Judgment and then executed God's judgment upon the wicked one. Remember that our weapons of warfare are not carnal, but spiritual with power to destroy principalities and powers (2 Cor. 10:4-6). Though they are spiritual, they are still weapons for the Church Army to use against all its enemies, whether they are natural or spiritual. By the time the Army of the Lord Movement comes forth and the Church has fulfilled the first phase of the doctrine of Resurrection Life and enters into the last of the six doctrines of Christ, eternal Judgment, the human race will be in a certain condition.

Everyone Will Be Either Divinely Possessed or Demon-Possessed. Jesus Christ, the Commander-in-Chief of His army, will arise within His Church as a Mighty Man of War. Jesus will be looking through the eyes of His saints at His enemy the devil. The great war against the demonized human race will be fought on earth by Christ as Head and commander of His Church/Army. It will be Christ fighting, not somewhere in the mystical realm, but "Christ in you, the hope of glory" will subdue all enemies under His feet, and His glory will fill the earth as the waters cover the sea (Col. 1:27).

What God Says About His Untouchable, Indestructible Army.

Behold, I give you the [power and] *authority to trample on serpents* [the devil and his evil angels] *and scorpions* [demons], *and over all the power of the enemy* [satan, whether in the spiritual or natural realm], *and nothing shall by any means hurt you* (Luke 10:19, NKJV).

Surely He shall deliver you from the snare of the fowler [the cunning devices of the devil] *and from the perilous pestilence. He shall cover you with His feathers, and under His wings you shall take refuge* [shielded by the force field of God's presence]*; His truth shall be your shield and buckler. You shall not be afraid of the terror by night* [a secret invasion], *nor for the arrow* [rocket, missile] *that flies by day, nor of the pestilence that walks in darkness* [germ warfare], *nor of the destruction that lays waste at noonday* [atomic warfare]. *A thousand may fall at your side, and ten thousand at your right hand; but it shall not come near you* [supernatural protection]. *Only with your eyes shall you look, and see the reward of the wicked. … No evil shall befall you, nor shall any plague come near your dwelling; for He shall give His angels charge over you, to keep you in all your ways* [a canopy of angels around us like a bubble]. *In their hands they shall bear you up, lest you dash your foot against a stone. You shall tread upon the lion* [the counterfeit of the Lion of Judah, the devil going about as a roaring lion] *and the cobra, the young lion and the serpent you shall trample under foot. "… I will be with him in trouble; I will deliver him and honor him. With long life* [resurrection life] *I will satisfy him, and show him My salvation* [deliverance and triumphant victory]*"* (Ps. 91, NKJV).

Preparation for the Army of the Lord Movement Is Taking Place Now.

Washington for Jesus, 1996. In April 20, 1996, John Giminez coordinated a Washington For Jesus rally. Approximately one quarter of a million Christians attended. The platform was on the front steps of the U.S. Capitol. Though it rained most of the day, God's purpose was accomplished. At 8:30 a.m., Cindy Jacobs prayed an intercessory prayer for America over those gigantic loud speakers. I gave a prophetic decree and prophecy to the nation concerning God's purpose and dealings with the U.S.A. One prophetic declaration was that God would move in His goodness, mercy and spiritual revival to turn this nation back to God and His righteousness. However, if the Church and America had not turned as God wanted it to by the year AD 2002, then He was going to stop defending America. This would cause great calamity and judgment to come upon America. If the Church and the nation does not turn around by His goodness, then it would turn by His severity.

Each group that participated made a prophetic sentence concerning a particular work of unrighteousness in the land. Those prophetic declarations of "guilty" with a prophetic declaration of destruction were established in the heavenlies and will be executed on the earth when the Army of the Lord Movement sweeps the earth.

New recruits are now being drafted and trained and older soldiers and generals are being updated on God's new revelations of our warfare weapons and prophetic-apostolic strategies. God's army cannot fight with the same weapons that past movements fought with, anymore than America could fight in the coming third world war and win with the same weapons they fought with in World War I. Many of the old apostolic generals will have to take time off to be taught in the strategies and advanced weapons that will be used in the Army of the Lord Movement. They are being rewired and updated with the Holy Spirit's latest technology with chips put in their old hard drive. They are being purified and tested to see if they have it yet. Everything that can be shaken is being shaken so that which cannot be shaken may remain (Heb. 12:27). These soldiers must be like an oiled machine with everything in perfect working order. Intensified test drives are being made to see if we can take the prolonged pressure and strain of God's spiritual "Indianapolis 500" race. God intends for His racers to be winners. The race is not won by the quick starters, but by those who can keep up the speed, avoid wrecking and not fall apart or break down while pressing on to win the race and receive the prize (Heb. 12:1).

The Church is being prepared, not for a skirmish or little war, but for the greatest battle and against the final enemy. They are now being equipped with the revelation and powerful authority to go against the most formidable fortress and wall that satan has ever built. Jesus paid the price for the redemption of our bodies and took the keys of death from the devil, taking them to heaven when He arose. Jesus has already provided everything for the full redemption of our spirit, soul and body. Yet there is no Church history account of even one member of the Body of Christ being able to appropriate Christ's victory over death. None of God's saints have gotten out of this world alive in their physical body. All have been taken out by the agent of death. Satan is determined that none will ever leave without dying, but Jesus has other plans (1 Cor. 15:51-54; 2 Cor. 5:4; 1 Thess. 4:13-18; 2 Thess. 1:5-11; Ps. 102:18-20; Rom. 8:23).

Somewhere between the Army of the Lord Movement and close to the end of the Kingdom Establishing Movement, Jesus will arise from His seat at the right hand of the Father. He will leap forth with His sword in His hand and give a shout that rings out to the ends of the universe and all over planet Earth. He will shout, "Devil, you have had it, and angel of death, your power over My Church is canceled and destroyed." He will have His archangels sounding the trumpet of the Lord as He shouts to His Church. "Delay shall not be one minute longer, for it is time for your final redemption and victory over death." As He is shouting this, He is descending from heaven faster than the speed of light. He brings with Him all the saints who have lost their bodies to death. As He comes into earth's atmosphere, He shouts again, and in a moment and the twinkling of an eye all the bodies of the saints ascend to meet the Lord and be joined with their spirit being. These bodies become eternally indestructible and never see death again. Then those saints who have been warring against death will finally win by Christ suddenly changing their bodies from mortal to immortal. Every cell in their body will be changed from corruptible to incorruptible cells. They will meet the Lord in the air, join with all the saints of the ages, and receive their strategies for finalizing God's purpose for the heavens and the earth.

God's Purpose for the Resurrection-Translation (R-T) of His Saints. We must realize that the Resurrection-Translation (R-T) of the saints does not take place because of a negative situation on earth. It is a positive event that takes place to fulfill God's timely purpose.

The R-T is not Christ coming like a heavenly helicopter to evacuate the saints out of the battle before they are overrun by the enemy. It is not the saints being ejected out before the plane crashes. It is not Jesus returning as an heavenly fireman to rescue the saints from a burning world. It is not the Church escaping out the back door before the devil breaks down the front door. It is not because of some evil beast or antichrist spirit activity. It is not Jesus being motivated to take action because of anything that the devil or the world system is doing on earth.

Jesus was not motivated to activate the R-T for His Church when millions were being martyred during the first three centuries of the Church. He didn't come back for His Church when the great falling away took place during the Dark Ages.

These were very negative forces taking place against and within His Church. However, He did activate the period of the "Great Reformation." He activated His Church into being a militant army to take back all that was lost during the Dark Ages. This restorational army will not only continue until all truth is restored, but will appropriate the last truth that will enable them to overcome the last enemy.

The positive purpose of the R-T is to enable the army of the Lord to finalize the war against all evil. The army of the Lord will progress on in the war until they have accomplished all they can in their limited mortal bodies. The R-T is for the purpose of immortalizing their bodies. This will remove all earthly limitations, thereby enabling the saints unlimited abilities. They will be able to travel in all space realms of the heavenlies the same as Jesus and the angels do now. They can move in and out of all dimensions of the natural and spiritual realms as Jesus did in His resurrected flesh-and-bone body.

There is a ministry to manifest and a battle to be won that can only be won by the last generation of the mortal Church. It is appointed to all humankind to die, but the prophetic scriptures declare that there is a generation of special people that will break the appointment with death (Ps. 102:18-20). There are millions of redeemed saints that have an end-time destiny to overcome death by participating in Christ's translation of His saints. It is not a fairy tale; it really is going to happen! However, it is not solely a sovereign act of God apart from divine revelation and faith appropriation of the saints. There are two Biblical examples of this end-time company that gains victory over the last enemy: Enoch and Elijah. Elijah had a revelation that he was going to be taken to heaven without going through the door of death. Enoch had a revelation of the end times when the Lord would come with ten thousands of

His saints to execute God's wrath and Judgment upon the wicked. This revelation probably included the understanding that God's people would be rescued from death. The scripture declares, "By faith Enoch was translated that he should not see death." This was not a faith revelation without living realities, for he had this testimony: that he walked with God and pleased Him in all His ways (Heb. 11:5; Gen. 5:24). The R-T is the fifth of the six doctrines of Christ (Heb. 6:1-2). The first four doctrines require faith, obedience and life participation to appropriate. The last two doctrines will require the same.

God Has Saved Us From His Wrath (Rom. 5:9). He has not appointed us to receive wrath but to co-labor with Him in executing His wrath upon the wicked of this world. The victorious, overcoming last-day army of the Lord saints will fulfill the numerous scriptures declaring the downfall of satan and all evil; the fall and destruction of Babylon; the subduing of all enemies under Christ's feet; etc.

Please keep in mind that Jesus and His Church are one, joint-heirs and co-sharers in all that Jesus shall ever do both now and throughout eternity. Jesus was joined with His Church on the day of Pentecost and the two became one corporate Body of Christ. Jesus is the Head of this Body consisting of multimillions of saints. Everything that God eternally ordained for Jesus to be, do and fulfill will be done with His Church. Everything you find Christ doing in the New Testament including the book of Revelation, He is doing with His Church. He personally fulfilled and accomplished all things in His personal mortal and resurrected body. Now it is His purpose, joy and delight to accomplish and fulfill all remaining things in, through, by and with His Church. It takes nothing from Christ's glory for the Church to be one with Him in all things. Jesus established the Church to "be to the praise of His glory" (Eph. 1:12). The Church is destined to go "from glory to glory" until it becomes the personification of His glory; "a glorious church" (2 Cor. 3:18; Eph. 5:27). The Church will always be the main manifestation of His glory. "Unto Him be glory in the church by Christ Jesus throughout all ages, world without end" (Eph. 3:21). His Church is the glory of the knowledge of the Lord that shall fill and cover the earth as the waters cover the sea (Isa. 11:9-10; Num. 14:21; Ps. 72:19).

There is one final restorational move of God that shall fill the earth with the Church of the Living God, and cause all the kingdoms of this world to become the kingdoms of our Lord Jesus and His anointed, joint-heir, co-laboring Church (Rev. 11:15).

Millions of Spirit-filled Christians believe there is an active army of the Lord in the Church today. They believe this army has a destiny in being instrumental in executing God's purposes and judgments upon earth. There are various opinions among them as to when, where and how this will take place. But there is no question that it is in the plans and purposes of God.

Whether a person is pre-, mid- or post-tribulation Rapture in their eschatological beliefs, they still believe that God's overcoming Church will be God's warriors that will co-reign with Christ, subduing and destroying all evil off His earth.

My Personal Belief and Attitude Is This. After ministering for almost half a century, I would love to take a seven-year sabbatical before fighting in the final battle. I would even take three years or five minutes. But if He so chooses to only give me the time of a twinkling of the eye, then I will stay one with my Jesus and follow my Mighty Warrior King until all enemies are under His feet and made His footstool.

Whether the process takes seven years, three-and-a-half, five minutes or one second, is not relevant. The fact still remains that Jesus has declared that He will raise up a Church Army that will be joint-heirs and co-laborers with Him in executing His Judgments until all enemies are under His feet where they are supposed to be. The majority of these things will be activated during the Army of the Lord Movement when the prepared saints enter into their Eternal Judgment ministry. This will take place before God's great white throne judgment for eternal sentencing of the unrighteous and handing out the rewards to the righteous overcomers. Let us press toward the mark for the prize that comes with reaching and fulfilling our high calling of God in Christ Jesus (Phil. 3:14). The sufferings and battles of this present life are not worthy to be compared with the glory that shall be revealed in us during the last two restorational movements of the mortal Church and into eternity (Rom. 8:18). We will now move to the final restorational move of God, which will activate God's plans for establishing His kingdom over all His earth.

—••••••——

18

THE KINGDOM ESTABLISHING MOVEMENT

—••••••——

Many books have been written on the kingdom of God. They cover both the spiritual kingdom of God that is in the Church, and the literal kingdom of God. The literal is called by some theologians, "The Kingdom Age," which follows the Church Age and covers the time of the millennial reign of Christ on earth for a thousand years. My purpose is to discover what activates the Kingdom Age other than just the sovereign coming of our Lord Jesus Christ. Is His Second Coming just a time and date that God preset in eternity past that will take place regardless of what is happening in heaven, in Israel, in the Church or in the world?

The Coming Kingdom Establishing Movement. Jesus mentioned several things in Matthew 24 that must take place before the end of mortal man comes. The one that directly involved the Church was verse 14. "And this gospel of the kingdom will be preached in all the world as a witness to all the nations, and then the end will come" (NKJV). The portrayal in the book of Acts reveals that "preaching" is more than a preacher standing before a group of people and talking

269

about his convictions and what the Bible says. Whether the New Testament ministers were preaching "the Gospel" or the "Gospel of the Kingdom," it was confirmed with supernatural signs and miraculous power. Many preachers have reduced preaching to the level of a politician giving a speech or a salesman making a presentation. Sometimes secular speakers put more fire and life into their speeches than historic and modernistic ministers put into their sermons.

Biblical preaching is proclaiming and demonstrating Jesus Christ as the only God and Savior for humankind, being accompanied with supernatural anointing and confirmed as truth by miraculous deeds. That's the reason Paul could say that the GOSPEL is the power of God unto salvation. The gospel is proclaiming God's plan of redemption through the death, burial and resurrection of Jesus Christ. But the gospel of the kingdom is more than John 3:16. The Bible did not say the gospel must first be preached to all people and then the end will come. According to scripture, this already happened in the first generation of the Church. The Holy Spirit inspired Paul to declare that the gospel "was preached to every creature which is under heaven" (Col. 1:23). That would include all humankind from every tribe and tongue on earth.

Therefore the declaration of Christ Jesus (that the gospel of the kingdom must be preached as a witness to all the nations before the end could come, Matt. 24:14) must have more meaning than preaching the gospel of Salvation. The Proclamation of the kingdom of God (the dominion of King Jesus over everything, including all the earth) will be demonstrated as a witness to all nations of the world, that Jesus has the right of rulership, ownership and Lordship of all the nations of the earth.

The Kingdom Establishing Movement will cause this to happen to the degree that God originally purposed when Jesus made this prophetic proclamation. The movement will not cease until all knees bow and every tongue confesses that Jesus is the true Lord God over all the earth. That does not imply that everyone who makes that confession or acknowledgment is saved. However, there will be such worldwide demonstration of God's power over the elements, people raised from the dead, miraculous control of natural catastrophes, miraculous prophetic words and endless supernatural manifestations, signs and wonders, until everyone will have to acknowledge that there is no god like Jesus Christ, the God of gods and Lord of lords.

A Biblical Example: In chapters 3 and 4 of Daniel we have two examples in Nebuchadnezzar, who was not only king of a nation but king of the whole Babylonian Empire consisting of many nations. The three Hebrew men, Shadrach, Meshach and Abednego, were thrown into the fiery furnace because they would not acknowledge any other god besides their eternal and invisible God, Jehovah. The king saw the power of their Most High God keep them in the midst of the fiery furnace without their hair or clothing being affected. Then he looked again and saw that a fourth man had joined them, having the form of the Son of Man.

This resulted in the king acknowledging that their God was the Most High God, and no god could deliver like Him. He then made a decree that if anyone throughout the Babylonian Empire said anything negative about the three Hebrews' God, they would be cut in pieces and all they owned burned. Talk about demonstrating the kingdom of God! It was in such a way that it made rulers acknowledge that there is only one true God. Can you imagine the open door this gave the Hebrews who wanted to establish synagogues for their God throughout the empire?

The second example is when Nebuchadnezzar had a dream that the Prophet Daniel interpreted for him. The prophetic application declared that the king was going to be humbled by being turned into a creature that was a combination of bird, animal and man. This would continue for seven years while he roamed the forests eating grass like an ox. When the seven years were ended, he would be restored. This was going to happen to him, "In order that the living may know that the Most High rules in the kingdom of men, [and] gives it to whomsoever He will..." (Dan. 4:17b, NKJV). When the king was restored, he wrote a long letter, addressing it "to all peoples, nations, and languages that dwell in all the earth: Peace be multiplied to you. I thought it good to declare the signs and wonders that the Most High God has worked for me. How great are His signs, and how mighty His wonders! His kingdom is an everlasting kingdom, and His dominion is from generation to generation" (Dan. 4:1-3, NKJV).

He then continues on to the end of chapter 4. Prophet Daniel gave him the possibility of this horrible ordeal not happening. He said to the king, "...break off your sins by being righteous, and your iniquities by showing mercy to the poor. Perhaps there may be a lengthening of your prosperity" (Dan. 4:27, NKJV).

However, a year later Nebuchadnezzar had not changed but became proud, taking all the glory for his great accomplishments to himself. "At the end of twelve months he was walking about the royal palace of Babylon. The king spoke, saying, 'Is not this great Babylon, that I have built for a royal dwelling by MY great power and for the honor of MY majesty?' While the word was still in the king's mouth, a voice fell from heaven..." (Dan. 4:29-31, NKJV). The voice repeated the seven-year judgment that Daniel had prophesied. At the end of his times of being a bird-man-beast creature who ate grass like an ox, then what he learned through the process would be revealed. Such things will happen to many rulers of nations during the Kingdom Establishing Movement. They will express the same things and proclaim it to the nations as this king did. The instant worldwide television communication systems will be in operation by that time.

And at the end of the time I, Nebuchadnezzar, lifted my eyes to heaven, and my understanding returned to me; and I blessed the Most High and praised and honored Him who lives forever: for His dominion is an everlasting dominion, and His kingdom is from generation to generation. All the inhabitants of the earth are reputed as nothing; He does according to His will in the army of heaven and among the inhabitants of the earth. No one can restrain His hand or say to Him, "What have you done?" (Dan. 4:34-35, NKJV)

He concludes his testimonial letter with these statements. "Now I, Nebuchadnezzar, praise and extol and honor the King of heaven, all of whose works are truth, and His ways justice. And those who walk in pride He is able to put down" (Dan. 4:37, NKJV). Amen and Amen!

It will be wonderful to read and listen to such testimonials from many of the rulers, kings and presidents of the nations of the world. These are the kinds of things that will happen as God's holy apostles and prophets and His army of apostolic and prophetic saints prophesy and decree such things and every detail will take place as was spoken. The kingdom of God will be demonstrated to every nation and will continue until every nation has properly responded and become a sheep nation, or rebelled, causing them to become a goat nation. When Jesus comes He will destroy all the goat nations off His earth and set His dominion over the sheep nations. Then Revelation 11:15 will finally be fulfilled as the kingdoms of nations that remain become the kingdoms of our Lord Jesus Christ and His anointed Church that co-labored with Him in bringing all of His predestined purposes to pass.

New Strategies for Winning and Subduing the Nations Unto Christ. Shall it be by evangelizing the people or converting the top leaders of nations? Both will be used, but the prophet's and apostle's anointings for affecting the leadership of nations are now being added. Past missionaries usually started with people of the lowest strata of society and gradually worked toward affecting the leadership of the nation. Evangelism has mostly reached the people in the nation. The Prophets and Apostles are starting at the top and working their way to the lowest. Because of the shortness of time left in the Dispensation or Covenant Age of the Church, things must be accelerated tremendously. For instance if the Church Age is a two thousand-year period, then more than ninety-eight percent of the Church Age has already come and gone. (The Church Age began in AD 30, plus two thousand years equals AD 2030, minus 1997, leaves thirty-three years in the Church Age. Thirty-three is less than two percent of two thousand.) If a two thousand-year period ends up being the allotted time for the mortal Church to accomplish God's purpose for its existence, then less than two percent of the original one hundred percent is left to finalize everything.

However, one encouraging thing concerning this subject is the fact that Jesus fulfilled more Messianic prophecies in His last twenty-four hour day than He did in His thirty-four years of being on earth, from His conception to the beginning of that last day. Like the Church, Samson started victoriously, but he began to flirt with the world until she took away his anointing. He then spent a long period of time going in a circle. His restoration began and continued until his hair was fully restored, and then he killed more of his enemies in his last supernatural move than he had throughout his lifetime. All things are possible with God.

Missionary Evangelism vs. Prophets/Apostles to the Nations. Missionaries and evangelists and the Saints Movement will reach multimillions of people in the nations of the world.

But how do we bring the nations under the dominion of the kingdom of God?

An Illustration for Comparison. Good reports are coming from the East that the underground church in China is winning twenty thousand a day to the Lord. That sounds great, but at that rate it will take one hundred thirty-five years to reach all the Chinese. To witness to the current population of one billion in twenty years, fifty million would have to be reached every year. That's over four million per month, one hundred thirty-seven thousand a day, if the current population stayed the same for the next twenty years.

However, if the apostles and prophets go to the Nebuchadnezzars of the world and get the same results as Prophet Daniel, then a whole nation could become a Christian nation. The Church would then have to follow up with personal and mass evangelism to reach the individuals. "Shall a nation be born at once?" (Isa. 66:8) The nation of the Church was born in one day, but I also believe an established nation can turn to God in one day.

Prophet Haggai prophetically declares, "For thus says the Lord of hosts: Once more...I will shake heaven and earth, the sea and dry land; and I will shake all nations, and they shall come to the Desire of All Nations [Jesus Christ the Lord]..." (Hag. 2:6-7, NKJV). We will preach and miraculously demonstrate Jesus Christ to all nations so that they may know and accept Him who is the hidden Desire of All Nations. This will escalate with each coming restorational movement, the Apostolic, the Saints, the Army of Lord, and lastly, the Kingdom Establishing Movement.

Has God preordained His Kingdom to be established on earth and continue forever? Prophet Daniel interpreted King Nebuchadnezzar's vision of the great image as four great Empires that would rule the world at different times. The king and his Babylonian Empire was the golden head. The rest of the interpretation was proved over the years to be the Babylonian Empire, the Medo-Persian Empire, the Roman Empire and then after that God would set up His Church-Kingdom Empire.

> *And in the days of these kings **the God of heaven will set up a kingdom which shall never be destroyed; and the kingdom shall not be left to other people; it shall break in pieces** and **consume all** these **kingdoms, and it shall stand forever. Inasmuch as you saw that the stone was cut out of the mountain without hands, and that it broke in pieces the iron, the bronze, the clay, the silver, and the gold**... [And the **stone** that struck the image became **a great mountain** and filled the whole earth, (verse 35)]. The dream is certain and its interpretation is sure* (Dan. 2:44-45, NKJV).

The Church is the stone that was cut out of the mountain without hands. Just as sure as these four empires arose, took over the world and passed from the scene except in history books, so shall God's Church Kingdom Empire **arise, take over all nations on earth**, and **never pass away** for **it shall stand forever**. "Then the kingdom and dominion, and the greatness of the kingdoms under the whole heaven, shall be given to the people, the saints of the Most High. **His kingdom is an everlasting kingdom, and all dominions shall serve and obey Him**" (Dan. 7:27, NKJV).

When the Kingdom Establishing Movement finalizes all things that God has purposed for His mortal Church, then the trumpet shall blow and Jesus shall excitedly shout forth "**It is finished!**" When He said that the first time, on the cross, He was saying that He had finished the work of redemption for the birthing of His Church. He said those words in great pain and agony with the last breath of life in His body. But now He will say it with a different finality. He will say it with an immortal body that is full of the everlasting breath of God and with the exceeding joy and confidence that He and His Church have finished everything that God the Father had ordained for them to do during the Age of the mortal Church. When the last note of the seventh trumpet is sounded, all the hosts of heaven begin to shout in unison with loud voices, "The kingdoms of this world have become the kingdoms of our Lord and His Christ, and He shall reign forever and forever!" (Rev. 11:15)

Let all Christendom begin to pray what Jesus said to pray. Pray it with greater understanding and faith. Jesus did not tell us to pray that we may leave this world and go to a space city in some far galaxy. But He did tell us to pray to Father God **"YOUR KINGDOM COME. Your will be done ON EARTH** as it is in heaven"** (Matt. 6:10, NKJV). We have prayed that prayer for the purpose of His kingdom life and attributes being established within our personal lives. Now let us begin to pray earnestly that the full dominion of His literal kingdom be established in all reality over all nations and people of the earth. Prophet Daniel discerned that it was time for the seventy years of Israel's captivity to be over. He began to do prophetic intercessory warfare prayer to activate that prophetic declaration into reality. Millions of Christians around the world will soon begin to prevail in prayer, declaring that it is God's predestinated time for the earth's captivity to satan and evil to be over. They will pray and declare that it is time for God's kingdom to be established over all the earth by the divine delegated authority and ministry of Christ's Church. God almighty declared that planet Earth would be filled with His glory as the waters cover the sea (Num. 14:21).

We are now in the transitional period of time like when John the Baptist and Jesus the Messiah were ministering on earth. Their ministries were closing out the Dispensation of the Law. They prepared the way and made ready a people to usher in the Church Age. Jesus' last acts of ministry on earth resulted in the beginning of the mortal Church.

The ministry of the prophet and apostle is destined to take the Church through this thirty- to forty-year transitional period that we are in now. These final moves of God will close out the Age of the mortal Church. The end result will be the beginning of the Resurrected-Translated Immortal Church and the restoration and establishment of King Jesus and His queen Church in dominion over all the earth (Rev. 5:10).

Thank God we are still in the time of grace and salvation. Multimillions can still come to Christ and become members in His Church kingdom and the Christ's Bride, the Church. The last thing said in the last chapter of the last book of the Bible is in the book of Revelation. Hear the final prophetic declarations and Jesus' last recorded statements:

> *"I, Jesus, have sent My angel to testify to you these things in the churches. I am the Root and the Offspring of David, the Bright and Morning Star." And the Spirit and the bride* [Church] *say, "Come!" And let him who hears say, "Come!" And let him who thirsts come. Whoever desires, let him take the water of life freely. ... He who testifies to these things says, "Surely I am coming quickly." Amen. Even so, come, Lord Jesus!* (Rev. 22:16-17,20, NKJV)

— ⋯•◐◑●◐◑•⋯ —

EXPLANATION AND DEFINITIONS OF PRESENT-TRUTH PROPHETIC & APOSTOLIC TERMS

— ⋯•◐◑●◐◑•⋯ —

FIVEFOLD MINISTERS / MINISTRIES

These are the fivefold ascension gift ministers as revealed in Ephesians 4:11—Apostle, Prophet, Evangelist, Pastor and Teacher. They are not gifts of the Holy Spirit per se, but an extension of Christ's headship ministry to the Church. Their primary ministry and function are to teach, train, activate and mature the saints for the work of their ministries (Eph. 4:12-13).

APOSTLE

One of the fivefold ministries of Ephesians 4:11. The Apostle is a foundation-laying ministry (Eph. 2:20) that we see in the New Testament establishing new churches (Paul's missionary journeys), correcting error by establishing proper order and structure (First Epistle to the Corinthians), and acting as an oversight ministry that fathers other ministries (1 Cor. 4:15; 2 Cor. 11:28). The New Testament Apostle has a revelatory anointing (Eph. 3:5). Some major characteristics are great patience and manifestations of signs, wonders and miracles. We will know more and see greater manifestations concerning the apostle during the peak of the Apostolic Movement.

PROPHET

He is a man of God whom Christ has given the ascension gift of a "prophet" (Eph. 4:11; 1 Cor. 12:28; 14:29; Acts 11:27; 13:1). A

prophet is one of the fivefold ascension gift ministers who are an exten-
sion of Christ's ministry to the Church. He is an anointed minister who
has the gifted ability to perceive and speak the specific mind of Christ
to individuals, churches, businesses and nations. **GREEK:** *"proph-*
etes" (prof-ay-tace) a foreteller, an inspired speaker (STRONG'S Con-
cordance, p. 62; VINE'S Concordance, p. 894). A proclaimer of a
divine message, denoted among the Greeks as an interpreter of the or-
acles of gods. In the Septuagint it is the translation of the word
"roeh"—a seer—indicating that the prophet was one who had imme-
diate intercourse with God (1 Sam. 9:9). It also translates the word
"nabhi," meaning either "one in whom the message from God springs
forth, or one to whom anything is secretly communicated" (Amos 3:7;
Eph. 3:5).

PROPHETESS

GREEK: *"prophetis"—the feminine of prophet (Gr. prophetes). A*
woman of God whom the Holy Spirit has given the divine prophetic
ability to perceive and speak the mind of Christ on specific matters to
particular people. STRONG'S: a "female foreteller or an inspired
woman." She is a specially called woman who functions like the New
Testament prophet to minister to the Body of Christ with inspired
speaking and prophetic utterance (Acts 2:17; 21:9; Luke 2:36; Isa.
8:3; 2 Chron. 34:22; Jude 4; Ex. 15:20). **Prophetess** *is the proper title*
for a woman with this ascension gift and calling. **Prophet** *is the proper*
title for a man with this ascension gift and calling.

EVANGELIST

The traditional view of the evangelist is a bearer of the "Good News,"
proclaiming the gospel to the unbelieving world. This is exemplified by
modern-day evangelists who preach the message of salvation in cru-
sades and the like. However, Philip, the New Testament Evangelist
mentioned in Acts 21:8, demonstrated a strong supernatural dimension
to the Evangelistic ministry. Philip preached the gospel to the lost (Acts
8:5), moved in miracles (8:6), delivered people from demons (8:7), re-
ceived instructions from an angel (8:26), had revelation knowledge
(8:29), and was supernaturally translated from Gaza to Azotus
(8:26,40). We are looking forward to the restoration of this type of Pro-
phetic Evangelist to the Body of Christ.

PASTOR

"Poiment, a shepherd, one who tends herds or flocks (not merely one who feeds them), is used metaphorically of Christian 'pastors'." Episkopeo (overseer, bishop) is an overseer, and Pesbuteros (elder) is another term for the same person as bishop or overseer (VINE'S). They normally give the title to the senior minister of the local church, regardless of his fivefold calling. It is a shepherding ministry to feed and care for the flock. Responsibilities that appear connected with pastoral ministry include oversight and care of the saints, providing spiritual food for their growth and development, leadership and guidance, and counsel. Prophetic pastors not only do the things normally associated with pastoring, but also move in supernatural graces and gifts of God (prophesying, word of knowledge, healing) and have the vision and willingness to develop the saints in their gifts and callings.

TEACHER

An instructor of truth. "All scripture is given by inspiration of God, and is profitable for doctrine, for reproof, for correction, for instruction in righteousness" (2 Tim. 3:16). A New Testament Apostolic-Prophetic Teacher is one who not only teaches the letter of the word, but also ministers with divine life and Holy Spirit anointing (2 Cor. 3:6). He exhibits keen spiritual discernment and divine insight into the Word of God and its personal application to believers.

APOSTOLIC-PROPHETIC MINISTERS

*Apostolic-Prophetic ministers are all other ministers who do not have the office of the "**prophet**," but who do hold another office of the fivefold ministry and believe that there are apostles and prophets in the Church today. They may move in prophetic ministry by prophesying with the gift of prophecy, or by giving personal prophecy with a prophetic presbytery, do prophetic counseling and ministry with gifts of the Holy Spirit, or minister in prophetic worship. All fivefold New Testament ministers in whichever office should be able to speak a **rhema** word revealing the mind and purpose of God for specific situations and people (2 Cor. 3:6; 1 Cor. 14:31). They should also manifest the miraculous.*

APOSTOLIC-PROPHETIC PEOPLE

They are the people of God who are full of the Holy Spirit and are fulfilling the scriptural command to "desire spiritual gifts, covet to prophesy" (1 Cor. 12:31; 14:1-2,39). They believe in, propagate and support the ministry of apostles and prophets in the church today. They are earnestly desiring gifts and are exercising their spiritual senses to be fully educated and activated in all the gifts of the Holy Spirit that Christ has ordained for them, including but not limited to the gift of prophecy and miracles. They are also submitted to divine authority and order (Heb. 5:14; 1 Cor. 12:1,7,11; 15:16).

APOSTOLIC-PROPHETIC MINISTRY

This includes all the methods by which the Holy Spirit makes known the heart and mind of Christ to people. Prophetic ministry includes the ministry of the prophet, prophetic ministers, and all prophetic people. It includes all the ministry and manifestations of the Holy Spirit and all the scriptural ways in which God can be praised. This includes prophetic worship with singing, praising, prophesying, song of the Lord, praise-dance, mime and sign language. In fact, it includes all dedicated physical expressions that may properly glorify God and edify the Church. Apostolic ministry is moving in the supernatural ministry with patience, while maintaining a proper relationship in the Body of Christ. It is those who have a burden for the great end-time harvest.

APOSTOLIC-PROPHETIC ANOINTING OR MANTLE

*An in-depth study of the word **anoint** reveals that it was used to consecrate people to a particular position or ministry. In ministering with an **apostolic-prophetic anointing**, it means one can minister with some blessings of that ministry. It is those who are ministering under the anointing of apostles and prophets. Prophet Isaiah declares that we destroy yokes because of the anointing (Isa. 10:27). In present-day application, this means the manifest presence of God upon a person to meet specific needs.*

*To say a person has an **apostolic** or **prophetic anointing** means that he or she has the calling to be anointed to minister at different times with the anointing of the prophet or apostle. It does not necessarily mean the person has the calling or office of a prophet or apostle. **Mantle** has a similar meaning. If someone has prophesied that you have a **prophetic mantle**, it implies that you can minister in prophetic ministry. To what realm will be determined by time and use (Ex. 28:41; Ps. 2:2; 23:5; 105:15; Zech. 4:6; Heb. 1:19).*

PROPHECY

GREEK: "propheteia," a noun that "signifies the speaking forth of the mind and counsel of God. It is the declaration of that which cannot be known by natural means. It is the forth-telling of the will of God, whether with reference to the past, the present, or the future" (VINE'S, p. 893). New Testament prophecy functions in three realms:

1.   *Jesus giving inspired testimony and praise through one of His saints by **prophetic utterance or song of the Lord** (Heb. 2:12; Rev. 19:10).*

2.   *One of the manifestations of the Holy Spirit called the **gift of prophecy**, which brings edification, exhortation and comfort to the Body of Christ (1 Cor. 12:10; Rom. 12:6).*

3.   *The **prophet speaking by divine utterance** the mind and counsels of God and giving a **rhema** word for edification, direction, correction, confirmation and instruction in righteousness (1 Cor. 14:29; 2 Tim. 3:16-17).*

   A truly, divinely inspired prophecy is the Holy Spirit expressing the thoughts and desires of Christ through a human voice.

PROPHETIC PRESBYTERY

Prophetic Presbytery is when two or more prophets and/or prophetic ministers lay hands on and prophesy over individuals at a specified time and place. Prophetic presbyteries are conducted for several reasons:

1.   *For revealing a church member's membership ministry in the Body of Christ.*

2.   *For ministering a prophetic rhema word of God to individuals.*

3.   *For impartation and activation of divinely ordained gifts, graces and callings.*

4.   *For the revelation, clarification and confirmation of leadership ministry in the local church.*

5.   *For the "laying on of hands and prophecy" over those called and properly prepared to be an ordained fivefold minister.*

PROPHETIC PRAYING

Basically, it is Spirit-directed praying. Praying with natural understanding is asking God's help about matters of which we have natural knowledge. Prophetic praying is prophesying with prayer phraseology.

It is praying out of one's spirit in his natural known tongue, flowing the same as one praying out of his spirit in unknown tongues. The prayer is on target and touches specific areas unknown in the natural to the one praying and uses prophetic motivation, word of knowledge, discerning of spirits, word of wisdom, etc. Intercessory prayer is much more effective when it moves into the realm of prophetic praying. In ministering to people in churches who do not understand or promote prophesying, prophetic ministry can still bless the people through prophetic praying. Instead of prophesying, "thus saith the Lord" or "the Lord shows me that...," you verbalize by saying, "Lord, we pray for this...." Jesus, You see what he or she has been going through regarding... or how difficult it has been in the area of...or overcoming...," etc.

APOSTOLIC-PROPHETIC COUNSELING
Apostolic-Prophetic counseling serves a little different purpose than the ministry of the prophet, prophetic presbytery or general counseling. It is one-on-one ministry to help people with scriptural wisdom and insight, but also with the gifts of the Holy Spirit to discover root problems and minister deliverance, inner healing, etc. The word of knowledge and discerning of spirits are two key gifts necessary to move in this realm effectively. It allows the counselor to cut through hours of discussion and look beyond the veil of human reasoning to get right to the heart of the matter and bring resolution. This is what makes Biblical counseling much more effective than that of the psychologist and psychiatrist who use only human wisdom and psychology. It deals with the root more than the fruit.

LOGOS
GREEK: "word"—the unchanging, inerrant, creative and inspired word of God. (See Psalm 119:89: "For ever, O Lord, Thy word [logos] is settled in heaven.") (See also Second Timothy 3:16 and First Corinthians 2:13.) Logos is the entire written Word of God—the Holy Bible. It is the complete revelation of God—His personage, character, plan and eternal purpose—as found in the Scriptures.

RHEMA
GREEK: "word"—derived from the verb "to speak." (See Romans 10:17: "So then faith cometh by hearing, and hearing by the word [rhema] of God.") A rhema is a word or an illustration God speaks

*directly to us, and it addresses our personal, particular situation. It is a timely, Holy Spirit-inspired Word from the **logos** that brings life, power and faith to perform and fulfill it. Its significance is exemplified in the injunction to take the "sword of the Spirit, which is the word [**rhema**] of God" (Eph. 6:17). It can be received through others such as by a prophetic word, or be an illumination given to one directly in their personal meditation time in the Bible or in prayer. The Logos is the fixed word of God—the Scriptures—and the **rhema** is a particular portion in line with the logos brought forth by the Spirit to be applied directly to something in our personal experience.*

PROPHETIC WARFARE PRAISE AND WORSHIP
They are Biblical expressions of praise and adoration (singing, clapping, dancing, lifting of hands, bowing, etc.) that are directed to God, inspired and directed by the Holy Spirit, and which come forth from the heart of man. Prophetic worship is where God's voice is heard and His presence felt as Christ begins to sing and express praise to the Father through His people (Heb. 2:12; Ps. 22:22; Rev. 19:10). These high praises of God both exalt the Lord and accomplish spiritual warfare in the heavenlies (Ps. 149:6-9; Eph. 6:12; 2 Cor. 10:4-6). It is worship that is expressed in obedience to a prompting of God that brings forth a prophetic word, mantle or anointing that results in the manifestation of God's power (2 Chron. 20:14-22; 2 Kings 3:15; 1 Sam. 10:5-6).

PROPHETIC SONG
A song that is inspired, anointed and directed by the Holy Spirit through an individual; usually spontaneous in nature, which expresses the mind of God in musical form. It is literally prophecy through song (referred to in the New Testament as spiritual songs). (See Colossians 3:16 and Ephesians 5:19.) These songs are directed to man for the purpose of edification, exhortation and comfort or may be directed to God as the Holy Spirit helps us express our deep devotion that we could not ordinarily express by ourselves (Heb. 2:12; Rom. 8:27; Zeph. 3:17: "The Lord thy God...will joy over [or through] thee with singing").

PROPHETIC PRAISE—DANCE AND SIGN
Physical movements that are inspirational and anointed by the Holy Spirit and many times accompanied by prophetic song (song of the Lord; spiritual songs). (See Exodus 15:20-21 and First Samuel 21:11.) It is used in praise, adoration and worship to God, which can in itself

release a prophetic anointing (1 Sam. 18:6). It may be spontaneous or choreographed (preplanned). At times, it may communicate divine thoughts, ideas and purposes—a visible expression of what God is saying (Acts 21:10-11; Job 42:5: "My ears had heard of you but now my eyes have seen you"[NIV]).

GRACE
Grace is God's divine unmerited enablements. It is God's free abilities (gifts, talents, etc.) being demonstrated through a human vessel in spite of sin and human frailties. It is having God's unearned supernatural ability to perform and execute whatever He has willed to the individual saint (Eph. 2:8-9).

ACTIVATION
To challenge God's people with the truth to receive and manifest the grace to do what the Bible says they can do. It is arousing, triggering, stirring and releasing God's abilities within the saints. Gifts are given by the Holy Spirit but activated by the faith of the believer. It is like the gift of Eternal Life, which is freely given, but is not activated within the individual until he believes in his heart and confesses with his mouth the Lord Jesus.

MEMBERSHIP MINISTRY
It is the individual members in the Body of Christ finding and manifesting their God-given talents, abilities and callings, so that "every joint" will supply according to God's plans and purposes (Eph. 4:16; 1 Cor. 12:7-11; 14:26; 1 Pet. 4:10). Every member in the Body of Christ has a ministry and needs to be educated and activated into it.

SCHOOL OF THE HOLY SPIRIT
It is a training time in which God's saints are discipled in a "hot house" environment to discern the language of the Holy Spirit and manifest the gifts of the Holy Spirit under proper oversight and care. It is a time and place to learn to discern between the human soul and the realm of the Holy Spirit (Heb. 5:14). It is a place where the saints allow the Holy Spirit and Word to operate in them, thereby causing them to Exercise their Spiritual Senses (E.S.S.) and Exercise their Spiritual Gifts (E.S.G.). But they are trained to know the difference between the natural mind and the Holy Spirit so that they do not move in the physic realm of E.S.P.

SHARING THE MIND OF CHRIST

(A Sanctified Thought): It is the ability of every believer to draw upon the indwelling Christ and then sharing without using Godhead terminology ("Thus saith the Lord, God says, or Thus saith the Spirit," etc.). It is what the Christian senses from his or her redeemed spirit where Christ dwells. It is the activation that prepares the believer to determine if he or she has the ability to give an accurate prophecy. This is based upon First Corinthians 2:16, Revelation 19:10 and Romans 12:6.)

COMPANY OF PROPHETS

This term today refers to the multitude of prophets God is raising up around the world in these last days to usher in the Second Coming of Jesus Christ. These prophets are being brought forth to be taught, trained and activated into their preordained ministry of "preparing the way for Jesus to return and establish His Kingdom over all the earth" (Isa. 40:3,5), as well as "making ready a people for Christ's return." They labor to purify the Church in righteousness and mature the saints for ministry, bridehood, co-laborship and co-reigning over God's vast domain (Luke 1:17; Eph. 4:11; 5:27).

SCHOOL OF PROPHETS (Sons of the Prophets)

Webster's Dictionary: "Among the ancient Israelites, a school or college in which young men were educated and trained to become teachers of religion among the people. These students were called 'Sons of the Prophets.' " This refers to a group of people who have the calling to prophetic ministry and have come together at one place to be schooled in hearing and recognizing the true voice of God and how to properly and timely minister that word with grace and wisdom for the greatest glory to God and good to mankind. Samuel is recognized as the founder of the School of Prophets, which was continued by such prophets as Elijah and Elisha. Based on First Samuel 19:18,24, regarding Saul, David and Samuel, the "school of the prophets" also serves as a covering for the Davidic company (the new order for ministry that God is raising up) to nurture and protect them from persecution of the old religious order (Saul's).

APOSTLE-PROPHET SEMINARS

These are seminars conducted to teach, train and activate saints concerning the gifts of the Spirit and prophetic-apostolic ministry in order to raise up a prophetic-apostolic people of the Lord. Our ministry emphasis is to help instruct and activate prophets and apostles into a powerful, proper and pure function in the Body through impartation of gifts, prophetic presbytery, anointed teaching and practical participation in training. There is helpful instruction for pastors and other five-fold ministers to enhance their functioning and relationship with the apostolic-prophetic ministry. Also, all in attendance receive a time of personal prophetic presbytery.

REGIONAL PROPHETS CONFERENCES
These are CI-sponsored prophets conferences held in different regions of the country in order to promote and propagate prophetic ministry in that area and to minister to a greater number of saints.

INTERNATIONAL GATHERING OF PROPHETS & APOSTLES
International Prophets Conferences are a gathering of prophets, apostles and other ministers and apostolic-prophetic people from around the world. Christian International sponsored the first such conference known in the annals of Church history in the fall of 1987. The events are designed as a vehicle for assisting in disseminating apostolic-prophetic ministry around the world that millions might be blessed and that a current consensus of what Christ is speaking to His Church may be attained and acted upon. Christian International conducts a IGAP Conference every year in October (usually in the third week) to bring maturity, unity and fruit to the work of restoration God is doing in the earth, especially dealing with the restoration of apostles and prophets.

APOSTOLIC-PROPHETIC CHURCHES
This is the term used to identify local churches within the Network of Prophetic Ministries and Churches. Those who qualify for recognition and promotion as a prophetic local church will have developed the following ministries within the church: qualified prophetic ministers and saints capable of forming prophetic presbytery; prophetic teams for healing, prophetic counseling, prophesying, and ministering God's grace and deliverance by the gifts of the Holy Spirit. The prophetic pastor needs sufficient experience and maturity to give proper oversight, structure, motivation and direction in order to maintain control without restricting the flow of the miraculous apostolic-prophetic ministry.

APOSTOLIC-PROPHETIC LIFESTYLE

These are the people who live their lives according to the logos and rhema word of God. The logos is their general standard for living and the rhema gives direction in specific areas of their lives. The fruit of the Holy Spirit is their characteristic motivation, and the gifts of the Spirit are their manifestation to meet the needs of mankind. They are allowing their lives to become a prophetic expression of Galatians 2:20: "I am crucified with Christ; nevertheless I live; yet not I, but Christ liveth in me: and the life which I now live in the flesh I live by the faith of the Son of God, who loved me, and gave Himself for me."

APOSTOLIC-PROPHETIC EVANGELISM

Evangelism is in the heart of God. Christ died to save sinners. Jesus came to seek and to save those who are lost (Matt. 18:11). Evangelism was restored in the Evangelical Movement during the 1600's and has taken on new dimensions with each additional move of God. The Prophetic-Apostolic Movement is likewise adding a new dimension to evangelism. Saints are being instructed and activated in the supernatural gifts of the Holy Spirit. They are being trained within the church but the goal is to send prophetic-apostolic evangelism teams into the highways and byways compelling the people to come into the kingdom of God with supernatural spiritual ministry. After the prophets and apostles are fully restored, there will three more restorational moves of God, which will cause more souls to be saved than have been saved since the Church began. The final move of God will finalize the fulfillment of all things that are necessary for Jesus to return and establish His kingdom over all the earth.

R-T

This is an abbreviated form for the Resurrection-Translation of the Saints. Some refer to this event as the "Rapture" or first resurrection of the saints.

Resources on Apostles and Apostolic Ministry

Cannistraci, David. *The Gift of the Apostle.* Ventura, California: Regal Books,1979.

Eckhardt, John. *The Apostolic Church.* Chicago, Illinois: Crusader Ministries, 1996.

Eckhardt, John. *The Ministry Anointing of the Apostle.* Chicago, Illinois: Crusaders Publications, 1993.

Hamon, Dr. Bill. *Prophets and the Prophetic Movement.* Shippensburg, Pennsylvania: Destiny Image, 1990.

Hamon, Dr. Bill. *Prophetic Destiny and the Apostolic Reformation.* Santa Rosa Beach, Florida: Chrisian International Publishing, 1997.

Hatwin, George R. "The Ministry of the Apostle." *The Sharon Star* (April/May 1951).

Lockyer, Herbert. *All the Apostles of the Bible.* Grand Rapids, Michigan: Zondervan Publishing, 1972.

McBirnie, William Steuart. *The Search for the Twelve Apostles.* Wheaton, Illinois: Tyndale House, 1978.

Sapp, Roger. *The Last Apostles on Earth.* Shippensburg, Pennsylvania: Companion Press, 1995.

Scheidler, Bill. *The New Testament Church and Its Ministries.* Portland, Oregon: Bible Temple, 1980.

Schultz, Steve. *Mentoring & Fathering.* Santa Rosa Beach, Florida: Companion Press, 1996.

Wyatt, Kenneth. *The Apostles.* Amarillo, Texas: Y-8 Publishing Company, 1989.

Resources on Prophets and Prophetic Ministry

Michael Abboud, Brooke Mackie and Victor Korabelnifkoff. *Canaan Land Prophetic Journal #94.* "Comest Thou in Peace?" Australia: Canaan Land Publications. 1994.

Basham, Don. *True and False Prophets.* Grand Rapids, Michigan: Chosen Books, 1986.

Crist, Terry. *Interceding Against the Powers of Darkness.* Tulsa, Oklahoma: Terry Crist Ministries, 1991.

Crist, Terry. *A Time of War.* Tulsa, Oklahoma: Terry Crist Ministries, 1986.

Crist, Terry. *Warring According To Prophecy.* Tulsa, Oklahoma: Whitaker House,1989.

Deere, Jack. *Surprised by the Voice of God.* Grand Rapids, Michigan: Zondervan Publishing, 1996.

Gay, Robert. *Silencing the Gates of the Enemy.* Lake Mary, Florida: Creation House, 1993.

Hamon, Dr. Bill. *Prophets and Personal Prophecy.* Shippensburg, Pennsylvania: Destiny Image, 1987.

Hamon, Dr. Bill. *Prophets and The Prophetic Movement.* Shippensburg, Pennsylvania: Destiny Image, 1990.

Hamon, Dr. Bill. *Prophets, Pitfalls and Principles.* Shippensburg, Pennsylvania: Destiny Image,1991.

Harfouche, Christian. *Authority Over the Powers of Darkness.* Shalimar, Florida: Christian Publications, 1993.

Harfouche, Christian. *The Miracle Ministry of the Prophet.* Shalimar, Florida: Christian Publications, 1993.

Jacobs, Cindy. *The Voice of God.* Ventura, California: Regal Books, 1995.

Pickett, Fuchsia. *Presenting the Holy Spirit.* Shippensburg, Pennsylvania: Destiny Image, 1994.

Schultz, Steve. *Restoration of the Modern-Day Prophet.* Santa Rosa Beach, Florida: D. Steven Schultz, 1990.

Schultz, Steve. *Radical Warriors Require Radical Training.* Santa Rosa Beach, Florida: D. Steven Schultz, 1991.

Sheets, Dutch. *Intercessory Prayer.* Ventura, California: Regal Books, 1996.

Stebbins, J.E. *Moses and the Prophets; Christ and the Apostles; Fathers & Martyrs.* Herlbut, Kellogg & Co., Hartford, Connecticut: American Subscription Publishing House, 1861.

Thigpen, Travis. *Prophetic Evangelism: A Course On Spirit-Led Witnessing. Richmond, Virginia:* Travis Thigpen, 1996.

Wagner, C. Peter. *Confronting the Powers.* Ventura, California: Regal Books, 1979.

Resources on Church Restoration, Refreshing and Destiny

Arnott, John. *The Father's Blessing.* Orlando, Florida: Creation House, 1995.

Chadwick, Henry. *The Early Church.* England: Penguin Books, 1967.

Conner, Kevin J. *The Church in the New Testament.* Australia: Acacia Press, 1982.

Hamon, Dr. Bill. *The Eternal Church.* Santa Rosa Beach, Florida: Christian International Publishers, 1981.

Hamon, Dr. Bill. *Prophetic Destiny and The Apostolic Reformation.* Santa Rosa Beach, Florida: Christian International Publishers, 1997.

Harrison, Everet F. *The Apostolic Church.* Grand Rapids, Michigan: Eerdmans, 1985.

Marocco, James. *The Invisible War.* Kahulu, Hawaii: Bartemaeus Publishing, 1992.

Pickett, Fuchsia. *The Next Move of God.* Orlando, Florida: Creation House, 1994.

Pickett, Fuchsia. *God's Dream.* Shippenburg, Pennsylvania: Destiny Image, 1991.

Pickett, Fuchsia. *For Such a Time as This.* Shippensburg, Pennsylvania: Destiny Image, 1992.

Wagner, C. Peter. "New Equipment for the Final Thrust," *Ministries Today* Orlando, Florida: Strang Communications. (January/February 1994).

Wagner, C. Peter. *Spreading the Fire.* Ventura, California: Regal Books, 1979.

Wagner, C. Peter. *Lighting the World.* Ventura, California: Regal Books, 1995.

Wagner, C. Peter. *Blazing the Way.* Ventura, California: Regal Books, 1995.

INDEX

Books on Prophets
Prophetic Movement & Ministry
by
Dr. Bill Hamon

"Prophets and Personal Prophecy" It is the biblical manual on prophets and prophetic ministry. Many scriptural proofs plus exciting biblical and life experiences revealing the proper guidelines for receiving, understanding and fulfilling God's personal words to individuals, churches and nations. More then 100,000 in print in eight different languages. 218 pages. **$13.99**

"Prophets and the Prophetic Movement" A complete overview of the Prophetic Movement, it's purpose and place in  Church history in fulfilling God's ultimate destiny for His Church. Only in this book do you find the all important Seven Principles for determining a true restorational move of God.

Standards are given for discerning the differences between supernatural manifestations of Church prophets and people involved in the New Age, occult and other groups which manifest the supernatural. 227 pages **$13.99**

 "Prophets Pitfalls and Principles" It reveals the pitfalls of weed seed attitudes, character flaws, and prophets syndromes found in the lives of several biblical prophets. The 10 M's for maintaining and maturing one's life and ministry are listed and explained. Answers are given to nineteen of the most common and complicated questions asked about prophets and personal prophecy. 224 pages. **$13.99**

Fulfilling Your Personal Prophecy

Pastors, make sure all of your leadership and members have their own copy of this vital booklet.

Everyone who thinks they have received a personal word from God needs this booklet.

Buy in quantity and give one to each person who receives a Personal Prophecy through your ministry.

SPECIAL VOLUME DISCOUNTS

Number of Copies	Price Per Copy	Approximate % Discount
1	$3.95	
2 to 10	$2.96	25% Discount
11 to 99	$2.40	40% Discount

IF YOU BUY A FULL CASE OF FULFILLING YOUR PERSOANL PROPHECY YOU MAY RECEIVE A 60% DISCOUNT.

The Coming Saints' Movement

• • • •

What's next for the Church? Essential insights concerning the next restorational move of God. A must for those who want to be a part of God's last moves. Revelation of God's purpose for the Saints' Movement and what it will accomplish in the Church and the world. **$10.00** (Two 90 minute tapes)

Dr. Bill Hamon's Tape Sets

T
h
e

10 M's

Principles to Live By

• • • •

Bishop Bill Hamon presents six major Biblical principles that have helped him fulfill 50 years of successful Christian living and 47 years of ministry. **$30.00** (Six 90 minute tapes)

This powerful series was developed to help you mature in and maintain your ministry. This series investigates 10 major areas of our personal lives which we need to continually examine and correct if we are to prove ourselves to be true ministers of God. **$15.00** (Three 60 minute tapes)

Plugging Into Your Spiritual Gifts

• • • • • •

CI's finest ministers in an array of teaching on the gifts of the Holy Spirit. This tape series will bring encouragement and build up your faith to manifest the gifts God has placed within you. **$30.00** (Six 60 minute tapes)

Prophetic Pitfalls

This exciting tape series is an in-depth look at the pitfalls that face today's Christians. Dr. Hamon uses biblical characters to disclose the subtle satanic pitfalls which can cause leadership and saints to fall. **$35.00** (Seven 60 minute tapes)

The Restoration and the Destination of the Church

A heavenly satellite overall view of the Church from its origination to its ultimate destination. The greatest information available on the progressive restoration of the Church unto its end time ministry and eternal destiny. The history and future of the Church from a Prophets view.

$50.00 (Ten 90 minute tapes)

• • • • • • • • • • • • • • • •

Jane Hamon's Books

Dreams and Visions

Jane Hamon gives us an understanding of the seemingly hidden messages of our dreams and visions. It's time we learn to discern the voice of the Lord as He communicates His mind, heart, purpose and plan to us through the language of dreams and visions. This is the most biblical and balanced presentation ever written by a proven Christian Prophetess. **$10.00**

The Deborah Company

God is releasing keys of revelation and spiritual principles that will unlock the latent potential of power on the Church and bring strategic breakthrough in these important days. Women will have a unique part to play in this last days army that God is assembling. The time is at hand in which God is activating the gifts which have been deposited by His Spirit into every blood-bought, Spirit-filled believer, regardless of gender. It is a day for women to step out from under their cloaks of inactivity and step into their God-ordained identities as active, vibrant members of the Body of Christ. **$10.00**

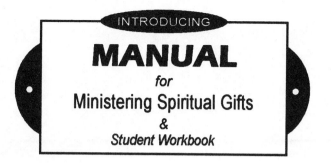

MANUAL

for

Ministering Spiritual Gifts

&

Student Workbook

"The Manual For Ministering Spiritual Gifts advances saints out of the realm of theory and brings them into a living experiential reality of God's graces. It is a manual designed for doing the Word, not just hearing it. This Manual helps teach, train, mature, and develop saints in their gifts of the Spirit while helping leadership to prepare qualified saints for use in various facets of team ministry."

by

Dr. Bill Hamon,
President & Founder of CI

Pastor, this manual will benefit your church and you...

* It will activate the gifts and ministries of the saints by providing 13 weekly sessions along with 16 corresponding spiritual exercises.

* It will stir and motivate your people towards spiritual ministry and their individual stewardship responsibilities of God's graces.

* It will build confidence and boldness in your saints by giving them opportunity to minister one to another.

* It will develop and mature your people in spiritual ministry without producing "spiritual spooks."

* It will deepen and strengthen your people's relationship with God as they are taught and challenged to hear His voice.

* It will furnish opportunity for church members to receive college credit for spiritual training through CI's School of Theology.

....

The *Manual for Ministering Spiritual Gifts* is available to those pastors who have become certified trainers. For information concerning certification for use of the *Manual for Ministering Spiritual Gifts* please call or write to:

CHRISTIAN INTERNATIONAL MINISTRIES NETWORK
P. O. Box 9000, Santa Rosa Beach, FL 32459-9000
(850) 231-2600 ext. 650

KNOW YOUR GOD AND YOURSELF

MTC

FULFILL YOUR DESTINY

Our Vision

Christian International **MINISTRY TRAINING COLLEGE'S** vision is to teach and equip students in a practical and experiential way for ministry. Our approach to teaching and learning is based on the Elijah - Elisha principle: the impartation of knowledge, experience and anointing through a mentor-student type relationship.

Receive

* A one or two year on-campus Ministry Training College Education, Degree Program.

* Powerful classroom teaching in vital areas like Prophetic Ministry, Leadership, Practical Theology, Pastoral Counseling, Worship, Apostolic miracles etc.

* Practical and supervised ministry training tracks with major personal emphasis with balance between acedemic and practical preparation for ministry!

FOR MORE INFORMATION CALL 850-231- 2683 OR 850-231-2682 OR WRITE CHRISTIAN INTERNATIONAL, MTC P.O. BOX 9000 SANTA ROSA BEACH, FL 32459

VISIT OUR WEB SITE: WWW.CIMN.NET/CI

CHRISTIAN INTERNATIONAL
BUSINESS NETWORK

Vision For Your Success

....

𝒯he vision of Christian International Business Network (**CIBN**) is to equip Christian business people to operate in the supernatural power of God and to practice biblical principles in the market place. In the day-to-day pressures of the business world, fortunes are made and lost based upon making the right decision at the right time. **CIBN** teaches, trains, activates, and mentors Christian business leaders in how to apply biblical decision making principles in this complex and stress-filled environment. **CIBN** also assists Christian business people in understanding their personal calling, and identifying their talents and gifts. Further, **CIBN** operates as a resource and networking center, bringing together Christian business people of like-vision and purpose in order to see the Kingdom of God established in the earth today.

CIBN offers opportunities for training and assistance in business through its newsletter (Christian Business Today), training seminars, local chapters, and consulting services.

Give us a call if you are interested in any of these resources at 850-231-2600 Ext 609 or write

Christian International Business Network

PO Box 9000, Santa Rosa Beach, Florida 32459
Fax: 850-231-1485 or www.CIMN.net

BOOKS BY DR. BILL HAMON

Apostles, Prophets and the Coming Moves of God	13.99
Prophets and Personal Prophecy	13.99
Prophets and The Prophetic Movement	13.99
Prophets Pitfalls and Principles	13.99
The Eternal Church	13.99
Teaching manuals and workbooks are also available.	
Prophetic Destiny and the Apostolic Reformation	6.95
Fulfilling Your Personal Prophecies	3.95

BOOKS BY EVELYN HAMON AND OTHER AUTHORS

The Spiritual Seasons of Life (Evelyn Hamon)	3.95
'NEW' God's Tests are Positive (Evelyn Hamon)	3.95
Redefining the Role of Women in the Church (Dr. Jim Davis)	7.95
Mentoring and Fathering (Steve Schultz)	9.50
Dreams and Visions (Jane Hamon)	10.00
The Deborah Company (Jane Hamon)	10.00

AUDIO TEACHING TAPE SERIES

Prophetic Pitfalls (Dr. Bill Hamon)	35.00
The 10 M's (Dr. Bill Hamon)	15.00
Plugging Into Your Spiritual Gifts (Dr. Bill Hamon and others)	30.00
The Coming Saints Movement (Dr. Bill Hamon)	10.00
Restoration and Destination of the Church (Dr. Bill Hamon)	50.00
Principles to Live By (Dr. Bill Hamon)	30.00
Handling Life's Realities (Evelyn Hamon)	20.00
Dealing With Life's Challenges (Evelyn Hamon)	20.00

PROPHETIC PRAISES CASSETTE TAPES AND CD'S

Show Your Power by Dean Mitchum (cassette)	10.95
Show Your Power by Dean Mitchum (CD)	14.95
Here's My Heart by Dean Mitchum (cassette)	10.95
Fan the Flame by Robert Gay (cassette)	10.95
Fan the Flame by Robert Gay (CD)	14.95

OTHER MATERIALS   Manual for Ministering Spiritual Gifts

Many more audio, video, cassettes, CD's and books available by other prophetic and apostolic ministers.